CHAUCER CRITICISM

VOLUME I

THE CANTERBURY TALES

An Anthology Edited by

RICHARD J. SCHOECK

AND JEROME TAYLOR

UNIVERSITY OF NOTRE DAME PRESS
NOTRE DAME   LONDON

Preface

Out of the diversity of authorship and approach represented in this anthology, a surprisingly consistent picture of Chaucer's art and spirit emerges. Of the eighteen selections, two are by poets as unlike as Cummings and Longfellow, sixteen by scholar-critics whose essays span half a century and whose critical approaches rest variously upon social history, literary history, rhetorical tradition, Biblical exegesis, or formal analysis of the text. A naive Chaucer—Chaucer as comic realist having his little jokes on contemporaries caught in his camera eye; Chaucer the benign indifferentist chuckling alike over good and evil, the happy ironist inspired by nothing so much as an incongruity; Matthew Arnold's Chaucer, lacking in "high and excellent seriousness"—does not exist for any writer represented here. It is difficult to see how the student or general reader could read far in this anthology without developing convictions about Chaucer as a poet of the most varied and sophisticated art—an art responsible to the moral and spiritual heart of man and human situations.

The interpretation of the *Canterbury Tales* and of Chaucer found in the essays is present, strikingly and emblematically, in the sonnets of Cummings and Longfellow, and it is for this reason that the two poems stand at the head of the collection. They are followed by two essays which deal with artistic problems arising in the General Prologue yet touching the *Tales* as a whole. Donaldson's essay, a delightful analysis of the narrative point of view provided by "Chaucer the Pilgrim," tells us that the most obvious function of the narrative *persona* is "to present a vision of the social world imposed on one of the moral world." Baldwin's essay finds the unity of the *Canterbury Tales* in a *sovrasenso* arising by "metaphorical pressure" from the springtime beginning, the pilgrimage, and the Parson's final call to penance.

The next three essays exemplify the use of historical scholarship in the interpretation of Chaucer's portraiture in the General Prologue. Beichner, by finding that hunting can be viewed as one of the "public relations" responsibilities of medieval monastic houses, makes it possible to read the General Prologue portrait of the Monk as a satire not on monastic abuses in general but, more specifically, on the monastic business administrator who has caught an "occupational disease." Williams, by identifying the traits of Chaucer's Friar with a series of Latin and vernacular attacks upon the mendicant orders, explains the absence of mitigating virtues in the portrait and enables one to "correlate Chaucer's artistic creation" with a partisan tradition. Horrell, who views the portrait of the Plowman against the background of social and economic tumult at the end of the fourteenth century, concludes that Chaucer shows a notable sympathy with the "character and human worth" of the peasantry and that he endows his Plowman with "a typal role" in his *comédie humaine*.

The ten essays which follow focus upon individual tales in an order corresponding to their appearance in Robinson's edition. Frost sees in the Knight's Tale "an idealized aristocratic universe, magnanimous, munificent, and ceremonial," yet threatened by forces of disorder and misery, and he suggests how the resulting tragic view of life is heightened by the fabliaux which follow in the first fragment. Beichner, concentrating on the art of the Miller's Tale, credits Chaucer with the deft creation of people "with whose characters the action of a borrowed plot would not be inconsistent." Kittredge, in the next selection, presents his famous case for the existence of a Marriage Group," while Sledd, redressing what he feels to be Kittredge's neglect of individual tales within this group, provides a witty formal analysis of the Clerk's Tale. Tatlock, too, focuses attention upon the Merchant's Tale not as a dramatic event in the "Marriage Group," but as Chaucer's farthest expression of "seriousness, disillusionment . . . hardly restrained emotion."

Sedgewick provides a useful review of the abundant scholarship on the Pardoner, and then offers what is substantially a refinement of Kittredge's dramatic interpretation of this figure and his tale—an interpretation given depth and added significance by Miller's exploration of the treatment of eunuchry in medieval Biblical exegesis. Miller's essay affords one of the best examples of what has been called the "neo-Augustinian" approach to medieval literature. The historical approach, earlier seen applied to characters from the General Prologue, is, in Schoeck's essay, applied to both the Prioress and her tale. Finally, Muscatine follows out the stylistic approach of his *Chaucer and the French Tradition* and, in his essay on the neglected Canon's Yeoman's Tale, goes beyond current interpretation of this tale as "autobiographical" or "journalistic" to find a realism which is ultimately symbolic of "the universe of technology"—and perhaps prophetic of technology's future.

The last two essays, though they look beyond the *Canterbury Tales* to the whole of the Chaucer canon, use individual tales in analyzing and appraising Chaucer's craft and the moral significance of his art.

Of the essays here presented, one (Beichner's on the Miller's Tale) has not been printed before; some have been revised by their authors with a view to their republication. Limitations of space and expense have made it necessary for the editors to eliminate a considerable portion of the original documentation, but notes identifying the source of quotations or essential to the argument have been retained. To aid the general reader, the editors have supplied translations of Latin, Old French, and Old English passages, placing these in the footnotes, or substituting them for the original in the text, whichever seemed best in particular cases. References to articles presenting notably contrary or qualifying points of view have also been added.

The editors are grateful for helpful comment on the selection of essays and for encouragement from Professors F. N. Robinson, Howard R. Patch, Kemp Malone, Morton Bloomfield, Charles W. Dunn, D. W. Robertson, Jr., Theodore Silverstein, Richard H. Green, T. A. Kirby, Charles Muscatine,

Hewette Joyce, and the late W. W. Lawrence. They also thank the contributors for their helpful advice and for the permissions which made this anthology possible. They wish to express particular gratitude to Mr. E. E. Cummings for permission to reprint his sonnet.

R. J. S.
J. T.

Notre Dame, Indiana
January 22, 1960

CONTENTS

honour corruption villainy holiness
riding in fragrance of sunlight(side by side
all in a singing wonder of blossoming yes
riding)to him who died that death should be dead

humblest and proudest eagerly wandering
(equally all alive in miraculous day)
merrily moving through sweet forgiveness of spring
(over the under the gift of the earth of the sky

knight and ploughman pardoner wife and nun
merchant frere clerk somnour miller and reve
and geoffrey and all)come up from the never of when
come into the now of forever come riding alive

down while crylessly drifting through vast most
nothing's own nothing children go of dust

—*E. E. Cummings*

CHAUCER

An old man in a lodge within a park;
   The chamber walls depicted all around
   With portraitures of huntsman, hawk, and hound,
   And the hurt deer. He listeneth to the lark,
Whose song comes with the sunshine through the dark
   Of painted glass in leaden lattice bound;
   He listeneth and he laugheth at the sound,
   Then writeth in a book like any clerk.
He is the poet of the dawn, who wrote
   The Canterbury Tales, and his old age
   Made beautiful with song; and as I read
I hear the crowing cock, I hear the note
   Of lark and linnet, and from every page
   Rise odors of ploughed field or flowery mead.

—Longfellow.

1

Chaucer the Pilgrim

E. TALBOT DONALDSON

VERISIMILITUDE IN A WORK of fiction is not without its attendant dangers, the chief of which is that the responses it stimulates in the reader may be those appropriate not so much to an imaginative production as to an historical one or to a piece of reporting. History and reporting are, of course, honorable in themselves, but if we react to a poet as though he were an historian or a reporter, we do him somewhat less than justice. I am under the impression that many readers, too much influenced by Chaucer's brilliant verisimilitude, tend to regard his famous pilgrimage to Canterbury as significant not because it is a great fiction, but because it seems to be a remarkable record of a fourteenth-century pilgrimage. A remarkable record it may be, but if we treat it too narrowly as such there are going to be certain casualties among the elements that make up the fiction. Perhaps first among these elements is the fictional reporter, Chaucer the pilgrim, and the role he plays in the Prologue to the

Reprinted, by permission of author and editor, from *Publications of the Modern Language Association*, LXIX (1954), 928-36. Cf. Ben Kimpel, "The Narrator of the *Canterbury Tales*," ELH, XX (1953), 77-96, which, like the present article, holds "there is no proof that the narrator in the *Canterbury Tales* is in any sense Chaucer," but which, in contrast with it, argues that the *CT* narrator lacks a definite personality.

Canterbury Tales and in the links between them. I think it time that he was rescued from the comparatively dull record of history and put back into his poem. He is not really Chaucer the poet—nor, for that matter, is either the poet, or the poem's protagonist, that Geoffrey Chaucer frequently mentioned in contemporary historical records as a distinguished civil servant, but never as a poet. The fact that these are three separate entities does not, naturally, exclude the probability—or rather the certainty—that they bore a close resemblance to one another, and that, indeed, they frequently got together in the same body. But that does not excuse us from keeping them distinct from one another, difficult as their close resemblance makes our task.

The natural tendency to confuse one thing with its like is perhaps best represented by a school of Chaucerian criticism, now outmoded, that pictured a single Chaucer under the guise of a wide-eyed, jolly, rolypoly little man who, on fine Spring mornings, used to get up early, while the dew was still on the grass, and go look at daisies. A charming portrait, this, so charming, indeed, that it was sometimes able to maintain itself to the exclusion of any Chaucerian other side. It has every reason to be charming, since it was lifted almost *in toto* from the version Chaucer gives of himself in the Prologue to the *Legend of Good Women*, though I imagine it owes some of its popularity to a rough analogy with Wordsworth—a sort of *Legend of Good Poets*. It was this version of Chaucer that Kittredge, in a page of great importance to Chaucer criticism, demolished with his assertion that "a naïf Collector of Customs would be a paradoxical monster." He might well have added that a naïve creator of old January would be even more monstrous.

Kittredge's pronouncement cleared the air, and most of us now accept the proposition that Chaucer was sophisticated as readily as we do the proposition that the whale is a mammal. But unhappily, now that we've got rid of the naïve fiction, it is easy to fall into the opposite sort of mistake. This is to envision, in the *Canterbury Tales*, a highly urbane, literal-historical Chaucer setting out from Southwark on a specific day of a specific year (we even argue somewhat acrimoniously about dates and routes), in company with a group of persons who existed in real life and whom Chaucer, his reporter's eye peeled for every idiosyncrasy, determined to get down on paper—down, that is, to the last wart—so that books might be written identifying them. Whenever this accurate reporter says something especially fatuous—which is not infrequently—it is either ascribed to an opinion peculiar to the Middle Ages (sometimes very peculiar), or else Chaucer's tongue is said to be in his cheek.

Now a Chaucer with tongue-in-cheek is a vast improvement over a simple-minded Chaucer when one is trying to define the whole man, but it must lead to a loss of critical perception, and in particular to a confused notion of Chaucerian irony, to see in the Prologue a reporter who is acutely aware of the significance of what he sees but who sometimes, for ironic emphasis, interprets the evidence presented by his observation in a fashion directly contrary to what we expect. The proposition ought to be expressed in reverse: the reporter is, usually, acutely unaware of the significance of what he sees, no matter how sharply he sees it. He is, to be sure, permitted his lucid intervals, but in general he is the victim of the poet's pervasive—not merely sporadic—irony. And as such he is also the chief agent by which the poet achieves his wonderfully complex, ironic, comic, serious vision of a world which is but a devious and confused, infinitely varied pilgrimage to a certain shrine. It is, as I hope to make clear, a good deal more than merely fitting that our guide on such a pilgrimage should be a man of such naïveté as the Chaucer who tells the tale of *Sir Thopas*. Let us accompany him a little distance.

It is often remarked that Chaucer really liked the Prioress very much, even though he satirized her gently—very gently. But this is an understatement: Chaucer the pilgrim may not be said merely to have liked the Prioress very much—he thought she was utterly charming. In the first twenty-odd lines of her portrait (A118 ff.) he employs, among other superlatives, the adverb *ful* seven times. Middle English uses *ful* where we use *very*, and if one translates the beginning of the portrait into a kind of basic English (which is what, in a way, it really is), one gets something like this: "There was also a Nun, a Prioress, who was very sincere and modest in the way she smiled; her biggest oath was only 'By saint Loy'; and she was called Madame Eglantine. She sang the divine service very well, intoning it in her nose very prettily, and she spoke French very nicely and elegantly"—and so on, down to the last gasp of sentimental appreciation. Indeed, the Prioress may be said to have transformed the rhetoric into something not unlike that of a very bright kindergarten child's descriptive theme. In his reaction to the Prioress Chaucer the pilgrim resembles another—if less—simple-hearted enthusiast: the Host, whose summons to her to tell a tale must be one of the politest speeches in the language. Not "My lady prioresse, a tale now!" but, "as curteisly as it had been a mayde,"

> My lady Prioresse, by youre leve,
> So that I wiste I sholde yow nat greve,
> I wolde demen that ye tellen sholde
> A tale next, if so were that ye wolde.
> Now wol ye vouche sauf, my lady deere? (B1636–41)

Where the Prioress reduced Chaucer to superlatives, she reduces the Host to subjunctives.

There is no need here to go deeply into the Prioress. Eileen Power's illustrations from contemporary episcopal records show with what extraordinary economy the portrait has been packed with abuses typical of fourteeth-century nuns. The abuses, to be sure, are mostly petty, but it is clear enough that the Prioress, while a perfect lady, is anything but a perfect nun; and attempts to whitewash her, of which there have been many, can only proceed from an innocence of heart equal to Chaucer the pilgrim's and undoubtedly directly influenced by it. For he, of course, is quite swept away by her irrelevant *sensibilité*, and as a result misses much of the point of what he sees. No doubt he feels that he has come a long way, socially speaking, since his encounter with the Black Knight in the forest, and he knows, or thinks he knows, a little more of what it's all about: in this case it seems to be mostly about good manners, kindness to animals, and female charm. Thus it has been argued that Chaucer's appreciation for the Prioress as a sort of heroine of courtly romance *manquée* actually reflects the sophistication of the living Chaucer, an urbane man who cared little whether amiable nuns were good nuns. But it seems a curious form of sophistication that permits itself to babble superlatives; and indeed, if this is sophistication, it is the kind generally seen in the least experienced people—one that reflects a wide-eyed wonder at the glamor of the great world. It is just what one might expect of a bourgeois exposed to the splendors of high society, whose values, such as they are, he eagerly accepts. And that is precisely what Chaucer the pilgrim is, and what he does.

If the Prioress's appeal to him is through elegant femininity, the Monk's is through imposing virility. Of this formidable and important prelate the pilgrim does not say, with Placebo,

> I woot wel that my lord kan moore than I:
> What that he seith, I holde it ferme and stable, (E1498–9)

but he acts Placebo's part to perfection. He is as impressed with the Monk as the Monk is, and accepts him on his own terms and at face value, never sensing that those terms imply complete condemnation of Monk *qua* Monk. The Host is also impressed by the Monk's virility, but having no sense of Placebonian propriety (he is himself a most virile man) he makes indecent jokes about it. This, naturally, offends the pilgrim's sense of decorum: there is a note of deferential commiseration in his comment, "This worthy Monk took al in pacience" (B3155.) Inevitably when the Monk establishes hunting as the highest activity of which religious man is capable, "I seyde his opinion was good" (A183). As one of the pilgrim's spiritual heirs was to say, Very like a whale; but not, of course, like a fish out of water.

Wholehearted approval for the values that important persons subscribe to is seen again in the portrait of the Friar. This amounts to a prolonged gratulation for the efficiency

the deplorable Hubert shows in undermining the fabric of the
Church by turning St. Francis' ideal inside out:

> Ful swetely herde he confessioun,
> And plesaunt was his absolucioun.
>
> For unto swich a worthy man as he
> Acorded nat, as by his facultee,
> To have with sike lazars aqueyntaunce.
>
> (A221–222, 243–245)

It is sometimes said that Chaucer did not like the Friar.
Whether Chaucer the man would have liked such a Friar is,
for our present purposes, irrelevant. But if the pilgrim does
not unequivocally express his liking for him, it is only because
in his humility he does not feel that, with important people,
his own likes and dislikes are material: such importance is
its own reward, and can gain no lustre from Geoffrey, who,
when the Friar is attacked by the Summoner, is ready to
show him the same sympathy he shows the Monk (see
D1265–67).

Once he has finished describing the really important peo-
ple on the pilgrimage the pilgrim's tone changes, for he can
now concern himself with the bourgeoisie, members of his
own class for whom he does not have to show such pro-
found respect. Indeed, he can even afford to be a little
patronizing at times, to have his little joke at the expense of
the too-busy lawyer. But such indirect assertions of his own
superiority do not prevent him from giving substance to the
old cynicism that the only motive recognized by the middle
class is the profit motive, for his interest and admiration for
the bourgeois pilgrims is centered mainly in their material
prosperity and their ability to increase it. He starts, properly
enough, with the out-and-out money-grubber, the Merchant,
and after turning aside for that *lusus naturae*, the non-profit-
motivated Clerk, proceeds to the Lawyer, who, despite the
pilgrim's little joke, is the best and best-paid ever; the
Franklin, twenty-one admiring lines on appetite, so expen-
sively catered to; the Gildsmen, cheered up the social lad-
der, "For catel hadde they ynogh and rente" (A373); and

the Physician, again the best and richest. In this series the portrait of the Clerk is generally held to be an ideal one, containing no irony; but while it is ideal, it seems to reflect the pilgrim's sense of values in his joke about the Clerk's failure to make money: is not this still typical of the half-patronizing, half-admiring *un*understanding that practical men of business display towards academics? But in any case the portrait is a fine companion-piece for those in which material prosperity is the main interest both of the characters described and of the describer.

Of course, this is not the sole interest of so gregarious—if shy—a person as Chaucer the pilgrim. Many of the characters have the additional advantage of being good companions, a faculty that receives a high valuation in the Prologue. To be good company might, indeed, atone for certain serious defects of character. Thus the Shipman, whose callous cruelty is duly noted, seems fairly well redeemed in the assertion, "And certeinly he was a good felawe" (A395). At this point an uneasy sensation that even tongue-in-cheek irony will not compensate for the lengths to which Chaucer is going in his approbation of this sinister seafarer sometimes causes editors to note that *a good felawe* means "a rascal." But I can find no evidence that it ever meant a rascal. Of course, all tritely approbative expressions enter easily into ironic connotation, but the phrase *means* a good companion, which is just what Chaucer means. And if, as he says of the Shipman, "Of nyce conscience took he no keep" (A398), Chaucer the pilgrim was doing the same with respect to him.

Nothing that has been said has been meant to imply that the pilgrim was unable to recognize, and deplore, a rascal when he saw one. He could, provided the rascality was situated in a member of the lower classes and provided it was, in any case, somewhat wider than a barn door: Miller, Manciple, Reeve, Summoner, and Pardoner are all acknowledged to be rascals. But rascality generally has, after all, the laudable object of making money, which gives it a kind of validity, if not dignity. These portraits, while in them the pilgrim, prioress-like conscious of the finer aspects of life, does deplore such matters as the Miller's indelicacy of lan-

guage, contain a note of ungrudging admiration for efficient
thievery. It is perhaps fortunate for the pilgrim's reputation
as a judge of men that he sees through the Pardoner, since
it is the Pardoner's particular tragedy that, except in Church,
every one can see through him at a glance; but in Church
he remains to the pilgrim "a noble ecclesiaste" (A708). The
equally repellent Summoner, a practicing bawd, is partially
redeemed by his also being a good fellow, "a gentil harlot
and a kynde" (A647), and by the fact that for a moderate
bribe he will neglect to summon: the pilgrim apparently
subscribes to the popular definition of the best policeman
as the one who acts the least policely.

Therefore Chaucer is tolerant, and has his little joke about
the Summoner's small Latin—a very small joke, though one
of the most amusing aspects of the pilgrim's character is the
pleasure he takes in his own jokes, however small. But the
Summoner goes too far when he cynically suggests that
purse is the Archdeacon's hell, causing Chaucer to respond
with a fine show of righteous respect for the instrument of
spiritual punishment. The only trouble is that his enthusiastic
defense of them carries *him* too far, so that after having
warned us that excommunication will indeed damn our
souls—

> But wel I woot he lyed right in dede:
> Of cursyng oghte ech gilty man him drede,
> For curs wol slee right as assoillyng savith— (A659–61)

he goes on to remind us that it will also cause considerable
inconvenience to our bodies: "And also war hym of a
Significavit" (A662). Since a *Significavit* is the writ accom-
plishing the imprisonment of the excommunicate, the line
provides perhaps the neatest—and most misunderstood—
Chaucerian anticlimax in the Prologue.

I have avoided mentioning, hitherto, the pilgrim's reac-
tions to the really good people on the journey—the Knight,
the Parson, the Plowman. One might reasonably ask how his
uncertain sense of values may be reconciled with the en-
thusiasm he shows for their rigorous integrity. The question
could, of course, be shrugged off with a remark on the ir-

relevance to art of exact consistency, even to art distinguished by its verisimilitude. But I am not sure that there is any basic inconsistency. It is the nature of the pilgrim to admire all kinds of superlatives, and the fact that he often admires superlatives devoid of—or opposed to—genuine virtue does not inhibit his equal admiration for virtue incarnate. He is not, after all, a bad man; he is, to place him in his literary tradition, merely an average man, or mankind: *homo,* not very *sapiens* to be sure, but with the very best intentions, making his pilgrimage through the world in search of what is good, and showing himself, too frequently, able to recognize the good only when it is spectacularly so. Spenser's Una glows with a kind of spontaneous incandescence, so that the Red Cross Knight, mankind in search of holiness, knows her as good; but he thinks that Duessa is good, too. Virtue concretely embodied in Una or the Parson presents no problems to the well-intentioned observer, but in a world consisting mostly of imperfections, accurate evaluations are difficult for a pilgrim who, like mankind, is naïve. The pilgrim's ready appreciation for the virtuous characters is perhaps the greatest tribute that could be paid to their virtue, and their spiritual simplicity is, I think, enhanced by the intellectual simplicity of the reporter.

The pilgrim belongs, of course, to a very old—and very new—tradition of the fallible first person singular. His most exact modern counterpart is perhaps Lemuel Gulliver who, in his search for the good, failed dismally to perceive the difference between the pursuit of reason and the pursuits of reasonable horses: one may be sure that the pilgrim would have whinnied with the best of them. In his own century he is related to Long Will of *Piers Plowman,* a more explicit seeker after the good, but just as unswerving in his inability correctly to evaluate what he sees. Another kinsman is the protagonist of the *Pearl,* mankind whose heart is set on a transitory good that has been lost—who, for very natural reasons, confuses earthly with spiritual values. Not entirely unrelated is the protagonist of Gower's *Confessio Amantis,* an old man seeking for an impossible earthly love that seems to him the only good. And in more subtle fashion there is the teller of Chaucer's story of *Troilus and Cressida,* who, while not a true protagonist, performs some of the same functions. For this unloved "servant of the servants of love" falls in love with Cressida so persuasively that almost every male reader of the poem imitates him, so that we all share the heartbreak of Troilus and sometimes, in the intensity of our heartbreak, fail to learn what Troilus did. Finally, of course, there is Dante of the *Divine Comedy,* the most exalted member of the family and perhaps the immediate original of these other first-person pilgrims.

Artistically the device of the *persona* has many functions, so integrated with one another that to try to sort them out produces both oversimplification and distortion. The most obvious, with which this paper has been dealing—distortedly, is to present a vision of the social world imposed on one of the moral world. Despite their verisimilitude most, if not all, of the characters described in the Prologue are taken directly from stock and recur again and again in medieval literature. Langland in his own Prologue and elsewhere de-picts many of them: the hunting monk, the avaricious friar, the thieving miller, the hypocritical pardoner, the unjust stewards, even, in little, the all-too-human nun. But while Langland uses the device of the *persona* with considerable skill in the conduct of his allegory, he uses it hardly at all in portraying the inhabitants of the social world: these are described directly, with the poet's own voice. It was left to Chaucer to turn the ancient stock satirical characters into real people assembled for a pilgrimage, and to have them described, with all their traditional faults upon them, by another pilgrim who records faithfully each fault without, for the most part, recognizing that it is a fault and frequently felicitating its possessor for possessing it. One result—though not the only result—is a moral realism much more significant than the literary realism which is a part of it and for which it is sometimes mistaken; this moral realism discloses a world in which humanity is prevented by its own myopia, the myopia of the describer, from seeing what the dazzlingly attractive externals of life really represent. In most of the analogues mentioned above the fallible first person receives, at the end of the book, the education he has needed: the pilgrim arrives somewhere. Chaucer never completed the *Canterbury Tales*, but in the Prologue to the *Parson's Tale* he seems to have been doing, rather hastily, what his contemporaries had done: when, with the sun nine-and-twenty degrees from the horizon, the twenty-nine pilgrims come to a certain—unnamed—*thropes ende* (I12), then the pilgrimage seems no longer to have Canterbury as its destination, but rather, I suspect, the Celestial City of which the Parson speaks.

If one insists that Chaucer was not a moralist but a comic writer (a distinction without a difference), then the device of the *persona* may be taken primarily as serving comedy. It has been said earlier that the several Chaucers must have inhabited one body, and in that sense the fictional first person probably always shared the personality of his creator: thus Dante of the *Divine Comedy* was physically Dante the Florentine; the John Gower of the *Confessio* was also Chaucer's friend John Gower; and Long Will was, I am sure, some one named William Langland, who was both long and wilful. And it is equally certain that Chaucer the pilgrim, "a popet in an arm t'enbrace" (B1891), was in every physical respect Chaucer the man, whom one can imagine reading his work to a courtly audience, as in the portrait appearing in one of the MSS. of *Troilus*. One can imagine also the delight of the audience which heard the Prologue read in this way, and which was aware of the similarities and dissimilarities between Chaucer, the man before them, and Chaucer the pilgrim, both of whom they could see with simultaneous vision. The Chaucer they knew was physically, one gathers, a little ludicrous; a bourgeois, but one who was known as a practical and successful man of the court; possessed perhaps of a certain diffidence of manner, reserved, deferential to the socially imposing persons with whom he was associated; a bit absent-minded, but affable and, one supposes, very good company—a good fellow; sagacious and highly perceptive. This Chaucer was telling them of another who, lacking some of his chief qualities, nevertheless possessed many of his characteristics, though in a different state of balance, and each one probably distorted just enough to become laughable without becoming unrecognizable: deference into a kind of snobbishness, affability into an over-readiness to please, practicality into Babbittry, perception into inspection, absence of mind into dimness of wit; a Chaucer acting in some respects just as Chaucer himself might have acted but unlike his creator the kind of man, withal, who could mistake a group of stock satirical types for living persons endowed with all sorts of superlative qualities. The constant interplay of these two Chaucers must have produced an exquisite and most ingratiating humor—as, to be sure, it still does. This comedy reaches its superb climax when Chaucer the pilgrim, resembling in so many ways Chaucer the poet, can answer the Host's demand for a story only with a rhyme he "lerned longe agoon" (B1899)—*Sir Thopas*, which bears the same complex relation to the kind of romance it satirizes and to Chaucer's own poetry as Chaucer the pilgrim does to the pilgrims he describes and to Chaucer the poet.

Earlier in this paper I proved myself no gentleman (though I hope a scholar) by being rude to the Prioress, and hence to the many who like her and think that Chaucer liked her too. It is now necessary to retract. Undoubtedly Chaucer the man would, like his fictional representative, have found her charming and looked on her with affection. To have got on so well in so changeable a world Chaucer must have got on well with the people in it, and it is doubtful that one may get on with people merely by pretending to like them: one's heart has to be in it. But the third entity, Chaucer the poet, operates in a realm which is above and subsumes those in which Chaucer the man and Chaucer the pilgrim have their being. In this realm prioresses may be simultaneously evaluated as marvelously amiable ladies and as prioresses. In his poem the poet arranges for the moralist to define austerely what ought to be and for his fictional representative—who, as the representative of all mankind, is no mere fiction—to go on affirming affectionately what is. The two points of view, in strict moral logic diametrically

opposed, are somehow made harmonious in Chaucer's won-
derfully comic attitude, that double vision that is his ironical
essence. The mere critic performs his etymological function
by taking the Prioress apart and clumsily separating her
good parts from her bad; but the poet's function is to build
her incongruous and inharmonious parts into an inseparable
whole which is infinitely greater than its parts. In this com-
plex structure both the latent moralist and the naïve reporter
have important positions, but I am not persuaded that in
every case it is possible to determine which of them has the
last word.[1]

[1] Quotations from Chaucer in this paper are made from F. N.
Robinson's text (Cambridge, Mass., n.d.). Books referred to or
cited are G. L. Kittredge, *Chaucer and His Poetry* (Cambridge,
Mass., 1915), p. 45; Eileen Power, *Medieval People* (London,
1924), pp. 59–84. Robinson's note to A650 records the opinion that
a good felawe means a 'rascal.' The medieval reader's expectation
that the first person in a work of fiction would represent mankind
generally and at the same time would physically resemble the
author is commented on by Leo Spitzer in an interesting note in
Traditio, IV (1946), 414–422.

2

The Unity of *The Canterbury Tales*

RALPH BALDWIN

IT IS ACCEPTED THAT *The Canterbury Tales* is not a whole, not an achieved work of art, but rather a truncated and aborted congeries of tales woven about a frame, the Pilgrimage from London to Canterbury. Although there is a closely articulated beginning, the *General Prologue,* and this beginning has, in turn, a beginning, a middle, and an end, the middle of the entire work reveals that the plan as presented by the Host is not even one-half realized on the outward journey, and as this study should demonstrate, no return talefest is even attempted. The ending seems to be a hastily subjoined recantation, tonally consorting with the *Parson's Tale* to which it is suffixed. It has been regarded as an anomalous and merely conventional appendage. It would appear then that an ending is nonexistent, because the pilgrimage is never brought back to the Tabard, the fund of stories never equates with the explicit number ordained by Harry Bailey, and the *motifs* released at the outset are never artistically concluded, never resolved.

Reprinted, by permission of author and publisher, from the mono-graph series *Anglistica,* ed. Torsten Dahl, Kemp Malone, and Geoffrey Tillotson, Vol. V (Copenhagen: Rosenkilde and Bagger, 1955), pp. 15–16, 19–20, 24–29, 47–52, 83–110. Excerpts have been retitled and renumbered consecutively.

It is true that the formal circularity that would have given the work that englobed and polished *ratio* lauded by the mediaeval literary theorists is lacking. "Whatever in the Middle Ages is not a long-rhymed story like Chrétien's *romans courtois*, has an additive and tell-as-you-go composition, not a shaded and circular or global composition. This certainly springs from the mediaeval *artes poeticae* and the mediaeval mind in general. What is elaborate in such works is the detailed *lexis*, the linguistic style, but not the larger *taxis;* the balanced composition is only found in works important in meaning, but not in trifling faits divers."[1]

But this apparent lack of balanced composition in the *Tales* would appear to result not from the surface tell-as-you-go tone, nor yet because it is a medley of "trifling faits divers," but rather because it is incomplete. In this respect it resembles in its building the mediaeval church. The master plan before them, its builders undertook work from the center outward, so to speak, and having provided walls and roof enough to shelter the sacrifice, they were sometimes content to leave the labor and expense of the rest of the building to posterity.

An examination of the beginning and the ending of the *Tales*, the only masonry of our edifice on which Chaucer labored without the help of his editors, reveals that they fulfill an architectonic function, hitherto overlooked, and that they sustain the story as they reinforce each other. They make the pilgrimage not a frame, but a dynamic entity. . . . By surveying the *Tales* from the vantage points of beginning and ending, the reader may see *The Canterbury Tales* from another perspective. . . .

A. THE BEGINNING (*GP*, 1–42)

The eleven lines which begin *The Canterbury Tales* are an elaborate rhetorical dating couched in the *high style*, and setting mid-April ("the yonge sonne/Hath in the Ram his halve cours yronne") as the date of a realistic fiction-pilgrimage in an undetermined year. Introduced by the subordinate temporal clause "Whan that," the first ten lines comprise an inaugural Spring metaphor that, it will be shown, does much more than draw us into the frame of the *Tales*. Compounded of the immemorial ingredients of the renascence —April and its frost-piercing showers, the mild west wind, the new sun, and the birds—the passage seems patly stylized and seasonal in an aureate troubadour fashion. . . .

Albert S. Cook,[2] in discussing the first eleven lines of the *GP*, seeks precedent or progenitive passages for them in Virgil, Lucretius, Aeschylus, and others; he detects special assimilations here to *Georgics* 2. 323–333. In these sources there are celebrated the embraces of Heaven and Earth, of Mater Terra and Pater Aether. But is it necessary to turn from the Middle Ages to such classical remoteness for what is an elemental and commonplace theme?

Skeat[3] traces the inspiration of this section to the opening lines of Book IV of Guido delle Colonne's prose treatise, *Historia Troiae*, and then goes on to observe that a passage in Vincent of Beauvais' *Speculum Naturale*, lib. xv. c. 66, entitled *De Vere*, somewhat resembles Chaucer's beginning. Other parallels have been found, such as the anonymous Latin poem of the second century A. D., *Pervigilium Veneris*.[4] But to comb verses 3–85 of the *PV* and relate a few disparate likenesses to Chaucer's eleven lines is a makeshift compression.

Basically, lines 1–11 are a type of *reverdie* or "chant of welcome to the Spring." The *reverdie* could be, and had been, from the mediaeval lyrics "Cuckoo Song" and "Alisoun" to Surrey's sonnet, "Description of Spring Wherein Each Thing Renews, Save only the Lover," acclimated to many *motifs*. However the poet may apply it, there is always the modal reaction to rebirth and renewal. It expresses one of the inherent, spontaneous rhythms of humankind. Certainly no more plangent note is struck in the mediaeval lyric than the nature pleasance or nature plaint. Furthermore, one can adduce and multiply such examples from classical, patristic and mediaeval continental literatures, and the attempt to pin any one of them down as at all prototypal for this passage has not so far been convincing. . . .

In short, spring was variously used to express psychological (and physiological), erotic, allegorical, and religious reawakenings, and the lover, the glossator, the allegorist, the mystic, even the satirist, again and again employ the counters of spring. But it is noteworthy that Chaucer alone made his *reverdie* the groundsong for a pilgrimage: there is, to my knowledge, no other such instance in continental literature prior to these lines opening *The Canterbury Tales:*

(1-11)   Whan that Aprille with his shoures sote
The droghte of Marche hath perced to the rote,
And bathed every veyne in swich licour,
Of which vertu engendred is the flour;
Whan Zephirus eek with his sweete breeth
Inspired hath in every holt and heeth
The tendre croppes, and the yonge sonne
Hath in the Ram his halve cours yronne,
And smale foweles maken melodye,
That slepen al the night with open ye,
(So priketh hem nature in hir corages)

That March and April were particularly synchronized with the redeeming rhythms and that the Easter season was especially imbued with the redemptive mysteries, are facts familiar to all students of mediaeval life and literature. The solar year was, and is, the vehicle by which the Church expresses Christian redemption. A glance at any liturgical calendar will demonstrate that the dates of the great Christian feasts are astronomical in origin, though there were also historical reasons for their choice, because the "8th Calends of January, April, July and October mark the official occurrences of the two solstices and two equinoxes according to Roman literature about the time of Christ."[5] The celestial and chthonic rhythms beat as triumphant cymbals, and symbols, of salvation, with the progressive dispersal of the darknesses by "Christus, sol," Christ, the sun, in the spring of the year.

Aelfric in his translation of *De Temporibus Anni* takes us back even farther into Christian credulity, to the acknowledged date of the origin of the world: "We secgath nu sceortlice thaet se forma daeg thyssere worulde is geteald to tham daege the we hatath quinta decima kalendas aprilis —thaes emnihtes daeg is gehaefd, swa swa Beda taecth, thaes on tham feorthan daege thaet is on duodecima Kalendas aprilis."⁶

We have then, behind the conventional spring beginning in mediaeval vernacular literature, an ancient Christian conviction that this time of year was not only the occasion for all natural and human beginnings, but the general date of the Redemption through the sacrifice of Good Friday:

> Without historical support, in the Gospels or elsewhere, the Western world came to accept December 25 as the Nativity because allegorically at the old Roman winter solstice Christ was born into a world of greatest darkness to bring light. So, too, the sacrifice at the Crucifixion brought greatest light to the world. The first day in the year when for twenty-four hours the world is flooded with light occurs at the full moon of the vernal equinox.⁷

It is a dependable moment for beginning anything, if we consider the mediaeval mind; and if we consider it from the liturgical point of view as that time of year in which man's chance for salvation is restored to him, it becomes inevitable that "thanne longen folk to goon on pilgrimages." The *Nun's Priest's Tale* demonstrates that Chaucer accepted, or at least regarded as a truism, the conviction of his time as regards Creation in the lines: "Whan that 'the month in which the world bigan,/ That highte March, whan God first maked man." It is possible that he is thinking of his pilgrimage, "Redy to wenden on *my* pilgrimage," likewise in the more extensive terms of his own time.

Beginning, pilgrimage, and regeneration then were for mediaeval man seasonally involved. March and April put a new face on the world, as one Goliard said it, "nova mundo reserat/Facies Aprilis"; and man, the microcosm, was tremulous with change, too. For the modern man, however, the same season has quite another aspect. To compare the openings of *The Canterbury Tales* and *The Wasteland* is by no means to define the ethos of either, but since in the twentieth century,

> April is the cruellest month, breeding
> Lilacs out of the dead land, mixing
> Memory and desire, stirring
> Dull roots with spring rain ...

it is obvious that a conventional literary theme has reappeared in a radically changed tradition. The *reverdie* in the age of Eliot celebrates the reanimation not of the living but of the dying. The poet is not responsible for, but responsive to, this mood. Neither Chaucer nor Eliot is doing this all by himself. Neither is "originating" an ethos. Each one bodies forth his own age, giving it form and feature, for in expressing himself he expresses his time. Eliot observes in this propos:

> The great poet, in writing himself, writes his time. Thus Dante, hardly knowing it, became the voice of the thirteenth century; Shakespeare, hardly knowing it, became the representative of the end of the sixteenth century, of a turning point in history. But you can hardly say that Dante believed, or did not believe, the Thomist philosophy; you can hardly say that Shakespeare believed, or did not believe, the mixed and muddled skepticism of the Renaissance. If Shakespeare had written according to a better philosophy, he would have written worse poetry; it was his business to express the greatest emotional intensity of his time, based on whatever his time happened to think.[8]

It is difficult, if not impossible, to recapture the attitudes of any era, but those of the Middle Ages especially elude us. The premises, the intellectual comfortables and furnishings of that theocentric epoch make on the whole no sense to the modern, yet the late mediaeval world which Chaucer inhabited had determinable lineaments which should not be blurred in any liberal and liberating attempt to repossess him on this side of the Renaissance, itself a late efflorescence of the mediaeval temper. It was a world which was in rather disturbing contiguity to the supernatural world, actual and present to it by prayer, by penance, by the mystical corporeity of those fraternally one in Christ. The City of God was quite as visible, quite as "palpable," as the City of London, and, in a sense, more real. London itself was a half-way house for the mediaeval Englishman, the caravanserai of Christ, sheltering overnight, until the dawn of eternity, the *societas peregrina* on its way to the City of God, to the *real* estate of the new Jerusalem. The City of God was not a metaphor or pious euphuism, but "a reality, an assembly and Church with its innumerable hosts of angels, not less but more actual than the commonwealth of men."⁹ And the only hostelry that welcomed man into this world and released him to the next, was the Church. All the foibles, floutings, blasphemies and malices of its members, of its weak and corrupted humanity, could not gainsay that simple, metatemporal, metapolitical fact.

The life of the mediaeval Christian, then, was framed by Creation and Doomsday, the covers for the *liber vitae* of mediaeval man. It should be no surprise to find that *The Canterbury Tales* is bound, metaphorically, in just that way. It is April, it is springtime, it is beginning;¹⁰ and we have a typical mediaeval *ab origine* commencement, not with the historical antecedence of *Sir Gawain and the Green Knight,* "After the siege and the assault had come to an end at Troy," but with the inchoative seasonal-moral, seasonal-religious metaphor, where the mirror of Nature could not but reflect the divine order.

What begins as the traditional image of artifice operates on a much deeper and more functional scale than is realized at a cursory reading. Spring not only "melts" vegetative and sentient nature, . . . but stirs the heart of man as well. For Chaucer the stimulation is not to pastourelle, nor to meditation, nor the lover's *planctus,* but to pilgrimage. The germination and wakening of all greenery and animals have their expansive and reparative effects upon man, too. The surge of spring, however, is deftly localized and made unmistakably English and unmistakably Catholic. This is the signal for the countrywide outpouring of the devout. The palmer or professional pilgrim and the folk "from every shires ende/Of Engelond, to Caunterbury they wende," to a shrine where *patria* is taken up into *ecclesia.*

The time is *solempne* in the truly mediaeval festal sense. The Venerable Bede, in the 64th chapter, "Typica Paschae Interpretatio," of his *De Temporum Ratione,* sums up the sentimental and the sacramental fusion of the season: "In primis namque aequinoctium transgredi in dominici paschae celebratione iuxta legis decreta curamus, ut videlicet solemnitas in qua mediator Dei et hominum destructa potestate tenebrarum mundo lucis iter aperuit, etiam temporis foras quid intus habeat ostendat. Et quae nobis aeternae beatitudinis lumen promittit tunc maxime celebretur, cum solis lumen annuo proficiens incremento primam sumit de noctis umbra victoriam."[11] Chaucer is heir to this tradition, established in and perpetuated from the fourth century; he can appropriate it with casual literacy. The "first victory" of the equinoctial sun over the shade of night is a promise of the everlasting splendor of beatitude. Christ is the Light of the World, and to set forth on a pilgrimage in the spring is to walk in the Way and in the Light.

It is therefore possible that the device of the pilgrimage was not merely a happy plot-strategem to provide a frame for the assembling of characters and the excuse for a story-telling congress. The usual explanation of the frame as an inspired catchall for a series of *faits divers* is inadequate, since the mediaeval frame story was apt to be carried on either as a serial, additive, *art pour l'art* composition, as Singleton has forcefully shown is the case with Boccaccio's *Decameron*, or as a unified, comprehensive, circular piece of literary art, significative, in short, as Dante's *Divina Comoedia* undoubtedly is. The balanced composition which yields a *sovrasenso* has never been urged of *The Canterbury Tales*, probably because it is left to us both incomplete and disarranged. The triune, almost mathematically precise englobement which goes to make up Dante's *Comoedia* achieves nearly perfect balance. At the same time, we must observe that the *Comoedia* is made out of just such serialized fragments and episodes as, disjunctive, disframed, would be mere *faits divers*. In short, the one is artistically subsumed in the other.

Though a much inferior work of art, *The Canterbury Tales* may be shown to possess, in a rough and unrealized state, a *sovrasenso* of its own, one that betrays a certain indecision of growth, and an artistic dubiety on the part of Chaucer, but which all in all is there, defined and prepared for, especially in the section intended to come at the end of the *Tales*. What we may come finally to respect most of all is the subtlety and competence of Chaucer, who in a disordered and unpolished work could leave so many traces of order and a *finis* that was ineluctably perceived in beginning.

B. Characterization (*GP*, 43–714)

. . . We do not find in Chaucer the density of specification which is so much a part of the naturalistic technique. For instance, the reasons each individual has for pilgrimage, save in the case of the Knight, are omitted after the initial, "That hem hath holpen whan that they were seeke" (*GP*, 18). Nor does he ever reveal anything more specific than that about motives, perhaps because the practice of visiting holy places as a form of religious exercise was its own accounting. *The Encyclopedia of Religion and Ethics* defines pilgrimage as follows:

> By this word most people understand a journey to a holy place or shrine, either in the pilgrim's native land or abroad. The object of pilgrimage is to obtain some benefit, material, moral or spiritual, which the sanctity of the chosen spot is thought to confer. It is true that pilgrimages may be undertaken because such a journey is regarded as meritorious, but the idea of the acquisition of divine favor directly or through a saint is seldom absent. All kinds of benefits may be asked in return for the labor and travail, from the healing of a bodily infirmity to the gift of everlasting life.[12]

The fact is that the mediaeval audience was well aware of the penitential nature of pilgrimage. It is not unreasonable to argue from our distance that it is spring which calls these people to the highway, but it is necessary to remember that the impulses of the mediaeval man were, unlike ours, conditioned by a tradition: a season of redemption, spring, is the time to move nearer to salvation, "ferne halwes," via a penitential exercise, pilgrimage.

It is interesting to recall in this context Miss Kate O. Petersen's quotation from *L'Ymage du Monde:* "Saint Pierre dit que nous sommes tous pelerins en ce monde cy et alons iour et nuyt sans arrester en nostre pays quie est au ciel. Et pour recreation auoir comment les pelerins qui parlent voulentiers en alant leur chemin aussi en alant a nostre pelerinage, cest en paradis, nous parlerons ong petit; car nous cheminons fort et nauons mais que trois iournees a cheminer: l'une des dictes trois iournees est Contrition et l'autre Confession, et la tierce est Satisfaction."[13] The homeland that lies beyond the "valley of the shadow" has only one access for the Christian: Contrition, Confession and Satisfaction. It is the conclusion of any pilgrimage as it is of any life; it is the end of the pilgrimage that is life. It is the last stop before viaticum. However obscure or mixed might be the motives of the pilgrims, the fact that they are at the Tabard, on their way to Canterbury, like Chaucer, with "ful devout corage," makes them participants not only in the fiction of pilgrimage but in the trope central to the fiction. Only one of the group that leaves the Tabard can be said to have a purely worldly reason for making the journey. The Host's emphatic lack of "ful devout corage," the typical impetus of the pilgrim, not only points up his characterization but may account for that secularity of tone which has permitted the Canterbury pilgrimage to be interpreted in a purely literal way.

We may now begin the more positive analysis of Chaucer's technique of characterization by restating that Chaucer's view of the world and of the human person was more uniform and more stratified than ours. Furthermore, in a way that post-Renaissance sophistication made much less possible, the furnishings of a man's life were then closely articulated metonymies for the man himself. His being in nature, and description in literature, were still supported by those modalities, and we thread our way to him through them.

Chaucer's innovation in [personal description] was the inorganic, disordered, and inconsequent piling-up of details. That he could do this while depending upon what was still a rigidly systematic social and sacramental order is a large part of his charm, and the source of his illusion. The rubric of classical biography is used to introduce each figure. The formulary *erat* or *fuit autem* persisted even to Chaucer's day: "A KNYGHT *there was* ..."; "A MONK *there was* ..."; "A FRERE *there was* ..."; "*There was* also a NONNE, a PRIORESS ..."; "A FRANKLYN *was* in his compaignye ..." and so on through the whole group, with slight verbal deviation. Only one paragraph is allotted each person described, which makes for an impressive straitening of presentation. And, for the most part, each description is intact, self-

enclosed, "framed" with very careful formality. There is a
studied perusal and putting-away of the one before another is
undertaken, and though they are grouped quite strategically,
as Malone has reminded us, they are severally self-contained
and complete from the point of view of a superficial order.
But that order is is one of succession, not of description, and
each person is a disarray of traits which, if we may use the
word, "repersonify," by virtue of several bold strokes or
catalytic agents.

We find first *the conscientious use of hyperbole.* Every
pilgrim is the best of his kind, and Chaucer scrupulously rein-
forces this by the pleonastic notation, such as "worthy" (five
times) for the Knight, and "ful" for the Prioress (ten times);
along with such superlatives as "wol," "fully" and "right"
which are variously, and frequently, attributed. By stippled
hyperbole, as in the Franklin's portrait, which is developed
with such phrases as: "and that a greet," (1. 339); "Seint
Julian he was in his contree," (1. 340); "was alweys after
oon," (1. 341); "A bettre envyned man was nowher noon,"
(1. 342); "It snewed in his hous .../Of alle deyntees" (345–
46); "Was nowher swich a worthy vavasour" (1. 360). By the
single hyperbolizing line, as the Frere's "Ther nas no man
nowher so vertuous," the Man of Law's "So greet a purchasour
was nowher noon," the Reeve's "Ther koude no man brynge
hym in arrerage," and the Manciple's "And yet this Manciple
sette hir aller cappe."

Next, *the radix trait.* Chaucer focuses on a central charac-
teristic, and moves toward, or away from that point in the
ensuing presentation. This radical characteristic may include
other traits, because the critic can no more exhaust the char-
acter of the Pardoner by saying he is a compensating eunuch,
than one can define Hamlet by terming him an Oedipus type.
But on the whole, except with the few subtly complex char-
acters, such as the Pardoner and the Wife of Bath, the
single capital trait, with room for future nuances, suffices.
Thus the Knight can be described by "worthynesse," the
Squire by "youth," the Yeoman by "forester," and the Prioress
by "noblesse oblige." The Wife of Bath may be summed up by
"archwife," of disposition, eye, and conversation; the Monk

by "game," and the pinguid animality bespoken by the epithet it attaches to him; the Friar by "wantonnesse," the Merchant by "facade," and the Parson by "pastoral activity." A single dominating characteristic epitomizes and epithetizes the person, although that characteristic may be a compound or hyphenated one. This serves to reduce him not to flatness or to "nonentity," but to essence or disposition, so that over most of the characters hovers the "style" of antonomasia, whereby the very name bequeaths a memorable equivalent for the sum of traits which constitute the character. . . .

Further, *the quick glimpse at the interior man*. This is the unexpected percipient thrust which throws the character into momentary bold relief, and reveals much, as with the Physician:

(443–44)   For gold in phisik is a cordial,
            Therefore he lovede gold in special;

the Merchant:

(279–80)   This worthy man ful well his wit bisette:
            Ther wiste no wight that he was in dette;

the Sergeant of the Law:

(321–22)   Nowher so bisy a man as he ther nas,
            And yet he semed bisier than he was;

and the Pardoner:

(691)   I trowe he were a geldyng or a mare.

These are not explosive culminations, but always quiet interpolations, casually, almost fitfully inserted, with the surprise of discovery upon them, as if, indeed, Chaucer had just had the intuition. It is the very bland fortuity of the description, unpremeditated, uttered as it hit the author, without the slightest hint of artistic calculation, that lures the reader, and that has tended to baffle the professional critic. The apparent haphazardness and easy variety of this method can pass for a lack of method.

But these lines above and others like them remain as touchstones for the characters they interpret. Inconsecutive as they seem, they actually contrive to glance off the character at his most vulnerable, and illuminable spot. The potable gold of the physician is a detail that points up the physician's greed in terms of his own medicines, the dram that distills the innermost dream. The Merchant, mediaeval tycoon that he was, usurer and money speculator "with his bargaynes and with his chevyssaunce," rehearsing *ad nauseam* his profits, is also betrayed from virtue by an excess of professional *virtu* in his risky investments. It is part of the artfulness of these lines that they demand that constructions be put upon them, and correlative qualities be adduced by those tacit prose completions that every poetic insight encourages. And again the character is coupled with his class, with its strivings, and failings, and professional ingenuities, and the character errs in the way that is possible, and likely, for one in his state of life.

The Sergeant of the Law is a man of affairs, caught up in the flux of his office and his forays into land speculation. But the core of aimlessness and faineance at the center of the whirlwind life is exposed by the terribly tolerant afterthought, "And yet he semed bisier than he was." "I trowe," Chaucer says of the Pardoner's abnormality, "I would say, that" or "In my opinion," he was a gelding or a mare, and with such personal and artistic diffidence the whole nature of the Pardoner and his desperate attempts at social justification are intimated.

Nowhere is an author's attitude toward people, and especially toward his own creatures, so revealingly brought out as in this flash-framing of the individual. Sentimentality, misanthropy, pique, overbearing subjectivity in drawing his characters, all may come through in the tone with which he makes his revelations. But uniformly with Chaucer there are affection, good will, and objectivity visited upon his characters, so that they get the chance to be what, independently, they *have* to be, given the working out of those characteristics with which they have been endowed. It is crass for the author to interfere in their lives, and the sign of the artist is the capacity for letting them alone. We have with Chaucer, especially in his handling of this facet of characterization, the release of the character without meddling or compulsion.

Finally, *the use of disparate detail*. Chaucer may concentrate largely on a radical trait, but there is no radial progression from that point. The usual procedure for the writer is to describe a person either through the order of organic contiguity, though without the rigors of the mediaeval *ordo effictionis*, or, having selected some prominent facial or physical trait or moral quality, to radiate from that by contiguity or association. But discontinuity and incongruity of detail are Chaucer's stock in trade. His technique is the loudest kind of objection to the method of his day. He jumps from head to foot, from practice to person, from horse to rider, and even, as in the case of the Cook, from shinbone to cookery without any warning at all:

(386–87) ... on his shyne a mormal hadde he.
            For blankmanger, that made he with the beste.

To his contemporaries it must have seemed a delirious garbling of detail. But, again, it works. The glaring couplet from the description of the Cook excepted because it is extreme, the technique, as Shelly has so well put it,[14] is the collusion of impression from collision of detail. It is a pre-impressionistic technique relying heavily on the accepted categories of person and society, both to contrast with its effects, and to provide the copulas, the middle terms which are so startlingly omitted. Whether by clash or correspondence, by type or antitype, the incontiguity of detail is given congruence by the wholeness of the man and the organization of the society from which these verbal snapshots are taken. A plethora of detail would have given us thick, unwieldy figures; the ordered fulsomeness of the accepted *descriptio* would have given us dull *simulacra*. With his technique of suggestiveness and contrapuntal detail, Chaucer has achieved those characters which are, on the whole, representative of their class and personal in their attributes, credible, natural, and, most of all, alive.

C. The Parson's Prologue

The principal investigations of the closing of the CT have been concerned with its authenticity, sources, and Biblical authority.[14] Let us consider rather its relevancy to the whole frame. It is generally agreed that the choice of the Knight as the first speaker had a certain social inevitability. On a purely social level the Knight is the only eminence from which an entertainment like the Pilgrimage could be launched. It seems hardly necessary to argue this point. The beginning of the CT then is congruous and calculated. It is curious that few have troubled to ask whether the same may be said of the ending. Malone, however, has made the point well. "Chaucer has saved the parson to the last. He is to bring the Tales of Canterbury to an end. And this end must be devotional, pious, edifying rather than entertaining. . . . And now the parson tells his tale, to knit up a great matter. And from a mediaeval point of view the matter was indeed knit up well."[15]

There are unmistakable signs that Chaucer has deliberately selected the Parson as the teller of the last tale. In order to reserve this position for him it has been necessary to have him discouraged from coming forward earlier. He does not refuse. His effort is postponed—and the headlink of his Tale indicates that he is to be the last of the pilgrims to speak. He is, however, "a good man of religioun"—not the most influential of the religious represented on the pilgrimage, but the good one. Given his calling, this endows him with an excellence akin to the Knight's. It is reasonable that he should build his tale on penitence as the Knight has built his on chivalry. The Middle Ages, which had seen an emperor stand barefoot in the snow awaiting the pardon of a pope, understood far better than we can the hierarchy of values represented here.

There are three critical sections in any mediaeval literary work: the beginning, middle, and end. In the unfinished but not wholly inconclusive work, *The Canterbury Tales*, the middle cannot be localized, but the work is carefully and artfully inaugurated. If we concede that Chaucer has staked out a conclusion as well as an introduction, we may assume that it will be just as cleverly worked out. And there is evidence in the text that he intended to end with the *Parson's Tale*, though whether his narration was to coincide with the arrival at Canterbury, or the return to the Tabard, cannot be said. . . . The topographic reference *placing* the Parson's Prologue, "As we were entryng at a thropes ende," is vague. The thorp or village, unnamed, has no value as a landmark. Chaucer may have intended to emend with more precision, although such indeterminacy in this final link hints at a designed vagueness.

It is certain that the Host's "Lordynges everichoon,/ Now lakketh us no tales mo than oon" [X (I) 15–16], represents an unprepared-for abandonment of the original plan:

[I (A) 791–94] "That ech of yow, to shorte with oure weye,
In this viage shal telle tales tweye
To Caunterbury-ward, I mene it so,
And homward he shal tellen othere two."

Most of the pilgrims so far have told but one tale (some, none), with the exception of Chaucer the Pilgrim, whose two stories, the one farcically secular, the other gravely moral, may be held to represent the two levels of joy of the pilgrimage, *myrthe* and *gaudium*. The ending's contravention of the beginning can be explained, if you will, by the literary difficulty of effecting the scheme originally projected, which may be attributed to the literal length of the journey, the sanguine character of the Host, or to the author's overconfident creativity. But assembling some one hundred and twenty stories was perhaps too ambitious an undertaking for a man of desultory writing habits. So much for the liberal approach. On a literary plane we may observe that it is in the nature of the construct that the Parson conclude the tales of a journey whose destination becomes thereby neither Southwark nor Canterbury, but the Holy City of Jerusalem.

The Host certainly seems satisfied that his "ordinaunce" will have been kept when they have heard from the Parson [X (I) 19], and in saying "Fulfilled is my sentence and my decree;/ I trowe that we han herd of ech degree" [X (I) 17–18], he congratulates the pilgrims and himself on squaring with an implicitly altered plan or an anticipatedly fulfilled one.

The Host then addresses the Parson, demanding his tale, "For every man, save thou, hath toold his tale" [X (I) 25], with the admonition, "breke thou nat oure pley." The Host's aversion to the homiletic, or dull, or "inartistic" tale asserts itself again when he chides the Parson, who has been depicted in the *GP* with such benignity and piety and discretion, by proffering him impossible alternatives.

First, the Host declares, "For, trewely, me thynketh by thy cheere/ Thou sholdest knytte up well a greet mateere" [X (I) 27–28], and although the expression of the Parson is not described in the *GP*, the devotion and humility of the man indirectly convey to us some notion of his "cheere." But the Host impishly qualifies this "knitting-up" and consummating tale by the demand that it be a "fable"—with the challenge of an impatient interjection: "Telle us a fable anon, for cokkes bones!" [X (I) 29].

The Parson's matter-of-fact simplicity and unsophisticated literacy rear up at this invitation. Once before his tale had been put off. Now he has the privilege and the power to speak as he must. The fabulous, the delusory, the "art-pour-l'art" tale will not come from him. He invokes St. Paul in his letters to Timothy which reprove the circulation of fables. The texts are worth recording, because a distinctive and crucial mediaeval question is at stake here. St. Paul entreats Timothy:[17] "Not to give heed to fables and genealogies endless: which furnish questions rather than the edification of God, which is in faith. . . . But avoid foolish and old wives' fables: and exercise thyself unto godliness." Again, St. Paul exhorts Timothy,[18] in the famous passage which is retained in the liturgy of the Mass to celebrate the Common of a Doctor:

1. I charge thee, before God and Jesus Christ, who shall judge the living and the dead, by his coming, and his kingdom:
2. Preach the word: be instant in season, out of season, reprove, entreat, rebuke in all patience and doctrine.
3. For there shall be a time, when they will not endure sound doctrine; but, according to their own desires, they will heap to themselves teachers, having itching ears:
4. And will indeed turn away their hearing from the truth, but will be turned unto fables.

The Parson has staunchly refused to tell a "fable." He is understandably suspicious of the work that is literary and not scriptural in import. The opposition between the religious and cultural, the classical and the Biblical, the secular and the Christian is keenly realized by this intellectual puritan, and he sets about earnestly to construct an edifying and corrective discourse. Chaucer, too, was poignantly aware of the problem. As artist and Christian he had the example of Boccaccio before him, who had in the framework of the *Decameron* made the "effort to justify and protect a new art, an art which simply in order to be, to exist, required the moment free of all other cares, the willingness to stop *going anywhere* (either toward God or toward philosophical truth),"[19] but who had later and rather surprisingly recanted. *The Retraction*, therefore, is no random appendage, but is indissolubly linked, as we shall see, with the problem both of character and of narrative art that the text presents at that juncture.

Anything that threatens to deviate from or waive ("weyven") truth ("soothfastnesse") for the pursuit of pleasure ("fables" and "swich wrechednesse") jeopardizes the Christian, and the Parson calls upon the apostolic injunctions against such behavior. He evokes the parable of the sower and his wheat and chaff to challenge the Host's command. For his part, if they will give him audience, the Parson is going to purvey "moralitee and vertuous mateere," and he is perfectly willing to add to their legitimate or permissible pleasure ("plesaunce leefful"), "at Christes reverence." . . . The Host had in the Tabard enjoined the group to be "myrie," presumably both in behavior and story-telling. The Shipman,[20] while elbowing out the Parson, had asserted that he would preserve the group from the Parson's preachments with a "mery" tale. And the Parson, boldly, drolly removing the context from recreation to edification, avers that he will tell them a "myrie tale in prose." . . . The "myrie tale" proves to be nothing less than a baldly homiletic, sober-sided preachment, a doctrinal sermon whose merriment can be called so only in Bernardian and ascetical terms, not in the lexicon of the Host at all. That is, since it purposes to predispose its hearers to the "knoweleche of hym (God)" and "to the blisful life that is

perdurable," then is it signally "myrie" with a celestial
gaudium. Such a denotation for merry was prevalent enough
during the period. The NED defines one meaning of *mirth*
as "pleasurable feeling, enjoyment, gratification; joy, happi-
ness. Often used of religious joy. *Obs.*" Then it cites under
this definition "1340 Hampole *Psalter* Prol., & oft sith in til
soun & myrth of heven." There are two entries under *merry*
that are apposite here: "c 1325 *Spec.* Gy Warw. 905 Hu
murie hit were, to have the siht off godes face, that is so
briht"; and "1435 Misyn *Fire of Love* 57 No thinge is meriar
then Ihesu to synge." . . .

Now Chaucer through the *Tales* has cunningly manipulated
the mediaeval sermon and the rhetorical *gradus* contained in
it. He expertly tailored the sermon to dramatic fit for the
Pardoner, retaining theme, exemplum, peroration, and closing
formula, all converging artistically to present and betray the
Pardoner's avarice, falsity, and malice through his own forte,
preaching. The sermon has been lifted into the Pardoner's
own story as a dramatic element. The Nun's Priest, also di-
rected to "telle us swich thyng as may oure hertes glade"
(VII 2811 B₂ 4001), delivers an *exemplum*, a sermon extract,
but closes with an earnest reminder that is for the most part
overlooked:

(VII 3438–43) "But ye that holden this tale a folye,
(B₂ 4628–33) As of a fox, or of a cok and hen,
            Taketh the moralite, goode men.
            For seint Paul seith that al that writen is,
            To oure doctrine it is ywrite, ywis;
            Taketh the fruyt, and lat the chaf be stille."

The moral, didactic, and even allegorical intentions here are
made quite clear; this also gives the tale body and complexity
by setting it dramatically.

The Parson's evangelical address, however, is more immedi-
ately and substantially the sermon than any of the sermon
fragments Chaucer has dramatically intermingled through the
Tales. But there is no reason to suppose that because it in-
cludes the theme, the dilatation or exposition of the text, and
the peroration or application, that there is no dramatic affinity
between it and the pilgrimage. As a matter of fact it is most

cunningly and artistically intervolved with the whole, as are the preceding tales with their dramatic links. As we confront this problem, however, there are a few almost paradigmatic impressions and suggestions which we should bring to bear on what is a peculiarly mediaeval *locus* and *ratio* of the *CT:* the Parson's *Prologue,* Parson's *Tale,* and Chaucer's *Retractation.*

First, the theorists of his day would bid Chaucer to terminate his work either on the subject itself, or by a proverb, or by a general idea, with, of course, the ineluctable expression of thanks for divine inspiration. In each case its intention is to summarize or reflect aphoristically the work at hand. Chaucer was, as we have seen, more apt to concur with large outlines of technique than with the cramping details which would tie fast his own talents. . . . Since any pilgrimage is of its essence a rehearsal for death and the judgment, it is fitting for Chaucer in this climactic place in the story, in the pilgrimage, to make the Parson the spokesman, the mediator, the scourge, and the ender of it all. Person and topic make a suitable mediaeval finish for the story.

Next, "in the end, as in the beginning, the only real terminal value admitted in the mediaeval world is God and the vision of God."[21] As the Christian approaches his last end he is, as mentioned above, more attracted to it. "The Christian on earth is a traveler, *viator,* who is advancing spiritually toward God. His spiritual advancement is made by more and more perfect acts of love, 'steps of love,' as St. Gregory says. We must conclude from this that charity on earth can and should always increase, otherwise the Christian would cease in a sense to be a *viator:* he would stop before reaching the end of his journey. The way is intended for travelers. . ."[22] This penultimate instruction must be true to the role of the Parson. He knew very well that the superlative and only genuine good for the Christian was the sight of God, face to face, immeasurably and ecstatically loved. The end is infinite, so is the desire; therefore all men are pilgrims of the Absolute.

Last, although there were admitted historical divagations, and unfortunate ones, from the professed *raison* of the pilgrimage in the later mediaeval period, it still existed basically

as a penitential, reparative, and propitiatory venture, as a
religious epitome and a sacramental symbol of the "pèlerinage
de la vie de l'homme." The moral and allegorical values in-
escapably present to such a *peregrinatio* would be well recog-
nized by Chaucer, and will be developed below. With such
foreshadowings for guidance, let us return to the text to see if
these implications are justified.

The Parson has insisted on relating "moralities and
vertuous mateere," regarding this as "lawfully pleasant," and
a "myrie tale" to boot. This merry tale in prose is calculated
to do two things: to "knytte up al this feeste," and [X (I) 47]
to "make an ende," to bring the affair to a close. In knitting,
that is, fusing or gathering together all the parts of this feast,
or merriment, the Parson feels himself morally obligated to
bring it to an end that is honorable, reverential, and merry,
not with a secular merriment, but with a supernal one. And
the inevitable metaphor to be translated by the Parson's
dedicated mind and tongue, to a moral, to a religious exhorta-
tion, is that of the pilgrimage. He says, unreservedly, that with
the influx of the grace of Christ he will summon up wit enough

[X (I) 49–51]   To shewe yow the way, in this viage,
                 Of thilke parfit glorious pilgrymage
                 That highte Jerusalem celestial.

Christian teaching has always regarded heaven by analogy
as a city—*Coelestis urbs Jerusalem*—housing the *Catholica
societas,* the congregation of men and angels, the City of the
saints. Augustine called it: "Tota ipsa redempta civitas, hoc
est congregatio societasque sanctorum."[22]

The wording does not seem merely coincidental. . . . This
very pilgrimage to Canterbury is to be the spiritual, that is,
anagogical, figure for the pilgrimage to the heavenly Jeru-
salem. We cannot argue for the full-fledged application of the
mediaeval "quaternity of reality" or "fourfold meaning" here,
but the deliberate statement of a present concern, the pil-
grimage to Canterbury, signifying what relates to eternal
glory, is certainly a metaphorical prosecution of the *sensus
anagogicus:* ". . . prout vero significant ea quae sunt in aeterna
gloria est *sensus anagogicus.*"[24] Here the Canterbury Pil-

grimage becomes by metaphorical "pressure" the pilgrimage
to the Celestial City. Canterbury, the destination of the pil-
grims, becomes the City of God; the *wey* to Canterbury be-
comes the way to the City of God; the pilgrims, wayfarers in
time, become *potius mystice quam chronice,* wayfarers to
eternity. Chaucer's Canterbury Pilgrimage becomes, and this
is the *sovrasenso,* the pilgrimage of the life of man. This
makes the diversity of the tales part of its structure. The way-
wardness and frailty of the characters, the too human gropings
and anguish, the tears and tumult, diversions and banter, the
self-indulgences and the heroism, tensions and tenderness,
the hypocrisies and rue: these are the actions of that feckless
creature man in his human comedy. And if the postlude to
this comedy is beatitude, the last scene is playable for the
mediaeval Christian only with that dramatic propriety sanc-
tioned by the Parson.

The Parson replaces the Host ultimately as docent because
this is the function of a priest, not an innkeeper, and all the
pilgrims to Canterbury in becoming pilgrims to the Heavenly
Jerusalem must take the *wey* or *via* of Penitence. . . . And so
it does not seem an exaggeration to say that the destination of
the pilgrimage becomes, by the interlocked metaphorical and
dramatic structure, not so much the Canterbury shrine as the
Parson's Tale, because it unfolds the *wey* to Him who is the
way, the truth, and the light. We have noticed that the Parson
has been silenced before this, not allowed to speak. The
theology is sound in this respect. The economy of grace, and
the form of the fiction, dictate that the assent to the Parson's
priestly and metaphorical solicitation be voluntary, that there
be a cooperation on the part of the pilgrims with grace. The
"heer" of the Shipman's denial in the Epilogue of the *Man of
Law's Tale,* "heer schal he nat preche;/He schal no gospel
glosen here ne teche." [II (B) 1179–80], was right, dramatic-
ally, structurally, and "morally." An appearance there would
have been crassly inopportune from a structural consideration.
The last place is and must be reserved for the Parson, for he
plays the intercessory and ecclesiastical role at the end, the
most vital spot in the work. . . .

From such considerations as these, habitual, reflexive to the

mediaeval person, we can say that it was indeed advisable
for Chaucer to end upon some virtuous or holy business. Like-
wise it was seemly to give that member of the group who was
best qualified to speak at the end of the Tales, "space and
audience" in order that he might counsel the pilgrims to pre-
dispose them for that end which is potentially, always, the
now for the Christian. If the pilgrims could forget themselves,
under the hearty encouragings of the Host, so far as to "pleye
by the weye," then it behooved the Parson, the professional
admonisher and mediator, to recall them to the realization
that the *weye* was a *via*, that play had to be remedied by a
Christian work, that *fable* had to give place to *morality*, that
the readiness is all; that death is precarious for the Christian
not so much in its inevitability as in its unexpectedness, be-
cause the state of grace must be maintained up to and at the
moment of death. The Parson becomes, supremely, the Pastor
in the actual as well as the parabolic sense. And he does it
with a gently insistent humor that is not mealy-mouthed.

The Parson circumvents the Host by appealing directly to
the company for sufferance for his "myrie tale in prose."

[X (I) 52–54] "And if ye vouche sauf, anon I shal
Bigynne upon my tale, for which I preye
Telle youre avys. . ."

Thus, it is the group that assents to the Parson's proposal,
"Upon this word we han assented soone" [X (I) 61], because
"as it seemed, it was for to doone,/ To enden in som vertuous
sentence" [X (I) 62–63]. There is no attempt to placate the
Host in his former status as arbiter. Instead the pilgrims in-
struct the Host to transmit their decision to the Parson:

[X (I)65–66] And bade oure Hoost he sholde to hym seye
That alle we to telle his tale hym preye.

. . . He demands a fable "for *cokkes bones!*" a corruption of
"for *Goddes bones!*" Though the Parson does not reprimand
the Host for swearing here, he gainsays his supremacy by
appeal to the pilgrims. As Malone has indicated,[25] this is un-
exampled in the *CT*. The Parson displaces the Host as sponsor

and steps into genuine spiritual leadership, "Upon this word we han assented soone." The response to the Parson as parson is as unanimous here as had been the acclaim of the Host as host after the dinner in the *GP*. And this scene once and for all accentuates the respective roles of Host and Parson, the one a guide in the ways of the world, the other a guide in the spiritual way.

That the ensuing tale was no mere routine tailoring of the *Tales* to a platitudinous symmetry, in keeping with the rhetorical expediency of the period, should be obvious at a reading. The pilgrims nowhere exhibit the modern unrest with the homiletic cast of the "tale." It is undiluted sermonizing, but they do not rebel at it, as at the Monk's unrelieved recital of misfortune. It is the longest piece in the *CT*, yet they hear it out unmurmuring. This may argue not so much that it was enjoyable, but that it was recognizably needful and in order, that whatever may have occurred before on the journey, here were sense, symmetry, and the soundness upon which to end the *Tales*.

D. THE PARSON'S TALE

. . . The Parson begins his "tale" as the mediaeval preacher began his sermon, with the Biblical text. The verse is Jeremias 6:16: "(Sic dominus dicit): State super vias, et videte, et interrogate de viis antiquis que sit via bona, et ambulate in ea; et inuenietis refrigerium animabus vestris, etc."[26] . . .

The text is especially revealing because here, at the terminus of the *CT*, and the terminus at least *ad quem* of the journey, is the time for recollection, the moment meant to qualify the pilgrims for their visit to Canterbury, and to enable them to "put their house in order. . . ." Here at last the metaphor is realized (it never hardens into allegory), because the Parson has expressly noted that he wishes to show them the way, "in this viage,"

[X (I) 51–52] Of thilke parfit glorious pilgrymage
                  That highte Jerusalem celestial.

At the Parson's behest they take their stand upon the ways. The Jerusalem of Jeremias and the Old Testament has been translated in glory to heaven; it has become by virtue of the promise and the pleroma the City of the Elect as it was the stronghold of the Chosen People here below. The pilgrims must take their stand upon the ways and consider, before they can make their way thither. . . . As they consider and "ask of the ancient ways what is the good way," they look back at their own way of life. With the preposition *super,* which may mean *above* or *upon,* the crossroads of decision are beheld from the remove of reflection. By that action the trip to Canterbury becomes an epitome of the *via vitae,* for there comes that moment in every Christian life when the vision of the *via vitae sempiternae* intersects with the daily round, and it is this that we encounter here. . . .

Since the refreshment is to be forgiveness of his sins, the only way for the mediaeval Christian to obtain that reinstatement among the heavenbound, is for his foot to be set anew upon the path, and this necessary redirection of the faithful the Parson undertakes with the zeal of Jeremias. He is well-informed on these matters. A Christian theology demands as its faith-bound first premise that God wills that no man perish, that is, be sentenced to the eternal pains of hell, though there is the mooted question of predestination that still troubles the professional theologians, as it did Chaucer, too, who has given it much speculative room in his work.

But all are agreed that God wills the salvation of every soul, though the *meritum de congruo* (congruous merit) exacts the cooperative worthiness of each soul and his readiness at the fatal, final moment. The Parson recalls this at the outset, and reinforces this truth of faith with the further received doctrine that God, by corollary, wills that we "comen alle to the knoweleche of hym, and to the blisful lif that is perdurable." All roads may lead to Rome, but not all ways lead to heaven. There is one imperial way, the way suitable for the Christian, says the Parson, "which may nat fayle to man ne to woman that thurgh syne hath mysgoon fro the righte wey of Jerusalem celestial." The answer is quite plain to the Parson: "and this wey is cleped Penitence, of which man sholde gladly herknen and enquere with al his herte"; and then follows a scholastic presentation of the *status quaestionis,* defining the lines of investigation to be followed in his homily.

The treatise is authoritative and orthodox. It is dull only to those who regard the posing and discussion of such questions as the sport of, in Bacon's phrase, *sectores cymini,* as a sophistry. It holds no general appeal for the modern reader, and even the Chaucerian scholar reads it for the most part out of a spirit of dedicated drudgery. The same contemptuous modernity is apt to dismiss mediaeval scholasticism as a bootless logic-chopping under the "angels-on-a-pin" absurdity, unmindful of the fact that the very question confronted, by analogy, the problem of the impenetrability of bodies—dynamic vs. static theories—which has been a major consideration of modern physics. This attitude may be reflected in the mentality that prefers to find the *Parson's Tale* spurious or un-Chaucerian, or, at best, a grubbing concession to his mediaeval auditors. But, word for word, principle for principle, it is not too much to say that Chaucer himself might have claimed it the most meaningful, and in a dialectical, perhaps even a dramatic sense, the most artistic of the *Tales.* To insist that a sermon is dramatic may seem at first blush tendentious, but the *Parson's Tale* can be considered non-dramatic only if it is regarded in itself, completely detached from the *Tales.* Yet such a reading of the *Parson's Tale,* or the complexus of the *Tales,* would pervert the work. For we know that Chaucer never allows us to forget for long that each story is part of a total situation, and if indices of structure, with emphatic expression of intent, mean anything, then the *Parson's Tale* is not only the capstone of edification but of drama as well. For when its pulsing relationship and organization with the rest of the Tales and the pilgrimage proper is marked, it becomes, in its own way, very dramatic. The *Parson's Tale,* or treatise, if you will, has been carefully articulated with the rest by Chaucer in its Prologue. Its importance and place have been emphasized. Implicitly it recapitulates and musters into dramatic unity all the silent symmetries of the other tales and the *viage* as such.

Every one of the pilgrims must recognize his sins, secret and public, as the Parson in the second part of the Tale treats of the seven mortal sins, "Sequitur de septem peccatis mortalibus et eorum dependenciis circumstanciis et speciebus." The first section of the homily had been given over to the need for Penitence and an inquiry into its salvific nature. To follow this incitation to Penance with an explanation of the sacrament of confession *(prima pars Penitentie)*, and then to climax the talk with the treatment of the seven deadly sins *(secunda pars Penitentie)*—which are matter for confession, their branches, and their remedies to be applied in following out the commandment of Christ, "Be ye perfect. . . ."—is to project the inner drama of the confessional against the cavalcade to Canterbury and eternity. That the tale and the scene it involves are not without drama is brought out most poignantly, because it even excites a public confession from Chaucer himself. Its spiritual, dramatic, and purgative effects cannot be gainsaid; the *Parson's Tale* marks the culmination of the pilgrimage, and Chaucer's immediate recantation is the denouement of the pilgrim-drama. Its very suddenness, without preparation, without explanations, except those latent in the drama, would be a turn of event quite understandable to the mediaeval mind acquainted with the mercurial nature of grace and with the Spirit that "bloweth where He listeth." Chaucer and his pilgrims realized that they have jollied one another, and bandied about triviality, entertainment, and bawdry on the journey. But the ever-present, ever-prescient *memento mori* sets a date of death upon every action, and signs it for all eternity. The terms and finalities of a sacramental system made the beginning of the end a somewhat more obtrusive daily fact than it is today. There is its warning to "learn to die daily," with the omnipresence of the Four Last Things: Death, Judgment, Hell, Heaven. There is the terrible knowledge that the soul is bound not by time but by state or condition, and the conviction that "a happy death is death in the state of grace, the death of the predestinate or elect." Finally, there is the realization that such a happy death is a special gift, that one cannot presume upon the providence of God, and that the person, either living or moribund, has no right to the grace of final perseverance. . . .

The Parson notes, "Soothly synnes been the weyes that

leden folk to helle" [X (I) 141], and here is the moment of recollection, and rerouting, for here they must stand upon the ways, and inquire of the ancient ways where lies the royal road to salvation. This, it should be pointed out, is no quixoticism of the faith, or the faithful. The Council of Trent, for example, has underscored the necessity of penance by decreeing that the sacrament of penance is no less necessary for clearing the way to salvation for those who have fallen into mortal sin after baptism, than baptism for those who have never been baptized. It is the pause preceding the step into heaven or hell.

The souls are enjoined to *"state super vias"* because the first step in rectifying the disobedience of the precept imposed upon every son of God, that of imitating the saints, is to consider the "diversas operationes bonorum et malorum ut utrorumque progressum et exitum videatis."[71] The *viae*, the various roads that all the pilgrims have traveled in their Specific Actions which severally comprise the Enveloping Action of the pilgrimage, must now be reconsidered from this spiritual vantage point. *"Stemus super vias,"* cries the Parson through the chastened lips of Jeremias, discalced of the sandals of vanity and ingratitude and iniquity which have retarded our progress, and let us stride forward on the way, freedmen, not bondmen.

Nor is the *Parson's Tale*, it must be remarked again, told in complete dissociation from the rest. Each pilgrim and his story combine with the Parson's homily to make a momentary —and moving—diptych, a story and gloss, action and passion. This confers a sense of completeness which such episodic fictions often lack. Though most is left unresolved, little is left "unexplained."

The Pardoner is avaricious and gluttonous, he is a blasphemer and a simonist. . . . Could the Pardoner have been unmoved by the return of his text? "After Accidie wol I speke of Avarice and of Coveitise, of which synne seith Seint Paul that 'the roote of alle harmes is Coveitise.' *Ad Thimotheum Sexto./* For soothly, whan the herte of a man is confounded in itself and troubled, and that the soule hath lost the confort of God, thanne seketh he an ydel solas of worldly thynges/" [X (I) 739–40]. Simony, "the grettest synne that may be, after the synne of Lucifer and Antecrist" [X (I) 788], pricks the conscience of him who had "in latoun a sholder-boon/ Which that was of an hooly Jewes sheep" [VI (C) 350–351]. The Parson further reproaches those "false en-chauntours or nigromanciens in bacyns ful of water, or in a bright swerd, in a cercle, in a fir, or in a schulderboon of a sheep" [X (I) 603].

The Wife of Bath is prideful, inobedient, and "likerous," a prattler and a scold. All these traits are castigated by the Parson. Did she not wince especially at these words of the Parson? "And yet is ther a privee spece of Pride, that waiteth first to be salewed er he wole salewe, al be he lasse worth than that oother is, peraventure; and eek he waiteth or desireth to sitte, or elles to goon above hym in the wey, or kisse pax, or been encensed, or goon to offryng biforn his neighebor,/ and swiche semblable thynges; agayns his duetee, peraventure, but that he hath his herte and his entente in swich a proud desir to be magnified and honoured biforn the peple" [X (I) 407–408]. She is the target for his extended comments in the discussion of *Remedium contra peccatum luxurie* [X (I) 914–955], with its incisive "ther neden none ensamples of this" [X (I) 927]. And as a classic shrew, per-haps her capital sin, she would have recognized the justness of the reproval of "chidynge." "And how that chidynge be a vileyns thyng bitwixe alle manere folk, yet is it certes moost uncovenable bitwixe a man and his wyf; for there is nevere reste" [X (I) 631].

The Monk had been twitted by the Host for his soundness of body. His devotion to its exercise in hunting and riding is reproached by the Parson: "As for to speken of heele of body, certes it passeth ful lightly, and eek it is ful ofte enchesoun of the siknesse of oure soule. For, God woot, the flessh is a ful greet enemy to the soule; and therfore, the moore that the body is hool, the moore be we in peril to falle./ . . . . And over al this, strengthe of body and worldly hardynesse causeth ful ofte many a man to peril and meschaunce" [X (I) 458–460]. The Monk too might be the target of the Parson's animadver-sions on richness of riding apparel and equipment: "Also the synne of aornement or of apparaille is in thynges that apertenen to ridynge, as in to manye delicat horses that been hoolden for delit, that been so faire, fatte, and costlewe;/ and also in many a vicious knave that it sustened by cause of hem; and in to curious harneys, as in sadeles, in crouperes, peytrels, and bridles covered with precious clothyng, and riche barres and plates of gold and of silver./ For which God seith by Zakarie the prophete, 'I wol confounde the rideres of swiche horses'" [X (I) 432–34].

The Merchant who was suspected of usury and who "wolde the see were kept for any thyng/ Bitwixe Middelburgh and Orewelle," is rebuffed with the observation: "Now comth deceite bitwixe marchaunt and marchant . . . . Of thilke bodily marchandise that is leveful and honest is this: that, there as God hath ordeyned that a regne or a contree is suffisaunt to hymself, thanne is it honest and leveful that of habundaunce of this contree, that men helpe another contree that is moore nedy . . . . That oother marchandise, that men haunten with fraude and trecherie and deceite, with lesynges and false othes, is cursed and dampnable" [X (I) 777–80].

The Franklin is the prime example of the sins of pride and gluttony. He in whose house it snowed of meat and drink is taken to task with clasping at least three of the five fingers of the devil's hand that "draweth folk to synne," according to St. Gregory's "speces of Glotonye." "The firste is for to ete biforn tyme to ete. The second is whan a man get hym to delicaat mete or drynke . . . . The fourthe is curiositee, with greet entente to maken and apparaillen his mete" [X (I) 828–29].

The Host has been rebuked by the Parson for his swearing earlier. Again, more formally, the Host hears: "For Christes sake, ne swereth nat so synfully in dismembrynge of Crist by soule, herte, bones, and body. For certes, it semeth that ye thynke that the cursede Jewes ne dismembred nat ynough the preciouse persone of Crist, but ye dismembre hym moore" [X (I) 591].

The Reeve and the Miller, the Friar and the Summoner are the quarrelsome pairs. Their strife is decried with "thanne stant Envye, and holdeth the hoote iren upon the herte of man with a peire of longe toonges of long rancour;/ and thanne stant the synne of Contumelie, or strif and cheeste, and bartereth and forgeth by vileyns reprevynges./ Certes, this cursed synne anoyeth bothe to the man hymself and eek to his neighebor. For soothly, almoost al the harm that any man dooth to his neighebor comth of wratthe" [X (I) 556–57].

The Miller's drunkenness, as well as the Cook's, is impugned as the "horrible sepulture of mannes resoun" [X (I) 822]. The Friar and the Summoner display not only envy and wrath [X (I) 491–92] but the Summoner is a lecher and a glutton, summarily dealt with under *gula* and *luxuria* in the Parson's catalogue. The Friar is a flatterer, and the Parson's "Flatereres been the develes chapellyns, that syngen evere *Placebo*" [X (I) 617] echoes the sentiments of the Friar in the *Summoner's Tale* who "Syngeth *Placebo*, and 'I shal, if I kan'/ But if it be unto a povre man" [III (D) 2075–76].

Every one of the sins has its perpetrators among the pilgrims. It is against the blandishments and entanglements threatening their souls at that moment that the Parson assiduously, spiritually struggles. And it is a struggle. If drama is basically a matter of conflict, then this is conflict of the gravest sort, because in context the Parson is battling not only against the "principalities and powers" behind all evil, but more specifically, and dramatically, against the weaknesses and sins which have been displayed *en route*, which call for correction and repentance. The various paths of the Tales are confronted with the Way; the many features of truth gaze on Truth itself; and the inner lights of the several pilgrims behold the Light. God is present throughout the *CT*, but nowhere is he so systematically presented as he is in the *Parson's Tale*. Not with sensationalism nor melodrama, nor even with overt drama, but with the starkness of the conflict of good and evil, for the stake of eternal happiness— that is the order of the drama earnestly performed by the humble Parson and his "parishioners"; one such as is understood beneath Sir Walter Raleigh's "The Pilgrimage" and St. Thomas More's *On The Four Last Things*.

. . . It is, we would say, dangerous in the sense of quite misleading to read Chaucer—and the temptation is stronger to read him this way than any other mediaeval English writer—with a post-Freudian, post-agnostic, post-materialistic twist to one' thinking. It appears that the mediaeval *morale* not only is hospitable to, but actually urges, the evaluation made above. For the Parson says in a remarkable summary paragraph, that points up the whole Tale, and tales, and pilgrimage, and Pilgrimage:

> Thanne shal men understonde what is the fruyt of penaunce; and, after the word of Jhesu Crist, it is the endelees blisse of hevene,/ ther joye hath no contrarioustee of wo ne grevaunce; ther alle harmes been passed of this present lyf; ther as is the sikernesse fro the peyne of helle; ther as is the blisful compaignye that rejoysen hem everemo, everich of otheres joye;/ ther as the body of man, that whilom was foul and derk, is moore cleer than the sonne; ther as the body that whilom was syk, freele, and fieble, and mortal, is inmortal, and so strong and so hool that ther may no thyng apeyren it;/ ther as ne is neither hunger, thurst, ne coold, but every soule replenyssed with the sighte of the parfit knowynge of God./ This blisful regne may men purchace by poverte espiritueel, and the glorie by lowenesse, the plentee of joye by hunger and thurst, and the reste by travaille, and the lyf by deeth and mortification of synne./ [X (I) 1076–80]

Here indeed the "endless bliss of heaven" is the "fruit of penance."

E. CHAUCER'S RETRACTION

... It has been clear that the man Chaucer has had some misgivings about the moral latitude and exemptions of the artist. In the *caveat* he issued to the reader in the Miller's *Prologue,* he displayed a certain chagrin, in a privative impersonal construction, "M'athynketh that I shal reherce it heere," that is, "I repent that," or "I regret that," or "it is displeasing to me that..." He has not been altogether easy in his mind on this matter. Also, later, in the Introduction to the *Man of Law's Tale,* when Chaucer has the Man of Law review his works, the lawyer attests to our author's refusal to tell repulsive or incestuous tales, the former first remarking "(Of swiche cursed stories I sey fy!)." This may well be a jibe at Gower, who treated such themes in his

Confessio Amantis, but it is also a deliberate rejection of such story matter by Chaucer himself, confirmed a few lines later. The Man of Law, who knows the value of testimony, says of Chaucer:

[II (B) 86–89] And therfore he, of ful avysement,
Nolde nevere write in none of his sermons
Of swiche unkynde abhomynacions,
Ne I wol noon reherce, if that I may.

The double standard quietly applied here seems to be that any *sermon,* preachment, harangue, discourse should offend in no manner, whereas the story told out of "game," "pleye," the sheerly recreative tale, might have broader acceptance. That has been the excuse of Chaucer the artist thus far in the *Tales.* We have dwelt upon the eschatological outlook of the mediaeval person, man and artist, and the fact that the end, like the beginning, is the eternal instant of the Christian comedy and the Christian tragedy. That moment is fraught with the *mysterium tremendens* of the conflict of good and evil, the instant of unalterable choice. It is in this mood that Chaucer then proceeds with his "confession."

First, if there is anything admirable, or likable, or stimulating to virtue for the auditors or readers of "this litel tretys," then thanks should be directed to "oure Lord Jhesu Crist," who is the author of all wit and goodness. All achievements are to be ascribed to Christ. Second, if there is anything unpleasant or censurable therein, it should be attributed to a defection of technique and ability, not to a perverse will. He, the author, is reprehensible for all failures and blemishes, and he is quite willing to take the blame. Third, because the bible ("oure book") says, "All that is written is written for our doctrine," and *"that is myn entente."* Therefore, as a result of these considerations, Chaucer beseeches their collective prayers that Christ have mercy upon him and forgive him his sins. His first solicitation is that they pray for the forgiveness of *all* his sins, but especially ("namely"): the translations and writings flawed by worldly vanities, which he hereby disavows. This is the sin of Chaucer the artist, who has presumed over Chaucer the man, and the only restitution is recantation—but, observe, a *recantation within a general and public confession.*

This is the prayer that Christ in His great mercy will forgive him that sin. If the Monk was a hedonist, if the Pardoner was a simoniac, if the Wife of Bath was a "wanderer by the way," if all were signed with their stigmas and their vices, they were not alone. The Chaucer of fiction here bows to Chaucer the man, the viator, who is answerable for his fictions. Yet, be it noted that of the *CT* he apologizes only for those tales that "sownen into synne," and this word *sownen* Professor Robinson translates as "tend toward."

Chaucer knew, with uncomfortable sensitivity, perhaps as only a mediaeval Christian could, the insuppressible arrogance, defiance, and libertinism that lurked in the artist. Though that part of his nature showed an admirable technical discipline, still any moral trespass must be acknowledged and repented for. And so we are asked to credit to the grace of Our Lord Jesus Christ what is good, and to blame what is displeasing on the limitations of his creature, Geoffrey Chaucer, "for. . . 'Al that is writen is writen for oure doctrine', and that is myn entente." Could an author be more specific?

With the ages of faith far behind us, it is easy to dismiss the "retraciouns" as a conventional and probably meaningless formula. Looking at the literature of the middle ages from any historical point of view it is inevitable that one reach such a conclusion. It has been stated as freely that spring is the conventional season for beginning a mediaeval work. But this answer is statistical rather than explanatory. Conventions arise out of convictions and the note of conviction is strong in this appendage to a treatise on Penance, which is appended in its turn to an account of a fictional penitential journey. Its tone is not literary, not rote-religious but confessional—and shows marked signs of the influence, if position and terminology are of any significance, of the *Parson's Tale* just concluded. Chaucer supplicates Christ, Our Lady, and the saints of heaven as intermediators with God, that henceforth, even to the end of his life, they should vouchsafe him the grace to suffer sorrow for his sins, to give heed

to the salvation of his soul, and grant him the triple repara-
tive grace of true penitence, confession, and satisfaction "to
doon in this present lyf," whose *gradus* had been developed
most minutely by the Parson in his tale. The very phraseology
of the Parson's treatise is repeated here, which seems to bring
the structures together in more than editorial juxtaposition.
This is for Chaucer the *Confessioun of Mouth* [X (I) 107]
necessary to "verray perfit Penitence." It is, if we accept the
Parson's Tale as representative of the theological thinking of
Chaucer's church, a type of "solempne penance" demanded
"when a man hath synned openly, of which synne the fame
is openly spoken in the contree" [X (I) 103]. For if there
were common talk of Gower's literary trespasses against the
decencies, we may reason that Chaucer's were subject to the
same kind of criticism.

. . . Chaucer has experienced contrition of heart and
confession of mouth. Some of the others would seem to have
been touched by it. The Reve is a pilgrim whose sardonic
disillusionment at life is a notable forerunner of the full-
fledged confessional prologues of the Wife of Bath and the
Pardoner, two of the most complex and fascinating char-
acters in all English literature, both of whom are colorful
and flagrant sinners. Yet the drama of their self-revelation
is enhanced by a rueful, unwilling, puzzled acknowledge-
ment that something is amiss. The Wife of Bath, with a mix-
ture of humor and compunction, remarks: "Allas! Allas!
that evere love was synne!" [III (D) 614]. Even the Par-
doner, though he recovers himself immediately, has one
flash of painful sincerity:

[VI (C) 916–18] And Jhesu Crist, that is oure soules leche,
So graunte yow his pardoun to receyve,
For that is best; I wol yow nat deceyve.

And the pardon of Jesus Christ can be received only by
those who fulfill the conditions for it.

L'Ymage du Monde has reminded us that we travel dili-
gently on this our pilgrimage since we have but "trois jour-
nees a cheminer: l'une des dictes trois journess est Contrition
et l'autre Confession, et la tierce est Satisfaction"—the com-

ponents of "verray Penitence." The Canterbury pilgrims ar-
rive not at a saint's shrine, but at a saint's convictions, and
Chaucer in his own voice then makes his public confession,
"so that I may been oon of hem at the day of doom that
shulle be saved" [X (I) 1091]. Then the narrator is iden-
tified, either by editorial rubric or by himself, for the first
time: "Heere is ended the book of the tales of Caunterbury,
compiled by Geffrey Chaucer, of whos soule Jhesus Crist
have mercy. Amen."

Yet with this word *compiled*, whoever is responsible for it,
Chaucer steps back into the frame, back into the character of
Chaucer the Pilgrim; and this is fitting, for if the motif of
pilgrimage has been resolved in the treatise on Penance,
the dual identity of Chaucer as author and pilgrim needs
resolution also. For though the *Canterbury Tales* is incom-
plete, it cannot be properly called unfinished. The ending is
as neatly calculated as the beginning. Even the conventional
metaphor, the springtime, has fostered one conspicuous, sym-
bolic tree, the tree of Penitence, whose roots thrust through
and whose branches overspread the world of the Canterbury
pilgrims.

Notes

[1] Helmut A. Hatzfeld, "Esthetic Criticism Applied to Medieval
Romance Literature," *RPh.*, I (1948), 324.

[2] Albert S. Cook, *Chaucerian Papers—I*, Transactions of the Con-
necticut Academy of Arts and Sciences (New Haven, 1919),
XXIII, pp. 5–10.

[3] *Notes to the Canterbury Tales*, Vol. V, *The Complete Works of
Geoffrey Chaucer*, ed. Walter W. Skeat (2d ed., Oxford, 1900),
pp. 1–2.

[4] John E. Hankins, "Chaucer and the *Pervigilium Veneris*,"
MLN, XLIV (1934), 80–83, Rosemond Tuve, "Spring in Chaucer
and Before Him," *MLN*, LII (1937), 9–16, comments upon
Hankins' article and urges that "Chaucer's seasons-descriptions,
particularly that in the Prologue, are a sort of amalgam, fusing
many lines of development." It was a complicated tradition that
included classical Latin and Carolingian poetry, encyclopaedists
and comput-writers, Old French lyric and romance, hymnwriters,
the *Horae* and the Psalters, zodiacal and astrological details, as
well as "*Venus-genetrix*-Goddess" and "*Natura-creatrix*-governess"
attitudes toward the Spring (*Ver.*). It would be virtually impossi-

ble, Miss Tuve argues here, to hit upon a single contributory source for the GP.

⁵ *Bedae Opera De Temporibus,* ed. C. W. Jones (Cambridge, 1943), pp. 6–7.

⁶ *Aelfric's De Temporibus Anni,* ed. Heinrich Henel, Early English Text Society, O. S. 213 (London, 1942), p. 18. ["In brief, the first day of this world is calculated to have been the day we call the fifteenth before the calends of April—the equinox takes place, as Bede teaches, the fourth day after, that is, on the twelfth day before the calends."]

⁷ Jones, p. 7.

⁸ T. S. Eliot, "Shakespeare and the Stoicism of Seneca," *Selected Essays* (3rd ed., London, 1951), p. 137.

⁹ T. S. Gregory, *The Unfinished Universe* (New York, 1936), p. 317.

¹⁰ *Byrthferth's Manual,* Vol. I, ed. S. J. Crawford, Early English Text Society, O. S. 177 (Oxford, 1929), p. 153. "*Aprilis quasi 'aperilis' dicitur.* April is so called because it is as it were the 'opener.' In its time the trees are opened to flower and plants to grow."

¹¹ Jones, pp. 286–87. [". . . we take care to approach the celebration of the Lord's pasch according to the provisions of the law, so that the solemnity in which the Mediator between God and man, having destroyed the power of darkness, opened the way of light to the world will, even in the season when it is held, show forth externally its inner value. The pasch, which offers to us the light of eternal blessedness, is celebrated at that special time when the light of the sun, in its yearly increase, has its first victory over the shadow of night."]

¹² "Pilgrimage," *Encyclopedia of Religion and Ethics,* Vol. X (New York, 1919), 12.

¹³ Kate O. Petersen, *The Sources of the Parson's Tale,* Radcliffe College Monographs, N. 12 (Boston, no date), p. 3, n. 5 ["St. Peter says that we are all pilgrims in this world and that we travel day and night, without ceasing, toward our native land, which is in heaven. And for recreation, like true pilgrims who gladly converse as they go their journey, we too talk a little in going our pilgrimage, which is to paradise. We travel hard and we have but three days on the road. Of these days, the first is contrition, the second is confession, the third is satisfaction."]

¹⁴ Percy Van Dyke Shelly, *The Living Chaucer* (Philadelphia, 1940), chapt. VIII, *passim.*

¹⁵ Emil Koeppel, "Ueber das Verhältnis von Chaucers Prosawerken zu seinen Dichtungen und die Echtheit der 'Parson's Tale,'" *Herrig's Archiv,* LXXXVII (1891), 33–54. Kate O. Petersen, *op. cit.*

¹⁶ Kemp Malone, *Chapters on Chaucer* (Baltimore, 1951), pp. 214–15.

¹⁷ *I Tim.* 1:4 and *I Tim.* 4:7.

¹⁸ *II Tim.* 4:1–4.

¹⁹ Charles Singleton, "On Meaning in the *Decameron,*" *Italica,* XXI (1944), 117–24.

²⁰ II (B) 1178–83. The mooted identity of the speaker has no bearing on the problem in context.

[21] Singleton, p. 119.

[22] Reginald Garrigou-LaGrange, O. P., *The Three Ages of the Interior Life*, Vol. I, trans. Sr. M. Timothea O'Doyle, O. P. (St. Louis, 1949), p. 130.

[23] St. Augustine, *De Civitate Dei, PL*, vol. 41, 284.

[24] *Summa Theologica*, I, 1, 10, *ad. resp.* [". . . insofar as things in eternal glory are signified, this is the anagogical sense."]

[25] *Chapters*, p. 215.

[26] ["Thus saith the Lord: Stand ye on the highways, and look about, and ask concerning the old ways, which is the good way, and walk ye in it; and ye shall find refreshment for your souls."]

[27] Sancti Thomae Aquinatis, *Opera Omnia*, Vol. XIV, *In Jeremiam* (New York, 1949), p. 595 [". . . the differing actions of good men and bad, so that you may see the development and final end of both"].

3

Daun Piers, Monk and Business Administrator

PAUL E. BEICHNER, C.S.C.

CERTAIN points concerning Chaucer's Monk need emphasis, or at least adequate consideration, lest one lose sight of a brilliant piece of character creation while following the scent of satire against particular abuses of monastic discipline.

Once Chaucer had decided to include a monastic character among his group of pilgrims, he wished, I think we can assume, to make him as interesting as possible. A cloisterer, whose horizons were limited to the routine monastic existence of chanting the Office and attending liturgical services at regular intervals throughout a day broken by periods of study or work in the scriptorium or monastic housework, would have been insipid fare. On the other hand, an abbot would have outranked everyone on the pilgrimage—a lord spiritual like a bishop but a feudal lord, nevertheless, who received homage and fealty (*homagia et fidelitates*) from his tenants, who had perhaps not only churches but also a monastic borough under his jurisdiction, "a lord of gret auctorite" able to exert influence in both church and state by his mere position. An abbot would not fit the plan for the pilgrimage unless an earl or count were included as a

Reprinted, by permission of author and editor, from *Speculum*, XXXIV (1959), 611–19.

balance. If both were included, each would have to be accompanied by an appropriate retinue. But the problem of tact would still remain. It would be better to have a monastic *official* wielding little or no spiritual authority. An outrider offered intriguing possibilities. He could be up-to-date, progressive, an "organization man" (monastic, of course), able to be an abbot as far as dealing with the world and getting along with people is concerned. He could speak his mind freely as an individual without the fear that his opinions might be taken as official pronouncements; he could have the expensive tastes of the wealthy; he could be a sportsman, the complete hunter. Chaucer knew what he was doing in selecting an outrider.

The key fact concerning the Monk, which is usually obscured by other considerations but in relation to which the details of the portraiture must be weighed, is that he is a member of the administration of his order—specifically the business administration. His duties and views are expected to be different from those of the simple monk of the cloister. Although readers sometimes forget it, even the Host knows that the Monk is

> No povre cloysterer, ne no novys,
> But a governour, wily and wys.[1]

We can regret that the Host's efforts failed to determine the exact office or offices the Monk held or to extract a monastic job-analysis from him:

> Upon my feith, thou art som officer,
> Som worthy sexteyn, or som celerer,
> For by my fader soule, as to my doom,
> Thou art a maister whan thou art at hoom.[2]

But we can be enlightened by considering as the Monk's modern parallel the business officer of a college or university, church-related or not, or the official in charge of fund raising or public relations. We do not expect such men to have the same ideas, even on education, as a freshman English teacher; and, privately or among others whose job for a nonacademic organization might be similar to their own, they can very easily speak what would sound like educational heresy to the teaching staff. They are more likely to be sports enthusiasts than education enthusiasts. Yet we must admit that they perform a useful function for the university of our time, even though such officials may not have been envisaged by the founding fathers of our older institutions.

According to the *Oxford English Dictionary*, an "outrider" was "an officer of an abbey or a convent, whose duty it was to attend to the external domestic requirements of the community, especially to look after the manors belonging to it." The word is used in the Scottish legend of St Theodora for the purchasing agent of a monastery. And Chaucer's Shipman says that the monk of his fabliau, because he was an officer and a man of high prudence, had received the permission of his abbot "out for to ryde as hym list"—to come and go as he saw fit—"to seen hir graunges and hire bernes wyde."[3] "Outrider" seems to be the vernacular for any monk who did monastery business with the world, regardless of his exact monastic office within the order. Although there is no Latin equivalent for "outrider," a number of obedientiaries or monastic officials could have been so designated. In his book, *The Religious Orders in England*, Dom David Knowles never uses the word. An outrider was a monk holding any monastic office, obedience, or job requiring travel on business, just as the modern term "traveling salesman" means the salesman who travels and is not confined to the home sales department, a "business cloister," if you like. To restrict an outrider's movements to the confines of the monastery would be tantamount to taking away his capacity to perform the job given to him by monastic superiors in virtue of obedience. It seems necessary to make this statement because there seems to be more familiarity nowadays with St Benedict's sixth-century Rule on the point of claustration than with monastic administration in the thirteenth and fourteenth centuries and the provisions of general or provincial chapters for administrators. Chaucer would have looked upon monks away from the cloister much as we should look upon military personnel away from their base; we presume that they have proper authorization to be where they are and not that they are A.W.O.L. until we are sure of the contrary. It is also well to keep in mind that Chaucer never had the opportunity to look into bishops' registers or monastic secret archives to determine abuses, just as we do not have access to the similar documents of our own day.

At this point it is well to dissociate the Monk on the pilgrimage from the monk in the *Shipman's Tale;* both are outriders, but for entirely different reasons. Having decided to use an ecclesiastic in the role of the deceiver in the *Shipman's Tale,* whose analogues in Boccaccio and Sercambi have a soldier in the same role, Chaucer would have seen immediately that an outrider would fit the basic plot with most plausibility. No one would raise an eyebrow about his comings and goings, his staying over night in the household of a merchant, and his need for a short-term loan to buy livestock. A friar, a mendicant, would have been incongruous in the same role, not from the point of view of absence from his convent but from the point of view of asking for a loan. He would have wanted an outright gift. The monk of the *Shipman's Tale* is an outrider because of plot requirements, but the Monk on the pilgrimage is an outrider for reasons of character portrayal.

Is the Monk more than an outrider? Is he a superior in charge of monks, or an official in charge of temporalities or property? By a nice ambiguity Chaucer gives the impression that he is the latter. He was certainly a fair prelate.[4] Although *prelatus* and *subditus* as correlative terms mean "superior" and "subject," taken alone *prelatus* or "prelate" means "dignitary." An outrider, an obedientary would qualify as a prelate. Thus Chaucer emphasizes that in his expensive clothes with marks of high fashion the Monk looks the dignitary. "Ther as this lord was kepere of the celle"[5] is sometimes used to prove that he was a prior, but here again the terminology is not clear-cut. If Chaucer had wished to emphasize that he was a prior, he would have called him a prior; he made certain that everyone understood that Madam Eglentyne was a prioress and not a mere official of her convent or order. "Keeper" means "custodian," "warden," someone in charge of some *thing* rather than some *one,* just as in

royal officialdom there were keepers of various things—the
seal, the wardrobe, etc. "Cell" usually means a dependent
religious house, the people rather than the property. The
monastic economy of the time, however, depended heavily
on scattered and parcelled estates administered by officials
with an independence checked by the necessity of rendering
accounts or turning over produce to the chief monastery;
and the impression Chaucer wishes to convey is that the
Monk thinks like an outrider in terms of monastic possessions.
At any rate, a keeper of a manor (not a keeper of a cell) in
the mind of John Peckham, O.F.M., archbishop of Canter-
bury, could not have been a prior but a supervisory official,
for he ordered the prior of Christ Church, Canterbury, not
to appoint monks as keepers of manors but, following his own
example, to appoint laymen. He gave as his reason that
monks should not be distracted by the custody of manors,
for a monk out of the monastery is like a fish out of water:
"Sicut enim piscis sine aqua, sic sine monasterio monachus
existere affirmatur."⁶ This is one version of the old bromide
for which Chaucer's Monk would not give an oyster.

Having established the point that Chaucer is preoccupied
with presenting a monastic official and not a cloisterer on a
holiday, we are in a position to examine the Monk's views
and attitudes. In the presentation in the *General Prologue*
Chaucer's fiction is that he is reporting the salient points of
an intimate conversation—a conversation which is as much the
Monk's apologia for his job and personal inclinations as the
Wife of Bath's prologue to her tale is an apologia for her
vocation as oft-wedded wife and for her inclinations. The
difference is that nobody could have presumed to telescope
her arguments. In both presentations, however, Chaucer
makes the character argue that he or she is within the letter
of the law, but with the subtle implication that in practice
the points may be stretched. The Wife should not be thinking
so much about the succeeding husband until the current one
is dead. Now the conversation of the Monk appears to have
made points like the following, though not necessarily in the
same order; and although my statement of them makes the
Monk appear argumentative and more respectful of the past

and the Rule than Chaucer's few choice remarks do, we must imagine a longer conversation from which those choice tidbits were extracted, if we are to understand the Monk's position:

> I am an outrider, sir, and therefore I travel a good deal. It is true that the Rules of St Benedict and St Maure are old and therefore strict, but centuries have passed since they were written and times and social conditions have changed. I believe that adaptations of the Rule to new conditions always have to be made. Take the rule of claustration in my case. Some folks will quote the old saw, "A monk out of the cloister is like a fish out of water"; it's not worth an oyster; it misses the point. Why, even the Constitutions of the General Chapter of 1351 made specific allowance for outriders to be out of the cloister' . . . . Manual labor as St Augustine bids? That, sir, was all right for him and the ancient monks of his time, but it doesn't take into consideration the agricultural and other advances of our day. Let Austin have his manual labor reserved for himself. Supervisory work is still necessary nowadays; that's my labor . . . . No, the monks at the monastery are not idle. In place of manual labor, according to their talents most are variously occupied with study, reading, or work in the scriptorium—copying, correcting, illuminating, glossing, or binding books.[8] The library is always in need of new books or additional copies of old ones; some service books have to be replaced occasionally; and of course some books are made to be sold. Good business, you know . . . . Me a scholar? Why should I drive myself mad poring over a book in the cloister? My talents lie in another direction, and they are used for the good of the monastery. I have already said that I am an outrider and spend most of my time away from the cloister overseeing manors or traveling between them . . . . Certainly I hunt. I consider it a part of my job to keep up good public relations with the local gentry or the visiting nobility by hunting with them. And I really enjoy it; but if you have enjoyable work, why not enjoy it? As for the saying that hunters are not holy men, it proves nothing—a mere slogan.[9] Somebody has to look after such matters. If our good neighbors and patrons come to hunt, I entertain them with a hunt and not with a chapel service. How shall the world be served? . . . Sure it's expensive. But you, sir, as a businessman know that you have to spend money to make money. Hunting pays off in benefactions.[10] But if you are going to hunt with such folk you may as well do things right, and also be able to take a hedge with the best hunter among them.

Such a line of argument made good business sense, and Chaucer was the first to say so. "And I seyde his opinion was good."[11] And what fund raiser or public relations officer of an American university would not say the same? Just as the Friar is the best beggar in his house, so too is the Monk the best outrider business official in his community; he understands the value of public relations. The deeper criticism is merely implied. The Monk has made his job his way of life, and not monasticism.[12] Although he has upper-class dignity, he has no asceticism, no detachment whatsoever, and he is as worldly in his fashion as the Wife of Bath is in hers. Both are rationalizing an extreme position, and they argue well. That is why it is fun to follow his summarized defense of the pursuit of the hare and her verbose defense of the pursuit of succeeding husbands.

Because so much is made of the Monk's hunting, further consideration of the sports might be useful. The mediaeval prohibition of hunting by clerics is still preserved in Canon 138 of the Code of Canon Law of today. The hunting envisaged is the chase, riding to horn and hounds, a social fox hunt for example. In the Middle Ages the chase, or such hunting, was a common sport of nobles and the wealthy. In effect, peasants or the poor out for a little fresh meat were not hunters but poachers. Clerics (monks included) were forbidden to indulge in the hunt because it was unbecoming their station in life. They were to live as poor and spiritual men, but hunting was expensive, fashionable, and worldly. Incidentally, a similar reason is given in the statutes of 1400 for New College, Oxford, for forbidding its scholars and fellows to keep a rabbit warren, a dog, ferrets, or any type of hunting bird—"because it is not fitting for the poor, especially those who live on alms, to give the bread of the children of men to dogs to eat."[13]

Among clerics the temptation to hunt was greatest for the upper ranks of monks and canons, that is, for the superiors and officials. Often enough they had, as I have implied, the reasonable excuse of good public relations with the nobility and neighboring gentry. They also had easy access to the means of hunting—large estates and good horses— since the great abbeys conducted large-scale commercial farming and sheep raising operations. On the other hand, one of the lower ranks, a cloisterer, would have had difficulty requisitioning a proper mount, even if he had given himself for the nonce a dispensation to hunt. In spite of drawbacks, the fascination of the sport might still get the better of some clerics in the lower ranks. At any rate, John Peckham learned on a visitation that the prior and canons of St Augustine at Coxford followed the hounds on foot. This conjures up a picture of them joining a party of hunters who crossed their land, which could be as amusing a burlesque of the hunt as *The Tournament of Tottenham* is of the knightly tourney. To correct a very undignified situation, Peckham assuming his full dignity as metropolitan and primate of all England, on 10 January 1281, wrote a letter of injunctions to the prior who had failed to correct delinquents, prevent scandal, and confine to the discipline of the cloister those canons prone to galavanting *(ad gyrovagationem pronos)*. "Wherefore," he says, "throughout the land scandal and ridicule arise from your subjects, because, through your negligence, by running after the hounds, attending the feasts, talking to maidservants, they make of their religious profession a laughing stock." Nevertheless, Peckham recognizes that there might be occasions when the prior himself would have a legitimate reason for hunting—but if he is going to hunt, he should do it right. "Although we wish you to guard your full liberty to hunt, we are unwilling for you or anyone of yours to follow the hounds on foot, but on horseback only, lest the opportunity for frivolity and suspect diversion be offered; nor do we permit any canon to indulge in this exercise unless when he accompanies the prior indulging in such at the time."[14] In his action Peckham tries to preserve three things: the dignity of the religious life, the position of the prior before secular society, and the dignity of the English hunt. This is all the more remarkable because Peckham in the same stern letter forbade the game of chess and "other like disreputable amusements."[15]

In a society which was still largely feudal it was impossible for superiors in charge of large monastic establishments to ignore the sport liked by so many of their lords and benefactors. No one wants to offend benefactors, past, present, or possible. Of the great Thomas de la Mare, abbot of St Alban's, 1349–1396, his chronicler wrote that he fled hawk-

ing and hunting like the plague. Yet he still had hunters and
hawkers from among the guards and other members of his
household to keep up his warren, to keep down destructive
beasts and birds, and to amuse his lords and friends. "But
he would not permit them to practice their art in his pres-
ence, or the monks to participate in any way, except monks
officially deputed to do so. This seemed very difficult but the
more meritorious for him because when he was a young
layman he had been very practiced in such things."[16]

Of William de Cloune, abbot of the Augustinian Canons
of Leicester, 1345–1378, Knighton says: "In hunting the
hare he was held the most famous and renowned among all
lords of the realm, so that the king himself and his son,
Prince Edward, and many lords of the realm were held by
an annual pension to hunt with him." He put on a good show
for public relations, for Knighton continues: "He would
frequently assert in private that he did not delight in such
frivolous hunting but only to show deference to the lords
of the realm, and to capture their kindness and gain their
favor in his business."[17] That his public relations were very
productive, the endowments, possessions, and privileges
granted to the abbey during his tenure are ample proof.[18]

To return to Chaucer's Monk and make an end. He has
many fine horses in the stables under his authority, but like
many a man of high position today, he has requisitioned the
best of the organization's property for his own use. He is
"pulling rank"; he is driving the monastery's Cadillac on the
pilgrimage—that horse as brown as a berry, with bridle and
bells. Though his arguments for his job are logical, he has
succumbed to the occupational disease of those religious who
deal with the worldly—worldliness; he has acquired the ex-
pensive tastes of his patrons—"men of distinction," who ap-
preciated fine fur and roast swan. But he is a gentleman: he
refuses to tell tales of hunting because it would involve his
lords and patrons.[19] The human nature which Chaucer put
into the Monk's character is so timeless that one can find his
reincarnation, *mutatis mutandis,* on many a pleasant Ameri-
can campus. To have created Daun Piers, monk and business

administrator, is a greater feat than to have written a caustic caricature.

Notes

[1] *Canterbury Tales,* vii, 1939–1940 (B², °3129–°3130). F. N. Robinson, ed., *The Works of Geoffrey Chaucer,* 2nd ed. (Boston, 1957).

[2] *CT,* vii, 1935–1938 (B², °3125–°3128).

[3] See *CT,* vii, 62–66 (B², °1252–°1256).

[4] See *CT,* i (A), 204.

[5] *CT,* i (A), 172.

[6] *Registrum Epistolarum Fratris Johannis Peckham, Archiepiscopi Cantuariensis,* ed. Sharles Trice Martin, 3 vols., Rolls Series, 77 (1882–85), i, 89–90, Ep. lxxiii.

[7] *Gesta Abbatum Monasterii Sancti Albani,* ed. Henry Thomas Riley, 3 vols., Rolls Series, 28, (1867–69), ii, 432. Constitutions of Abbot Thomas de la Mare published in the General Chapter of the Benedictines, 1351, cap. xi.

[8] *Documents Illustrating the Activities of the General and Provincial Chapters of the English Black Monks, 1215–1540,* ed. William Abel Pantin, 3 vols., Camden Society Third Series, 45, 47, 54 (1931–37), ii, 51. Statutes of 1343, xiv, *De occupacione.*

[9] For the development of the saying see Rudolph Willard, "Chaucer's 'text that seith that hunters ben nat hooly men.'" *University of Texas Studies in English,* 1947, 209–251.

Although the saying was frequently quoted in support of the prohibition of hunting by clerics, hunting in itself is a morally indifferent act becoming morally good if performed with a good intention and in legitimate circumstances. The attitude of laymen was that the hunt is a good invigorating sport, and since the Monk is dealing with laymen, he takes the secular attitude towards the saying. The ceremonial and seriousness surrounding the hunt were analogous to those of chivalry, and books on hunting have a moral purpose or contain instructions in morality to a degree that would astonish a modern sportsman. Gaston Phoebus, comte de Foix, in the preface of his very famous book, *La Chasse* (begun in 1387), draws up an extended argument to show that the true sportsman has the best of both the here and the hereafter—he avoids the works of the seven deadly sins and goes "tout droit en paradis." "On desire en ce monde a viure longuement en sante et en ioye et apres la fin la salutation de lame, et veneurs ont tout cela. Donc soyez tous veneurs et vous feres que saigez." (*Phebus des deduitz de la chasse des bestes souuaiges Et des oyseaulx de proye.* Nouuellement imprime. [Paris, Jean Trepperel, about 1505–07; 2nd ed.] folio A iii recto, col. 2). *La Chasse* was translated between 1406 and 1413 by Edward, second duke of York, in the *Master of Game,* the oldest book on hunting in English, edited by William A. and F. Baillie-Grohman, with a foreword by Theodore Roosevelt (London, 1909). The second duke of York was the grandson of Edward III, who used to hunt with Abbot William de Cloune (see below), and one of the five original chapters he added in the *Master of Game* is on hunting the hare. From the preface: "Furthermore I will prove by sundry reasons in this little prologue, that the life of no man that useth gentle game and disport be less displeasable unto God than the life of a perfect and skilful hunter, or from which more good cometh. The first reason is that hunting causeth a man to eschew the seven deadly sins . . . in short and long all good customs and manners cometh thereof, and the health of man and of his soul. For he that fleeth the seven deadly sins as we believe, he shall be saved, therefore a good hunter shall be saved, and in this world have joy enough and of gladness and of solace, so that he keep himself from two things. One is that he leave not the knowledge nor the service of God, from whom all good cometh, for his hunting. The second that he lose not the service of his master for his hunting, nor his own duties which might profit him most (pp. 4–5) . . . . Therefore be ye all hunters and ye shall do as wise men" (p. 12). . . .

[10] See below William de Cloune and n. 18.

[11] *Canterbury Tales,* I (A), 183.

[12] Mediaeval Benedictines were well aware of this constant danger. Statutes of 1343, cap. iii, *De obedienciariis* (Pantin, op, cit. [n. 8 above], II, 36–37).

[13] *Statutes of St. Mary's College of Winchester in Oxford; or New College, in Statutes of the Colleges of Oxford,* 3 vols. (Oxford, 1858), I, 48.

[14] Martin, *Reg. Epist. Peckham,* I, 162–163, Ep.cxxxvii.

[15] *Ibid.,* I, 165.

[16] Riley, *GAMSA* (n. 7 above), III, 401–402. The monk-officials deputed to participate in the hunt would also be able to prevent a certain amount of damage to hedges, fences, levees, etc., or report afterwards so that damage could be repaired. John of Gaunt took similar measures for the protection of his property when he allowed others to hunt on it. *John of Gaunt's Register, 1379–1383,* ed. Eleanor C. Lodge and Robert Somerville, 2 vols., Camden Society Third Series, 56, 57 (1937), I, 83, No. 252. See also p. 210, No. 645.

[17] *Chronicon Henrici Knighton,* ed. Joseph Rawson Lumby, 2 vols., Rolls Series, 92 (1889–95), II, 127.

[18] *Ibid.,* II, 126–127.

[19] The tale which the Monk tells is safe and rather appropriate for an outrider, dealing as it does with the great ones of this world—"de casibus virorum illustrium." When he mentions that he has a hundred tragedies in his cell and then gives a bookish definition of tragedy, he reminds one of the modern busy administrator who still keeps his anthology of English literature and can still quote a definition from college days.

4

Chaucer and the Friars

ARNOLD WILLIAMS

AMONG the many unlovely characters in the General Prologue to the *Canterbury Tales*, the Friar is one of the rather small group with no mitigating virtues. Whenever Chaucer has occasion to mention friars, we get the same characterization, of unextenuated hypocritical villainy. Besides the sketch of Huberd the Friar in the Prologue, there is the Summoner's Prologue and Tale and the remark of the Wife of Bath that since the banishment of fairies,

> Wommen may go saufly vp and doun
> In euery bussh or vnder euery tree
> Ther is noon oother incubus but

the friar on his 'lymytacioun,' who after all, 'ne wol doon hem but dishonour.'[1]

This attitude towards the friars is superficially all the more surprising when contrasted with Chaucer's pictures of other clerics, with the possible exception of the Canon, who is not so much a cleric as an alchemist. The worst that can be said of the Monk is that he found the wrong situation in life. His vices would not be vices in the Franklin, the Physician,

Reprinted, by permission of author and editor, from *Speculum*, XXVIII (1953), 499–513.

or the Man of Law. On the positive side, he is something of
a scholar, albeit a tedious one. Daun John, the monk of the
Shipman's Tale, partly because of the fabliau morality of
the piece, does not strike us as an evil man—a trickster and
a lecher, perhaps, but certainly not a hypocrite. The Parson,
Chaucerian scholars have long recognized, is an idealized
portrait.

If Chaucer could be so liberal in his depiction of the
secular clergy, if he could pass the monks by with no greater
castigation than that they were worldly, why is he apparently
so hard on a way of life founded by Dominic and Francis,
which gave the world Thomas Aquinas, Bonaventure, and
Roger Bacon? Why is the poor Parson the concrete realiza-
tion of the religious spirit, and the Friar its utter negation?
Surely, at the least, Chaucer could have given us a friar no
farther from Francis or Dominic than the Monk is from
Benedict or Bernard.

The problem of Chaucer's friars, stated as I have stated it,
has gone largely unrecognized in Chaucerian criticism. The
standard comment is that the mendicant orders had rapidly
degenerated from the ideals of their founders, Francis and
Dominic, and were by Chaucer's time, not yet two centuries
later and scarcely a century from their golden age, hopelessly
corrupt.[2] This explanation probably reflects a somewhat un-
critical acceptance of the widespread criticism of the friars
in the vernacular literature of the fourteenth and early fif-
teenth centuries.

Alternatively, other critics view the Friar rather as an
individual than as a representative of his order; he is, they
tacitly assume or frankly state, an unlovely individual who
happens to be a friar.[3] In general, critics have not applied
historical scholarship to the problem, or sought the sources
of Chaucer's characterization, or correlated Chaucer's artistic
creation with prevalent social attitudes.

It was only in the decade before the war that the his-
torians exhumed, edited, and published enough of the docu-
ments of the famous mediaeval controversy over the men-
dicant orders to indicate to the literary critics the true genesis
and real nature of Chaucer's attack on the friars. We now

know that the attack started within three decades of the foundation of the two chief orders, that it had been going on a century and a half before Chaucer began work on the *Canterbury Tales,* and that it assumed complex and varied forms. By Chaucer's time both the secular clergy and the monks had attacked the friars; the various orders of friars, especially the Franciscan and Dominican, were attacking one another; the Franciscan order had split into several factions and the dominant faction had involved itself in a contest with the papacy; and a number of special interests had become attached to one or other of the several sides in this most confusing struggle.

With the exception of the contest of the Franciscans with the papacy, all these quarrels and dissensions are somehow represented in Chaucer's picture of the Friar and in the Prologue and Tale of the Summoner. Hence a brief summary of the history of the mendicant orders is necessary even in a periodical article.

The two leading orders of friars, the Franciscan and the Dominican, were founded early in the thirteenth century; two others, the Austin Friars and the Carmelites, somewhat later, though the former alleged Augustine as their founder and the latter Elijah. These 'four orders' embodied at least three practices sure to excite hostility: 'evangelical poverty,' which meant that the friars owned nothing, either individually or in common, but begged their living; the parochial work of preaching and hearing confessions, formerly the undisputed province of the parochial clergy; and learning, for the friars soon came to dominate the universities.

For convenience, we may divide the attacks on the mendicant orders into three historical periods: (1) that which commenced in the 1240's at the University of Paris and spread to England somewhat later; (2) that initiated by Richard FitzRalph, Archbishop of Armagh, in the 1350's; and (3) that by Wyclif and his followers in the 1380's. The first phase is largely continental, though Englishmen were involved; the second and third phases are purely English; and, of course, there is much overlapping and one phase fades into another.

The Dominican and Franciscan orders were scarcely established at the University of Paris before the secular clergy, who until then had enjoyed a monopoly on instruction, attacked them. Matthew Paris speaks of contentions between seculars and regulars in the 1240's.[4] The chief interest of the Chaucerian scholar is that this quarrel produced a document of extreme importance, William of St Amour's *De periculis novissimorum temporum*, written in 1256. William was a secular clerk and teacher; and one suspects that his indignation was caused primarily by the competition of such teachers as Thomas Aquinas and Bonaventure. For his argument, however, he selected a particularly vulnerable spot, the apocalyptic speculations which were apparently rife among a wing of the Franciscans. These were based on the work of Joachim, abbot of Fiore, which had been developed by Burgo of Santo Donnini in the famous *Introductorius* to the 'Eternal Gospel.' No copy of this has survived, but we know that the *Introductorius* saw the world as divided into three great periods, that of the Old Law ('the gospel of the Father'), that of the New ('the gospel of the Son'), and that of the 'Eternal Gospel' ('the gospel of the Holy Ghost'). The third period was expected to begin in 1260. As the Old Law had been superseded by the New, so the New was now to be superseded by the 'Eternal Gospel.' The friars, particularly the Franciscans, were the forerunners of this third age, as John the Baptist had been of the second.[5]

This wild speculation gave William of St Amour his opening. The world, he says, is indeed nearing its end, for the perils foretold in II Timothy, iii, 1–10, are upon us. The friars are the deceivers of whom Paul here speaks. A series of signs by which the false apostles whom Paul prophesied may be known form the basis of most of the charges subsequently made against the friars, even by so unapocalyptic an author as Chaucer. The chief ones are that the friars preach without a calling, that they cultivate friends in the world, especially among the rich and powerful, and that they capitivate weak women whose consciences are burdened by sin.[6]

The *De periculis* was composed between the months of March and September 1256. The counterattack of the friars was both political and literary. Pope Alexander IV condemned *De periculis* and ordered it burned. William of St Amour was exiled from France. An anonymous author, probably a Franciscan, answered William in a tract called *Manus quae Omnipotentem tenditur*. Gerard of Abbeville continued the attack of the seculars in *Contra adversarium perfectionis*,[7] which, in its turn, was answered by two leading figures among the friars, Thomas Aquinas in *Contra impugnantes*[8] and Bonaventure in at least three separate tracts.[9] The prominent English Franciscan, John Pecham, subsequently archbishop of Canterbury, wrote a prose tract, *Tractatus pauperis*, and a debate in Latin quatrains called *Defensio fratrum mendicantium*,[10] in which Mundus and Religio argue the issue before the Pope, who decides in Religio's favor. All this, which we may call the academic debate, was carried on in Latin and, except for Pecham's *Defensio*, in the prose of scholastic argument. Two important French poets, Rutebeuf and Jean de Meung, took up the cause of William of St Amour in the vernacular.[11]

This struggle ebbed and flowed until the first quarter of the fourteenth century, when a state of equilibrium seems to have been reached with the publication of Boniface VIII's bull *Super cathedram* in 1300, which, though emasculated by Benedict XI in 1304, was reinstated in full vigor by the Council of Vienne in 1311. *Super cathedram* established a workable compromise by which the mendicant orders (1) retained their confessional powers, but had to be licensed by the bishop of the diocese, who could limit the number of friars confessors and supervise their activity; (2) kept their rights to bury the dead, but had to give to the parish priest one fourth of both canonical dues and any bequest; and (3) could preach, but not in competition with the secular clergy.

This settlement should have satisfied the economic and jurisdictional demands of the secular clergy. In fact, it seems to have for a time. The early part of the fourteenth century is not notable so much for any conflict between seculars and mendicants as for struggle within and between the mendicant orders. The chief events of these years are the controversy between Franciscans and Dominicans over the exact mean-

ing of evangelical poverty and the splits within the Francis-
can order. Both of these events are of importance for the
subsequent English attacks on the friars. The 'spiritual' wing
of the Franciscans, with its insistence on maintenance of the
Rule of Francis in its full severity, provided much material
for later propagandists like the author of *Piers Plowman* and
Wyclif. In the contest about evangelical poverty the Domini-
cans eventually won. In 1332 Pope John XXII sanctioned
their interpretation by refusing to remain steward of Fran-
ciscan property, as required by the rule of the order. The
effect of this, too, was to encourage within the Franciscan
order those worldly tendencies which anti-mendicant forces
would denounce.

In the 1350's a far more formidable antagonist appeared
than any hitherto. Richard FitzRalph had been chancellor
of Oxford (1332–1334), was an eminent theologian and a
popular preacher, and when he began his attacks on the
friars was archbishop of Armagh and primate of Ireland. In
a Latin sermon, preached according to the rubric on the
manuscript, before Pope Clement VI in 1350, he opened his
offensive.[12] In 1356 he preached four sermons in the vernacu-
lar in London.[13] Then he took his cause to the papal curia,
where he presented it in a document generally known as the
Defensio curatorum, which was translated into English by
Chaucer's contemporary, Trevisa.[14]

In all these works the argument is substantially the same.
Though he gives some attention to mendicancy, which he
condemns, his main attack is directed against the usurpation
of the rights of the parish clergy: burying, preaching, and
hearing confessions. Why, he asks, of all the functions of the
clergy do they select these to invade? Why of all sacraments
do they administer only penance? Obviously because these
are the lucrative ministrations. FitzRalph's argument against
confessional practice of the friars is eminently practical: it
weakens the power of the parish clergy and the hierarchy.
It provides the sinner an easy escape from the discipline
which the curate and bishop would enforce. . . .

One would suppose that the mendicants replied vigorously
to these attacks. Apparently they did preach against Fitz-

Ralph in London, but there are only two extant answers.[15] One is by Roger Conway, general of the English province of Franciscans, who defended the mendicant orders at the Curia.[16] To the modern reader it is a rather disappointing performance, for Conway sticks to the canon law, the papal bulls and decrees which undoubtedly gave the friars the privileges which FitzRalph protested. To higher considerations of morality or discipline Conway gives no attention. The Pope, he argues, is the supreme priest; he can delegate his powers to whomever he chooses, as he has done to the friars. Apparently this line of argument was appropriate to the circumstances. FitzRalph lost his case, though he himself died before the decision was handed down.

A more thorough treatment is that of William of Woodford (or Wydford), another English Franciscan, whose work *Defensio fratrum mendicantium contra Rich. Armachanum* is extant in full in two manuscripts and in summary in a third.[17] Woodford canvasses the whole field of attacks on the friars. He tries to answer FitzRalph point by point in the method of scholastic argument, and he lists forty-one errors in FitzRalph's various works against the mendicants. Though the work lacks the intensity of Aquinas' defense and the verve of Bonaventure's tracts, it is an adequate presentation of the mendicant case. There is, however, no reason to suppose that it reached a large audience.

FitzRalph's writings remained a weapon in the continuing campaign against the friars, which reached new intensity in the 1380's. Over a dozen manuscripts of the late fourteenth or early fifteenth century contain one or more of FitzRalph's works against the mendicants, to which one should add the five manuscripts of Trevisa's translation of the *Defensio curatorum*. 'Armachan' furnished arguments to Wyclif and his followers, indeed to all enemies of the friars. 'Armachan destroy hem,' cries one anonymous versifier, 'if it is Goddes will.'[18]

The agitation aroused by FitzRalph's sermons had scarcely died down when a new attack on the friars was launched by Wyclif, who took over the principal charges of William of St Amour and of FitzRalph and added some of his own. In

the twenty or thirty years after 1380 one can distinguish
two simultaneous attacks on the friars, one the Wycliffite
and the other a mere continuation of the old one, which was
still using *De periculis* and FitzRalph's works as its main
documents. The Wycliffite attack is usually quite distin-
guishable. Wyclif often linked the friars with the 'Caesarian'
secular clergy and the wealthy monks; he and his followers
called the friars a 'new sect,' different from the 'sect' of
Christ; and they often named as the chief offense of the friars
their persecution of the true gospel. In addition, various of
the heterodox doctrines of Wyclif get into the attacks on
the friars, attacks on transubstantiation and the worship of
images, for instance. There is no evidence of the peculiarly
Wycliffite point of view in Chaucer's jabs at the friars; and
it is certainly a mistake to use Wycliffite documents to illus-
trate Chaucer's friar.

On the other hand, the Wycliffites shared hatred of the
friars with many who were orthodox. Hence, the vehemence
of the Wycliffite attack doubtless had the effect of keeping
the older secular agitation going too. Certainly there was a
multiplication of manuscripts of William of St Amour and
FitzRalph between 1380 and 1420, as well as the composi-
tion of several pieces, in both Latin and English, which are
not specifically Wycliffite in doctrine or tone.

It is against this long attack on the friars that both the
portrait of the Friar in the Prologue and the Summoner's
Prologue and Tale must be viewed. The surest way to dem-
onstrate that both these pieces derive ultimately from the
charges made by the principal opponents of the friars is to
compare point by point Chaucer's work with the chief docu-
ments in the attack. From an examination of manuscript re-
sources it is easy to say that these documents were William
of St Amour's *De periculis,* much of which was repeated in
Jean de Meung's portion of the *Roman de la Rose,* and the
various works of FitzRalph. A few minor points will be illus-
trated by other documents.

Confession was the source of the friars' power and men-
dicancy the source of their livelihood and their riches. These
are the two practices of the mendicant orders which receive

the hardest blows from FitzRalph, and we are not surprised to see that they bulk large in Chaucer's handling. Huberd, the friar of the Prologue, is described as having, or asserting, a power of confession beyond that of a curate. He is licenciate of his order, that is, he either has or usurps the right of forgiving 'reserved cases,' the more serious sins, partially enumerated by FitzRalph above, which the parish clergy cannot forgive, but must refer to their bishops. The meddling of the friars in these reserved cases was precisely what aroused FitzRalph's ire. When he charges that of two thousand excommunicates in his diocese, scarcely forty come to him or his penitentiaries for absolution, the rest going to the friars, he is hitting at exactly the 'license' which Huberd boasts of possessing. False-Semblaunt in the *Roman de la Rose* pretends to a similar power:

> I may assoil, and I may shryve,
> That no prelat may lette me,
> All folk, where evere thei founde be.
> I not no prelat may don so,
> But it the pope be, and no mo.[19]

The second item in Huberd's confessional technique is that he is an 'esy man to yeue penaunce,' that as long as the penitent shows his contrition by a donation 'vnto a poure ordre,' Huberd is willing to overlook 'wepynge and preyeres.' This accusation is most violently made in a vernacular poem of the 1380's, probably by a secular priest:

> ffor sixe pens er þai fayle
> Sle thi fadre & iape thi modre & þai wyl þe assoile.[20]

In more dignified language FitzRalph says that the desire of the friars to become confessors must be ascribed to avarice. The parishioner, he says, argues 'Why wolde þis begger sitte & here my schrifte & leue his beggyng and getyng of his liflode, but he hope to haue of me siche maner help. . . . Þanne hit folewiþ, þat for all maner synnes, he wole ioyne me almes dede for to releue his owne beggerie.'[21]

Since, then, the real reason for the friars' resented power of confession was their mendicant life, the attack on their confessional powers is accompanied by one on begging, the very foundation principle of the mendicant orders. William of St Amour listed as one of the forty points by which true apostles could be told from false that true apostles do not go about soliciting temporal goods.[21] Gerard of Abbeville devoted one of the three books of his *Contra adversarium* to an attack on mendicancy, and FitzRalph a whole work, *De pauperie Salvatoris,* which attempted to prove that Christ was not entirely without possessions, that he never begged voluntarily or spontaneously (i.e., without immediate necessity), and that hence the friars were not following the higher perfection of his example. FitzRalph's first London sermon, on the text 'Dirigite viam Domini' (John, i, 23) and much of the second, 'Quodcunque dixerit vobis facite' (John, ii, 5), is devoted to proving these points, which appear in briefer form in *Defensio curatorum:* 'Oure Lord Ihesus, in his conuersacioun of manhed, alwey was pore, nouȝt for he wolde & loued pouert by-cause of hitsilf. . . . Oure Lord Ihesus neuer beggide wilfulliche. . . . Christ neuer tauȝt willfulliche to begge. . . . Oure Lord Ihesus tauȝte þat no man schuld wilfulliche begge. . . . no man may redlich & holiliche wilful beggyng vppon hym take, euermore to holde.'[22] The apostles were commonly said, as in the *Roman de la Rose,* to have earned their living by their hands: 'And with travel, and ellis nought/They wonnen all her sustenaunce' (ll. 6566–67; 11310–11). The law of Justinian which prohibited begging by able bodied men was often cited.

Now, Huberd was the 'best beggere in his house,' who got more 'by his purchas than by his rent.' His ways were so beguiling, so pleasant was his 'in principio,' that he would have a farthing from a poor widow without a shoe. The phrase is an apt characterization of the mendicant from the point of view of the secular clergy, the monk, and the layman, for the friar must get all by his purchase, his daily winnings at beggary, and nothing from his rent, or permanent income from investment or land. The *Summoner's Tale* is in great part an illustration of the methods of the begging friar. After preaching he goes from house to house:

Yif vs a busshel whete malt or reye
A goddes kechyl or a tryp of chese
Or ellis what yow list we may nat chese
A goddes hal peny or a messe peny
Or yif vs of youre brawn if ye haue any (D, 1746–50)

A fellow friar has a pair of ivory tables in which he enters the names of donors, but as soon as they are out of sight, he rubs the names off his table.

With the two mendicants also went a "sturdy harlot," who bears a sack into which go the receipts of the begging. This servant is surely a relic of the *bursarius*, or spiritual friend, who received goods and especially money, which the Franciscans were forbidden to touch. It is interesting to note that this practice, little commented on by the secular critics of the mendicants, drew vigorous fire from the Spiritual Franciscans, who wished to restore the order to what they claimed was the primitive simplicity of Francis. Ubertini da Casale and Peter Olive both condemn the *bursarius* along with such devices as handling money with sticks (to avoid touching it) as evidence of laxity and hypocrisy. The spirituals seem to have passed on to the later secular attackers of the mendicants this scorn of the *bursarius*. FitzRalph includes it in a list of how the friars break their own rules. The Rule of St Francis, he charges, prohibits friars from receiving either for themselves or for others any money; yet now they journey through country and town, accompanied by a fellow who collects pennies."

Hypocrisy is, of course, the favorite charge against the friars. William of St Amour reiterates it. 'Pseudo' and 'hypocrite' are two most frequent terms in his work. A common form of the allegation was to call attention to the disparity between the boastful profession of absolute poverty and the riches of the friars' clothing, diet, and buildings; their pleasure in the companionship of the rich and powerful; and their desire for worldly recognition and fame. So Huberd will have nothing to do with lepers or beggars:

It is nat honeste it may nat auance
For to deelen with no swich poraille
But al with riche and selleres of vitaille. (A, 246–48)

And we see the friar of the *Summoner's Tale* likewise favoring the well-to-do with his company.

William of St Amour devotes much space to such charges. True apostles, he writes, do not seek more opulent lodgings or better fare. They are false preachers who seek lodgings where they are better fed and receive money of rich, evil men.[25] Jean de Meung echoes these sentiments. Poor folk, he makes False-Semblaunt say, "that gone by strete/That have no gold, ne sommes grete/Hem wolde I lete to her prelates,"[26] and elsewhere:

> I love bettir th'acqueyntaunce
> Ten tymes, of the kyng of Fraunce
> Than of a poore man of mylde mod,
> Though that his soule be also god. (ll. 6491–94; 11241–44)

Friars love rich food and good entertainment, the charge proceeds. True apostles are satisfied with the food and drink offered. Those who are offended when sumptuous fare is not provided are false, writes William.[27] So the friar of the *Summoner's Tale* hypocritically specifies capon's liver, a 'shyvere' of soft bread and a roasted pig's head—nothing elegant, since, as he says, he is a man of 'little substenaunce' whose spirit 'hath his fostering in the Bible' rather than on worldly food.[28] As another sample of luxury Huberd's cope is explicitly described:

> For ther he was not lyk a cloystrer
> With a thredbare cope as is a pour scoler
> But he was lyk a maister or a pope
> Of double worstede was his semycope
> That rounded as a belle out of the presse. (A, 259–63)

The general effect of this description is to continue the contrast between profession and practice. FitzRalph mentions costly apparel as one of the ways in which the friars break their rule.[29]

But it may also have a more specific implication. In the attack of the Spiritual Franciscans on their laxer brethren clothing, especially the hood or cope, assumes a symbolic significance. A very interesting document dating from about 1340 centers the whole case of the Spirituals on the material and pattern of their habits. Upholding the earlier insistence on vile clothing, sparse and patched, the anonymous author condemns the ostentatious habits of contemporary Franciscans, with their fullness of material and their pleats and creases. The true garb of the Minor is short and but a single fold, such as the old pictures show Francis wearing.[30] If Chaucer knew of the Spiritual propaganda (as Wyclif and the author of *Piers Plowman* did), then his lines about Huberd's semicope may well be a subtle calling attention to the degeneration of the friars of his day from their first perfection.

Long before such degeneration could have progressed very far, however, the mendicants were accused of seeking high place and worldly honor and of busying themselves in secular affairs. William of St Amour devotes several of his forty points to such accusations. True apostles do not seek the favor of the world, nor to please men. They flee the solemnities of men, their salutations, banquets, and offices. Nor do true apostles frequent the tables of strangers and become flatterers. In a sermon he cites the text 'You are not to claim the title of Rabbi' (Matthew, xxiii, 8) against the friars. The *Roman de la Rose* echoes this allegation. Friars

> loven setes at the table,
> The first and most honourable;
> And for to han the first chaieris
> In synagogis, to hem full deere is;
> And willen that folk hem loute and grete,
> Whanne that they passen thurgh the strete,
> And wolen be cleped 'maister' also. (ll. 6913–19; 11627–33)

Both Huberd and the friar of the *Summoner's Tale* are walking pictures of these charges. Huberd is 'curteis' and 'lowely of seruyse'; he was also 'lyk a maister or a pope.' He lisped 'to make his Englisshe swete vp on his tonge.' He practised such social arts as singing and playing on a rote. He was familiar with franklins, that is, with the best people, over all his country. The friar of the *Summoner's Tale* is such another. After Thomas' insult he goes to a house.

> Wher as ther woned a man of greet honour
> To whom that he was alwey confessour
> This worthy man was lord of that village. (D, 2163–65)

On being called 'maister' he admits the justice of the title, but coyly rejects it:

No maister sire quod he but seruytour
Thogh I haue had in scole that honour
God liketh it nat that Raby men vs calle. (D, 2185–87)

At least William of St Amour had had that effect: one friar
acknowledges the justice of the complaint, though evading
its spirit.

Meddling in secular affairs is another common accusation.
Chaucer hints this when he says of Huberd: 'In louedayes
ther koude he muchel helpe' (A. 258.) Jean de Meung lists
some of the pieces of business undertaken by friars: they
make peace and arrange marriages, serve as executors, pro-
curators, and messengers, act in inquests. William includes
among his points that false apostles sojourn in courts of
princes and magistrates, where worldly business is trans-
acted, that they procure themselves friends in this world,
and that they use their influence with the powerful to make
trouble for their enemies. This last is just what the friar of
the *Summoner's Tale* does when he takes his grievance
against Thomas to the lord of the village. True apostles,
on the other hand, hate no one, not even their enemies.

This unwillingness to brook correction meekly, this hatred
of opponents is often developed in attacks on the mendicant
orders. True apostles, writes William, are not contentious,
but if any are unwilling to hear them, they shake the dust
of the city off their feet, as Christ commands in Matthew **x**,
14. Those who will not suffer correction are false apostles.
Jean de Meung repeats this accusation:

Another custom use we:
Of hem that wole ayens us be,
We hate hem deedly everichone,
And we wole werrey hem, as oon.
Hym that oon hatith, hate we alle. (ll. 6923–27; 11637–41)

Certain other faults alleged by their enemies also appear
prominently in Chaucer's friars. One is the commendation
of themselves and their works, of which so much is made in
the *Summoner's Tale*, where the friar expostulates at length
on the superior holiness of his order, who 'live in poverte
and in abstinence.' Thus their prayers are more effective
than those of 'burel folk,' and to them are granted miraculous

visions. When the wife tells of her child's death, the friar answers that he saw the child's salvation in a vision, as did also the sexton and the infirmarian of his convent.[31] These details, as we should expect, are concrete presentations of William's general charges. True apostles, he writes, do not commend themselves, or say their usages are better than those of others. Nor do they glory in the miracles the Lord performs through them. Only false apostles glory in the special favors God shows them.

Among the minor irritations, especially complained of by the monks, is the assertion that the two minor orders of friars traced their foundations to Augustine for the Austin Friars and to Elijah for the Carmelites. This annoyed the Augustinian Canons, who also held Augustine as their founder, and the Benedictines, who because of their sixth century foundation held all other orders to be upstarts. The friar of the *Summoner's Tale* seem to have been a Carmelite, for he tells us 'But sith Elye was or Elise/Han freres been that fynde I of record' (D. 2116-173, a story which even the other three orders rarely accepted. Two manuscripts of the late fourteenth century attack such presumptions. In the one the author, apparently an Augustinian canon, writes some verses and a dialogue of several folios to prove that Augustine founded no order of hermits, such as the Austin friars claimed to be.[32] A monastic chronicler of St Albans adduces a good bit of historical data to show that the first friars were the Franciscans, founded in 1206, and that attempts to claim Augustine, Elijah, or Jacob as founders are clearly mendacious.[33] In view of this monastic attack on the friars, it is interesting to note that the friar of the *Summoner's Tale* has a disparaging word for the monks 'that swymmen in possessioun/Fy on hir pomp and on hir glotonye' (D. 1926-27). Chaucer very probably knew of these contemporary squabbles and worked them into his picture.

This is only a side issue. As we have seen, the main attack of the seculars was against the confessional power of the friars and their freedom from discipline by the hierarchy. It is therefore significant that Chaucer touches both issues. In both the Prologue and the *Summoner's Tale* we see the friars trying to steal the confessional business of the parish clergy. Huberd says that he has more power than a curate, and the friar of the *Summoner's Tale* assures the wife that

> Thise curatz been ful necligent and slowe
> To grope tendrely a conscience
> In shrift. (D, 1816–18)

The jurisdictional quarrel between the seculars and mendicants has already been introduced in the *Friar's Tale*. When the Summoner, who represents the secular clergy, since he is a process server in an ecclesiastical court, becomes angry, Huberd boasts that

> We been out of his correcioun
> They han of vs no iurisdiccioun
> Ne neuere shullen terme of all hir lyues. (D, 1339–31)

'They' surely means the whole secular clergy: priests, bishops, and archbishops, as well as the Summoner. In fact, the whole quarrel between the Friar and the Summoner is a sort of miniature of the larger one between mendicants and seculars, and the friar's arrogance is probably meant to be that of his whole profession, who had not long since beaten back the most determined of the assaults on them, that of Fitz-Ralph, and were then engaged in meeting the less formidable attack of the Lollards.

In a number of smaller matters, too, Chaucer's picture of the friar in the *Summoner's Tale* can be illustrated from the literature produced by the attack on the mendicants. There is, for instance, the rather fervid rhetoric of the friar. William of St Amour had included as one of his points against the friars that they studied eloquence in the composition of words, and the friar of the *Summoner's Tale* with his artificial hortatory style and his long list of exempla gives us a good idea of what William was talking about. He also illustrates a remark of FitzRalph that when he challenged the friars to produce one scriptural text commanding poverty or proving that Christ even begged voluntarily or spontaneously, they complained that he respected only the text of Scripture, not the gloss. The friar of the *Summoner's Tale* finds himself in exactly this difficulty:

> I ne haue no text of it as I suppose
> But I shal fynde it in a maner glose
> That specially oure swete lord Iesus
> Spak this by freres whan he seyde thus
> Blessed be they that poure in spirit been. (D, 1919–23)

In only one important matter does Chaucer seem to depart widely from the lines laid down by William of St Amour and FitzRalph, that is, from the more serious, academic attack on the friars, as represented in the Latin documents, rather than in contemporary vernacular squibs. Chaucer implies, though perhaps he does not clearly state, that friars are as loose about their vow of chastity as about their other vow of poverty. Huberd, we are told, 'hadde maad ful many a mariage/Of yonge wommen at his owene cost' (A, 212–13). More directly, the Wife of Bath says that, since the banishment of fairies, there is now no threat to a woman's chastity except from the limiter: 'Ther is noon oother incubus but he/And he ne wol doon hem but dishonour' (D, 880–81). The *Summoner's Tale* lacks such direct statements, though the greeting which the friar gives the wife is capable, at least, of giving scandal:

> The frere ariseth vp ful curteisly
> And hire embraceth in his armes narwe
> And kiste hir swete and chirketh as a sparwe. (D, 1802–04)

The *Summoner's Tale* is here more representative of William of St Amour and his followers than the other two passages. Allegations of unchastity are extremely rare in the Latin documents. What is to be found is the common exegesis of II Timothy, iii, the warning against deceivers who will come in the last times. This was William's primary text, which gave the title to *De periculis novissimorum temporum*. Verses six and seven characterize the deceivers as 'men that will make their way into house after house, captivating weak women whose consciences are burdened by sin: women swayed by shifting passions, who are ever inquiring, yet never attain to recognition of truth.' This passage figures largely in all William's attacks on the friars; phrases from it are reiterated. As William glosses the text, 'making their way into house after house' means entering into consciences by hearing confessions, and 'captivating weak women' means seducing them to sin, as the serpent seduced Eve and then Eve seduced Adam. This text and this gloss are hammered home, and the first of the forty signs of *De periculis* is that true apostles do not creep into houses and lead weak women astray.[34]

Probably as a consequence of this approach by William, a great deal of the succeeding literature abounds in charges that friars particularly seek out women and *spiritually* seduce them. Women are often pictured as being most receptive to friars. Sometimes one sees statements that friars give cause for scandal by their frequent and close association with women as confessors and counselors. A compilation of canon law and practical theology, made probably by a Cistercian monk towards the middle of the fourteenth century, levies exactly this charge. Mendicants, the author writes, freely converse with women, noble and common, both secular and religious (i.e., nuns), and so give rise to grave scandal. To be always with women is to revive the dead. A marginal note directs this aphorism to the attention of 'you flattering mendicant friars conversing every day with women.'[35] The author, who was surely no friend of the friars, gives no sign of believing the charges of unchastity; what he objects to is that a basis for making them should exist.

Familiarity with attacks on the friars suggests strongly that the association of friars with women comes originally from William of St Amour. It is not hard to see how charges of spiritual seduction would become charges of bodily seduction. And, of course, appearances made the charge believable. The friar, who travelled about a great deal and met many women, was as natural a magnet to attract stories of seduction as were the ice man and the travelling salesman in more recent times. The nature of the stories about friars leads one to suspect that the role of lover usually assigned the clerk in the earlier Goliardic story and poem (exemplified in Chaucer's *Miller's Tale*) eventually became attached to the friar. Doubtless there were enough actual instances—only a few suffice—to render the convention credible.

And so the allegation of unchastity becomes most common

in the vernacular poetry and story of the fourteenth and fifteenth centuries. Some anonymous verses probably of the 1380's will serve as representative of the whole genre:

> Were j a man þat hous held
> If any woman with me dwelde
> þer is no frere bot he were gelde
>   Schulde com with jn my wones
> For may he til a woman wynne
> In preuyte he wyl not blynne
> Er he a childe put hir with jnne
>   & perchaunce two at ones.[36]

Chaucer thus expresses both attitudes, that of the more popular vernacular literature in the Prologue and the *Wife of Bath's Tale*, that of the more academic Latin documents in the *Summoner's Tale*. In the last the situation of the friar using his influence with the wife to gain the confidence, and the money, of the husband is precisely paralleled in William of St Amour.

In fact, the attitude of the whole of Chaucer's treatment of the friars is paralleled in the writings of William and Fitz-Ralph. What Chaucer did, it is clear, was merely to give artistic form to the most important of the charges against the friars made by William, repeated in every generation over a century and a quarter, and naturalized in England, stripped of their apocalyptic costume, by FitzRalph. With such evidence, we can hardly accept as adequate and complete the explanation that Chaucer faithfully reflected the degeneration of the mendicant orders in his time. Clearly, we are dealing with an *ex parte* presentation. Chaucer accepts and reflects the attitude of the secular party—and no wonder, for the secular clergy must have dominated the thinking of the upper-class, governmental circles in which Chaucer moved. Until the historians furnish us with more evidence, from less biased sources than the natural enemies of the mendicant orders, we should no more take Chaucer's friars as representative of the mendicant orders as a whole than we take his Parson as typical of the parochial clergy. Too many vested interests are at stake, too many social attitudes are in conflict to take the word of Chaucer, or that of any other poet, without further investigation.

Notes

[1] *Canterbury Tales*, D, 877–879. I quote the *Canterbury Tales* from the Manly-Ricket edition (Chicago: University of Chicago Press, 1940).

[2] Muriel Bowden, *A Commentary on the General Prologue to the Canterbury Tales* (New York: Macmillan, 1948), pp. 119–41, esp. pp. 119–123, summarizes, with documentation, this point of view.

[3] *Ibid.*, 139–141.

[4] *Chronica majora*, tr. J. A. Giles (London: Bohn, 1853), esp. year 1246, II, 135–140.

[5] For a useful summary see Ernest Langlois' notes to his edition of *Roman de la Rose* (for the Société des anciens textes français), III, 325–326.

[6] The *De periculis* is printed in William of St. Amour, *Opera* (Constance [Paris?], 1632; also (though anonymously) in Ortwin Gratius' *Fasciculum rerum expetendarum*, ed. Edward Brown (London, 1690), pp. 18–41. All references in this paper are to the *Opera*.

[7] Ed. Sophronius Clasen, O.F.M., *Archivum Franciscanum Historicum*, XXXI (1938), 276–329; XXXII (1939), 89–200.

[8] Opusculum I (Parma ed.), tr. John Proctor, O.P., *An Apology for the Religious Orders* (London, 1910).

[9] Opuscula XII–XIV, *Opera Omnia* (Quaracchi ed.), VIII, 331–385.

[10] Both are edited by C. L. Kingsford, A. G. Little and F. Tocco, *British Society of Franciscan Studies*, II (1910).

[11] See *Roman de la Rose* (ed. cit.),'ll. 11483–508; English translation in Robinson's edition of Chaucer (Cambridge: Houghton Mifflin, 1933), ll. 6759–80. Hereafter, references to the *Roman* will be given in the English translation with the lines of the French following. See also on Jean de Meung and Rutebeuf, T. Denkinger, 'Die Bettelorden in der französischen didaktischen Literatur des 13. Jahrhunderts, in besondere bei Rutebeuf und im Roman de la Rose,' *Franziskanische Studien*, II (1915), 63–109, 286–313.

[12] Ed. L. L. Hammerich, 'The Beginning of the Strife between Richard FitzRalph and the Mendicants,' *Det Kgl. Danske Videnskabernes Solsob*, Historisk-filologiske Meddelelser, XXVI (1933), 3.

[13] There is no modern text of the sermons. The only printed text is in *Summa Domini Armacani in quaestionibus Armenorum . . . cum aliquibus sermonibus* [Paris, 1512], sigs Dii^r–Fiv^r. Since this text is quite unsatisfactory I shall cite that in BM MS. Lansdowne 393. For an account of the manuscripts see Aubrey Gwynn, S.J., 'The Sermon Diary of Richard FitzRalph, Archbishop of Armagh,' *Proceedings of the Royal Irish Academy*, XLIV (1937–1938), Section C, 1–57. On the career of FitzRalph see a series of articles by Gwynn in *Studies, an Irish Quarterly*, XXII (1933), 389, 591–607; XXIII (1934), 395–411; XXIV (1935), 558–372; XXV (1936), 81–96, XXVI (1937), 50–67.

[14] Latin text in Gratius, II, 466–486; and in Melchoir Goldast,

Monarchia (Hanover, 1612), II, 1392–1410; English translation ed. A. J. Perry, EETS, O.S., 167, pp. 39–93.

[15] Since writing this study, I have discovered a third: G. Meersseman, O.P., 'La défense des ordres mendiants contre Richard Fitz Ralph par Barthélemy de Bolsenheim O.P.,' *Archivum Fratrum Praedicatorum*, v (1935), 124–173. I have not yet studied this.

[16] In Goldast, II, 1410–1444.

[17] Complete in Cambridge University MS.Ff. I. 21 and Magdalen College (Oxford) MS Latin 75; summarized in New College MS. 290, fols. 58r–61).

[18] In Thomas Wright, *Political Poems and Songs* (Rolls Series), I, 269.

[19] Ll. 6364–68. For the French text see Langlois ed., III, 311.

[20] In Wright, I, 270. Both murder and rape were, by the way, normally reserved cases.

[21] *Defensio curatorum*, pp. 47–48; *Nemo vos seducat*, B. M. MS. Lansdowne 393, fol. 133 . Cp. also William of St. Amour, *De periculis*, ch. 5 (*Opera*, pp. 32–34).

[22] Point 11 (*Opera*, pp. 60–61).

[23] Pp. 39–40.

[24] 'Regula Beati Francisci precipit ne fratres recipiant per se vel per alios denarios vel pecuniam nullo modo, et vix transit [frater] per patriam aut per villam, qui socium ducat ad colligendum denarios.' B. M. MS Lansdowne 393, fol. 131.

[25] Points 26, 28 (*Opera*, pp. 66–67).

[26] Ll. 6454–56. For the French text see Langlois ed., IV, 314, ll. 81–85.

[27] Point 24 (*Opera*, p. 65). Cp. *Roman de la Rose*, ll. 6483–90 (11234–40). Bonaventure comes close to conceding the truth of these charges, for he does not deny them, but explains that friars seek the friendship of the great because they can do more good than the poor, witness the effects of the conversion of Constantine. Friars sometime fare sumptuously because they eat whatever is put before them, and that is sometimes elegant fare.

[28] D, 1839–45. Cp. *Roman de la Rose*, ll. 8738–48 (11740–56).

[29] B. M. MS. Lansdowne, fol. 131 .

[30] *Decalogus evangelice paupertatis*, ed. Michael Bihl, O. F. M., *Archivum Franciscanum Historicum*, XXXII (1939), 330–411, esp. pp. 330–332, 342–345.

[31] D, 1854–1860.

[32] British Museum MS. Add. 38,665, fols. 5r–13.

[33] British Museum MS. Cotton Claudius E. IV, fols. 322–23r. The Dominicans, often called 'Jacobins' after their convent of St. James near Paris, must be the order to claim foundation by Jacob, but I have never seen the assertion made.

[34] Ch. 5 (*Opera*, pp. 32–34) and point 1 (*Opera*, p. 57).

[35] British Museum MS. Royal 6. E. VI, fols. 50r–50v.

[36] Wright, I, 269.

5

Chaucer's Symbolic Plowman

JOSEPH HORRELL

> I have, God woot, a large feeld to ere,
> And wayke been the oxen in my plough.

THE neglect by scholars of Chaucer's Plowman is surprising
in view of the quantity of Chaucerian scholarship. The
reprobate Cook has been showered with an academic gloss
out of all proportion to his spiritual impulses. The dubious
morality of the Eternal Wife has elicited charges and counter-
charges from the ranks of the learned. From the concavity of
the eighth sphere, where he can hear the heavenly harmony
and view the erratic stars, Chaucer must ring out peals of
celestial laughter when he considers that his Plowman, his
only perfect Christian among the lay pilgrims, has received
from scholars the usual rewards of piety. Skeat has a few notes

Reprinted, by permission of author and editor, from *Speculum*,
XIV (1939), 82–92, with revisions by the author. Cf. Gardiner
Stillwell, "Chaucer's Plowman and the Contemporary English
Peasant," *ELH*, VI (1939), where it is argued that Chaucer's
"evident affection for the ideal peasant suggests an antagonism
toward the actual peasant," and that because "the real plowman
of the time was revolting against everything that Chaucer stood
for," Chaucer was expressing in this portrait the character he
believed the contemporary plowman did not, but ought to, possess.

on him; Manly's are briefer; Hinckley's are conspicuous by their absence.

Yet of the characters described in the General Prologue, only a few are more revealingly described. This Plowman is not dim and uncharacterized like the Burgesses or shadowily set forth like the Manciple. He is a man with a *typal* rôle in Chaucer's *comédie humaine*.

II

The Plowman's inclusion in the *Canterbury Tales* suggests that the class represented by him had achieved some sort of autonomy. We can mention only the important historical events and forces that furnish his background.

The most important single event of economic and social significance in Chaucer's age was the Peasants' Revolt. The swiftly moving developments, according to Professor Trevelyan, 'give a human and spiritual interest to the economic facts of the period, showing the peasant as a man, half beast and half angel, not a mere item in the bailiffs' books.'[1] Long before the Black Death, the Peasants' Revolt, and Chaucer's Plowman, the services of villains had been commutable for money payments. From the latter half of the thirteenth century forward, landowners were gradually turning away from labor-rents because they needed cash to meet the rising standards of living and the royal tax collectors; and the laborers were glad to commute for money payments, since this allowed them more independence in the cultivation of their own holdings. It was first the office of herdsman and next that of plowman that came to be filled with hired laborers. The plowman was usually expected to furnish his own team of cattle or horses. Plowing was naturally an essential operation on the demesne and was considered one of the skilled labors. It was some time before less necessary work was performed for money payments.

Before the Peasants' Revolt, the Black Death fell upon the land in a series of devastating onslaughts that hit most heavily the ranks of laborers. Consequently, the slowly developing agricultural revolution was hurried; the laborer was brought into a new position of prominence; and there came about a recognition of distinct classes, laboring and capitalist. On the heels of the Black Death and in the same year, 1349, came a startling increase in wages; so startling that, after a royal proclamation had failed, the manorial lords of Parliament enacted the Statute of Laborers the following year. The plowman is the only specific type of laborer mentioned in the law.[2] There followed the intolerable poll taxes, the preaching of the 'Great Society,' and finally, in 1381, the revolt. How the revolution failed, how the head of Wat Tyler ultimately replaced that of the Primate over London Bridge, is too long a story to occupy us here. We must note, however, that the revolt enhanced the prestige of the lowly workers; particularly that of the plowman, because of the nature of the prevailing economy. We must also note that the widespread and dramatic violence of the Peasants' Revolt gave it great symbolic significance.

The plowman's lot was still not a happy one. By a statute of 1495 men worked from five in the morning to between seven and nine in the evening, with a half-hour off for breakfast and one hour and a half for dinner and midday sleep—this from the middle of March to the middle of September. The avenues to independence were open, but the emancipation itself was to take time. The slow process found sustenance in the growing democratic sentiment. Not only did political and social agitators like John Ball pose the question,

> When Adam delved and Evé span,
> Who was then a gentleman?

but even a conservative like John Gower found himself arguing in strong terms for the original equality of men.

> Tous suismes d'un Adam issuz,
> Combien que l'un soit au dessus
> En halt estat, et l'autre en bass;
> Et tous au mond nasquismes nudz,
> Car ja nasquist si riches nuls
> Qui de nature ot un pigas.
> Ô tu q'en servitute m'as,
> Si je meinz ay et tu plus as
> Richesce, et soietz sanz vertus,
> Si tu malfais et je bien fas,
> Dieus changera tes sis en as,
> Tu meinz aras et j'aray plus.[3]

In this period of social and economic flux Chaucer surveyed mankind as a whole for types of men to represent it, and saw fit to include a plowman among the pilgrims journeying loquaciously to Canterbury.

III

But the treatment of the plowman at the hands of four-teenth-century writers was not always gentle. Simply as a mediaeval subject he was more often treated contemptuously.[4] In his orderings of the *états du monde*, Gower describes plowmen as persons lazy and avaricious, despite the fact that they are under divine commission to Adam to cultivate the soil. They are few in number; they ask exorbitant wages; one used to do as much work as three now.[5] This may be regarded as typical. On the other hand, despite some rebukes to plow-men, Langland portrays the saintly figure on the Malvern Hills with deep sympathy. He recognizes the vantage of a plowman, humble and living close to the soil, as most favor-able for a critical view of society. Piers the Plowman is a man conscientious in fulfilling his obligations to truth and duty, and we feel that with him Chaucer's Plowman has much in common.

Chaucer indicates some of the labors which engaged the Plowman's time. He carried many a load of manure, and the threshing and diking and delving that he would graciously do for his neighbors were doubtless a part of his own work. A good early account of the 'office of plowman' is found in the anonymous *Seneschaucie*, probably of the reign of Edward I:

> The ploughmen ought to be men of intelligence, and ought to know how to sow, and how to repair and mend broken ploughs and harrows, and to till the land well, and crop it rightly; and they ought to know also how to yoke and drive the oxen, without beating or hurting them, and they ought to forage them well, and look well after the forage that it be not stolen nor carried off; and they ought to keep them safely in meadows and several pastures, and other beasts which are found therein they ought to impound. And they and the keepers must make ditches and build and remove the earth, and ditch it so that the ground may dry and the water be drained. And they must not flay any beast until some one has inspected it, and inquired

by what default it died. And they must not carry fire into byres for light, or to warm themselves, and have no candle there, or light unless it be a lantern, and for great need and peril.[6]

Another interesting account similar to this one is found in the thirteenth-century *Fleta:*

> The *Plough-driver's* art consisteth herein, that he drive the yoked oxen evenly, neither smiting nor pricking nor grieving them. Such should not be melancholy or wrathful, but cheerful, jocund and full of song, that by their melody and song the oxen may in a manner rejoice in their labour. Such a ploughman should bring the fodder with his own hands, and love his oxen and sleep with them by night, tickling and combing and rubbing them with straw; keeping them well in all respects, and guarding their forage or provender from theft. . . . If he find other beasts in their pasture, he must impound them. He and the hands, when plough-time is over, must dike and delve, thresh, fence, clean the water-courses, and do other such-like profitable works.[7]

The particular tasks of threshing and diking and delving mentioned by Chaucer were the usual duties of plowmen in his day.

Concerning the Plowman's personal appearance our information is meagre. Chaucer simply tells us that he wore a tabard and rode upon a mare. The tabard was originally an elaborate coat worn by nobles, but there is evidence indicating that by Chaucer's time it was the usual dress of plowmen—doubtless a rude imitation of its aristocratic prototype. Our plowman's garment was probably a loose-fitting overcoat, either sleeveless or with loose, wide sleeves open at the sides. As for the Plowman's mount, the mare was usually ridden by one of humble station; indeed, it indicated humility, or often humiliation. No person of social standing would have condescended to ride such a steed. There is a Latin poem on the execution of Archbishop Scrope in 1405 which describes the ignominy of being led to death mounted on a mare. So far as Chaucer's specific statements enlighten us, the Plowman is quite conventional in his bearing and doubtless typical of the class he represents.

But despite this dearth of information, there are literary

portraits to which we may look for a more complete, picture of this pilgrim. A not too dispassionate one of about 1394 is in *Pierce the Ploughmans Crede,* a Wycliffite poem:

> And as y wente be þe waie · wepynge for sorowe,
> [I] seiȝ a sely man me by · opon þe plow hongen.
> His cote was of a cloute · þat cary was y-called,
> His hod was full of holes · & his heer oute,
> Wiþ his knopped schon · clouted full þykke;
> His ton toteden out · as he þe londe treddede,
> His hosen ouerhongen his hokschynes · on eueriche a side,
> Al beslombred in fen · as he þe plow folwede;
> Twey myteynes, as mete · maad all of cloutes;
> Þe fyngers weren for-werd · & cul of fen honged.
> Þis whit waselede in þe [fen] · almost to þe ancle,
> Foure roþeren hym by-forn · þat feble were [worþen];
> Men myȝte reken ich a ryb · so reufull þey weren,[8]

However much this portrait may be overdrawn, the plowman's life was certainly not one of many comforts. His fare was usually as rude as his person; breakfast a scant meal taken early, dinner at noon, supper perhaps not until the day's work was done. From *Piers the Plowman* we learn that the principal food was beans and bacon, with variations in fare before and after harvest time. Dependent upon his own produce, the plowman found some months in the year pretty lean. Listen to Piers' bitter reply to Hunger, which contains other information pertinent here:

> 'I haue no peny,' quod peres · 'poletes forto bigge,
> Ne neyther gees ne grys · but two grene cheses,
> A fewe cruddes and creem · and an hauer cake,
> And two loues of benes and bran · y-bake for my fauntis.
> And ȝet I sey, by me soule · I haue no salt bacoun,
> Ne no kokeney, bi cryst · coloppes forto maken.
> Ac I haue percil and porettes · and many koleplantes,
> And eke a cow and a kalf · and a cart-mare
> To drawe a-felde my donge · þe while þe drought lasteth.
> And bi þis lyflode we mot lyue · til lammasse tyme;
> And bi þat, I hope to haue · heruest in my croft;
> And þanne may I diȝte þi dyner · as me dere liketh.'
> Alle þe pore peple þo · pesecoddes fetten,
> Benes and baken apples · þei brouȝte in her lappes,
> Chibolles and cheruelles · and ripe chiries manye,
> And profred peres þis present · to plese with hunger.[9]

A following passage tells us that after harvest conditions were all for the better. Then laborers with no lands to live on save their hands would disdain to breakfast on herbs a night old. No penny ale or bacon for them; nay, nothing less than fresh flesh or fish, fried or baked, and that *chaud* or *plus chaud* against the cold in their maw. And if the laborer is not paid a good price for his work, he will complain and bemoan the time he was made a laborer. More than that, he talks against Cato's admonition, 'Paupertatis onus pacienter ferre memento,' complains against God and Reason, and curses the King and all his council for making laws to vex laborers. There was, however, a harsh reality which often suppressed this out-spokenness in hard seasons; and the very lives of plowmen doubtless furnished the pathos of these following lines, remarkable in their poetic quality:

Ac whiles hunger was her maister · þere wolde none of hem chyde,
Ne stryue aȝeines his statut · So sterneliche he loked.[10]

The character of the Plowman, as we shall see, hardly allows us to associate him closely with these malcontents; yet they are none the less helpful in our efforts to determine roughly his economic status. . . . We have already seen that many laborers of this time, like those in *Piers the Plowman,* toiled for wages and even had personal holdings. The general interpretation of the Plowman holds that he was a free laborer and property owner, or perhaps a tenant farmer. Indeed, the readiness with which he would charitably go to to the aid of 'every povre wight,' 'withouten hire,' 'For Cristes sake,' suggests the freedom of his position and the lack of any except religious obligation.

Chaucer implies that the Plowman owns property in his statement that he pays his tithes fairly and well 'Bothe of his propre swynk and his catel.' The usual interpretation of 'catel' has been property, or, more generally, goods, though it has also been interpreted simply as cattle. Whatever the interpretation may be, the Plowman paid tithes fairly on his 'catel' as well as his proper work; and Chaucer doubtless knew that many persons of his time could not have made this claim. . . . In Chaucer's own day, 1385, John de Burgo exhorts the clergy to be wary that tithes of *all* income be collected, as he instructs them in the duties of their profession in his *Pupilla Oculi*: 'Let peasants and serfs be questioned [in the confessional] whether they have defrauded by withholding or diminishing their tithes, either of produce or personal labour. . . .' But the Plowman was not one to circumvent a clearly religious obligation, as Chaucer's delineation of him as the ideal Christian among the lay pilgrims finally indicates.

IV

The Plowman was a laborer far down, economically speaking, in the scale of laboring men; and to understand him as an ideal Christian we must know something of the mediaeval attitude towards poverty. Of all ages Chaucer's certainly had its share of Jeremiahs to deplore the decay of life through defections in the estates. This was a favorite and nearly a stock theme with many moralists and poets. Usk, Langland, Gower, and Scogan, to mention only a few, raised their voices in this chorus of complaint against the times. Wyclif again and again leveled his fire on the Church for its oppression of the poor. In his tract *Of Clerks Possessioners* he berates the clerks for their departure from abstinence, poverty, and labor—the way of life they formerly chose.[11] He argues that all truly religious men should love poverty. We see that the scriptural warnings of the difficulty of a rich man's getting into Heaven were not lost upon him in his insistence that poverty is the status of life most conducive to true religion. He had ample support from the Bible and many religionists for the contention that God loves the poor.

It is with this idea that God loves the poor, and that the poor can best lead the true Christian life, that we are most concerned. Wyclif's ideas on poverty correlated well with his theory of dominion. He declares that the unrighteous man has no right to lordship, for the right to possess comes from righteousness.[12] Since dominion is by God's grant, the righteous man is lord of all things, having charity, which is God, and grace, which is the Holy Spirit. With this general idea

Wyclif proceeds to show that the righteous man, by the fact of his surrender of all earthly things for Christ, has a more real possession of all things. But this idea of poverty, taking its origin ultimately in the Scriptures, goes back much farther than Wyclif. The well known Rule of St Benedict had stipulated poverty for monks as one of the grades of humility, a poverty that would cause the monk to consider himself 'as a poor and unworthy workman.' The Rule of St Francis of Assisi also extolled 'lofty poverty'; there need be no shame in it, 'for the Lord made Himself poor for us in this world.' The Church assimilated this idea of poverty and continually expounded it as the rule of the noblest Christian life.

Aquinas reasoned the matter at great length. A beatitude, because it belongs to the perfection of spiritual life, he considers to be an act of perfect virtue; a perfection requiring 'that whoever would strive to obtain a perfect share of spiritual goods, needs to begin by despising earthly goods'—the renunciation of earthly goods being not perfection but the way to it.[13] This does not mean that any sort of poverty is worthy. In the same manner that riches incur pride, so does begging occasion lying and perjury. Poverty is a sign of great humility when one, like Christ, is poor willingly.[14] In general, the Middle Ages conceived of two kinds of poverty, willful and impatient. It is the former that is extolled as a virtue and a part of the ascetic life. But impatient poverty, poverty of grumbling and complaint, was despised as a vice.[15]

These ideas of poverty were current in Chaucer's day. How else would that experienced lady of secular mind, the Wife of Bath, know about them? It is related in her tale:

> And ther as ye of poverte me repreeve,
> The hye God, on whom that we beleeve,
> In wilful poverty chees to lyve his lyf.
> And certes every man, mayden, or wyf,
> May understonde that Jhesus, hevene, kyng,
> Ne wolde nat chese a vicious lyvyng.[16]

In the spurious *Ploughman's Tale*, which was tagged on the *Canterbury Tales* and attributed to the Plowman, we read that a tiller at the plow knows nothing of the Pope. His creed is sufficient for him, and he can tell a cardinal by his hat. Such as he are the men and women of poverty "That been Christes awne likeness." Behind this and other plowmen is, of course, the Christ-like figure of Piers, the rude toiler in the dream of William who had a vision of the world while asleep on the Malvern Hills. After Langland's poem the plowman, as Wright says, 'had been adopted as the representative of religious and political purity . . . the embodiment of the pure democratic principle which lay at the bottom of the opinions which now agitated the world.'⁸ So Chaucer, surveying the mass of mankind for an ideal Christian layman, chose the Plowman as a symbol of the rude, anonymous folk who might lead the beatific life.

V

This true and good worker lived in 'pees and parfit charite.' Chaucer was fully aware of the high compliment he was paying the Plowman. The religious treatises of the age were full of encomiums of charity and exhortations for its practice. But we cannot justly appraise the religious temper of this rude fellow until we understand what it was in mediaeval times to possess perfect charity.

The best exposition of the scholastic virtues is naturally found in Aquinas. He reasons from Aristotle's idea of two principles of human action, intellect and appetite. Every human virtue is of necessity a perfection of one of these principles; thus derive moral virtue, perfecting the appetitive faculty, and intellectual virtue, perfecting the intellectual faculty. So much, then, for the human virtues. But to the question as to whether virtues can be adequately divided into moral and intellectual there is raised the objection that faith, hope, and charity are indeed virtues, yet of neither of these two sorts. To this objection Aquinas answers that 'faith, hope, and charity are *superhuman* virtues'—the virtues of man as sharing the grace of God, or theological virtues. So man's happiness is twofold. One part has to do with his human nature, the happiness he can attain by natural principles. The other is a happiness beyond man's nature obtained only by the power of God. It is here that only the theological virtues can be efficacious: their object is God and they direct man to God; they are infused into man by God and made known to man by Divine revelation.

A question is raised as to the precedence of the theological virtues of faith, hope, and charity. This order is held to be twofold, the order of generation and the order of perfection. In the order of generation, just as matter precedes form, or the imperfect the perfect, so does faith precede hope, and hope charity. But in the order of perfection charity comes before faith and hope, because these latter are quickened by charity and receive their full complement as virtues from it. Aquinas concludes that 'charity is the mother and the root of all the virtues.' This conclusion he deduces from his Aristotelian principle of matter and form, charity being the form of, and giving form to, all virtues. The definition of every virtue must include charity, not because charity is every virtue, but because every virtue depends upon it.[19]

Wyclif, too, thought charity the sum of all the virtues. It is not strange that he considered it at some length when we recall that he bases dominion, or lordship—a concept of great ideological importance in the age—upon charity. Charity is to be recognized in a person by his preference for the eternal good to the temporal.[20]

But our Plowman lived in *perfect* charity; and Aquinas has more to say about that. The title of one of his articles is: 'Whether Charity can be perfect in this Life?' That man has perfect charity who loves as much as he can; and, on earth, perfect charity obtains to him when he 'makes an earnest endeavor to give his time to God and Divine things, while scorning other things except in so far as the needs of the present life demand. This is the perfection of charity that is possible to a wayfarer; but it is not common to all who have charity.'[21] From the unknown writer of the *Vices and Virtues* of about 1200, and before him, down to encyclopaedic Gower and others later, the virtue charity was praised. Chaucer would not have unknowingly given his lowly Plowman this crown.

With all the love of his fellow men that would naturally emanate from his bounty of charity, the Plowman yet loved God best of all and with his whole heart, at all times, no matter what his fortunes might be. And after that, he loved his neighbor just as himself. Indeed there is more than mere sociability in this plowman. He has the deep and sincere, the heavenly religious feeling of his brother the Parson, who is of like humility. Aquinas and Wyclif agree that man should love God out of charity above all others, because He is the cause of happiness; whereas one's neighbor is loved out of charity as a fellow-participant in that happiness. The 'pees' that the Plowman enjoys may simply be a consequence of charity. Although peace is not in itself a separate virtue, the conditions for it are provided by charity: 'Since then charity causes peace precisely because it is love of God and of our neighbour, . . . there is no other virtue except charity whose proper act is peace. . . .'[22]

The Plowman is always ready to aid his fellows—to thresh and dike and delve gratis, for any poor man, if he is able—and he does his good turns 'For Cristes sake.' In the practical expression of love for his neighbor, the Plowman may even be religiously exact in doing acts of charity for Christ's sake; for Aquinas had contended that '. . . God is the principal object of charity for God's sake.'

These niceties might very well alarm Chaucer, more probably would amuse him. The ideological elements of his age were less consciously present in his mind than they are consciously absent from ours. As a poet he was not primarily interested in abstractions. He found in the Plowman a convenient symbol; and he crowned this lowliest of the pilgrims with the highest of Christian virtues. The Plowman's social and economic background shows us, in a general way, the forces that brought him into prominence in the flux of fourteenth-century life. His cultural background shows us that literary and religious men, often the same, were aware of him as a convenient representative of the stirring masses of lowly workers. Behind him lay a long tradition exalting the poverty he found his lot.[23] And in singling out this obscure man as a symbol of the lower fringe of humanity seeking emancipation from economic and social servitude, Chaucer is again revealing a deeply sympathetic regard for character and human worth in an age when others might have more gladly cracked a pate.

Notes

[1] For discussions of the Peasants' Revolt see G. M. Trevelyan, *England in the Age of Wycliffe* (London, 1915), pp. 183–255; Bernard L. Manning, *Camb. Med. Hist.* (New York, 1932), VII, 460–465; special works cited here.

[2] Statute of Laborers, *Select Historical Documents of the Middle Ages*, trans. and ed. E. F. Henderson (London, 1892), p. 165.

[3] *Mirour de l'Omme*, ll. 23389–400, in *The Complete Works of John Gower*, ed. G. G. Macaulay (Oxford, 1899), Vol. I. Cf. further for numerous citations G. M. Vogt, 'Gleanings for the History of a Sentiment: *Generositas Virtus, non Sanguis*,' *JEGP*, XXIV (1925), 102–123. ["We have all sprung from the one Adam, even though one may be above in high estate, the other below. And all were born naked into the world, for never was anyone born so rich as to possess his finery by nature. O, you who hold me in bondage, if I have less riches and you more, and if you are without virtues and do evil while I do good, God will change your pieces-of-six into mere pennies, and you shall have less, I more."]

[4] Cf. Robinson, *op. cit.*, notes to A, 529–541.

[5] *Vox Clamantis*, v, ix *passim*, in Gower, *Complete Works, op. cit.*, Vol. IV. Cf. also Ruth Mohl, *The Three Estates in Medieval and Renaissance Literature* (New York, 1933), pp. 27 ff, and *passim*. For two interesting sixteenth-century accounts of the origin of the rank of plowman see Alexander Barclay's fifth eclogue, ed. Beatrice White, *The Eclogues of Alexander Barclay*, EETS, CLXXV (London, 1928), 194 ff.

[6] *Walter of Henley's Husbandry*, trans. and ed. Elizabeth Lamond (London, 1890), p. 110.

[7] *Fleta*, ed. John Selden, 1647; quoted from *Social Life in Britain from the Conquest to the Reformation*, ed. G.G. Coulton (Cambridge, 1918), p. 166.

[8] *Op. cit.*, ll. 418–30 ["And as I went along the road, weeping for sorrow, I saw nearby a simple man clinging to a plow. His coat was of a ragged cloth called cary, his hood full of holes, his hair sticking through them, his shoes knobbed and wrapped thickly in rags. His toes protruded as he trod the earth. His hose hung down from his thighs all about his shins, and were caked with filth as he followed the plow. Two mittens he had, made all of rags; the fingers were out and cold and dirty. This man tramped in the muck almost ankle-deep, four oxen before him, feeble grown; one could count each rib, so pitiful were the beasts."]

[9] *Op. cit.*, VII, 282–97 [" 'I haven't a penny,' said Piers, 'to buy chickens or geese or pigs; I have only two green cheeses, a few curds and cream, and an oaten cake, and two loaves of beans and bran baked for my children. Nay, by my soul, I have no salt bacon; no hen's eggs, by Christ, with which to make collops. But I have

parsley and leeks and many cabbages, and a cow and a calf and a cart-mare to draw manure to the field, while the drought lasts. These must be our livelihood till Lammastide. By then I hope to have my harvest in the barn, and then I may make your dinner in the way I'd dearly like.' Then all the poor folk came bringing peas in the pod. Beans and dried apples they brought in their aprons, and onions and herbs and many ripe cherries, and gave these to Piers as presents to allay his hunger."]

[10] *Ibid.*, 304–5 ["But while hunger was their master, no one of them would grumble or rebel against his rule, so grim was his visage."]

[11] Cf. *The English Works of Wyclif*, ed. F. D. Matthew, EETS, OS 74 (London, 1902), cap 34 and *passim*.

[12] Iohannis Wycliffe, *De civili dominio*, ed. R. L. Poole, Wyclif Society (London, 1885), I, i. and *passim*.

[13] *Summa Theologica*, trans. Fathers of the English Dominican Province (London, 1917), II–II, xix, 12, *ad* 1.

[14] *Ibid.*, III, xl, 3, *ad* 3.

[15] Cf. Frederick Tupper, 'Wilful and Impatient Poverty,' *The Nation*, XCIX (1914), 41. See also on poverty Dan Michel, *Ayenbite of Inwyt*, ed. Richard Morris, EETS, OS 23 (London, 1895) pp. 138–139.

[16] D, 1177–82.

[17] Ll. 453 ff., in *Oxford Chaucer*, Supplement.

[18] *Political Poems, op. cit.*, I, lxxviii.

[19] See *Summa Theologica*, II–I, lviii, 4; II–I, lviii, 3, *ad* 3; II–I, lxii, I, c; II–I, lxii, 4, c; II–II, xxiii, 8, c; II–II, xxiii, 4, *ad* 1.

[20] *De civili dominio*, I, xv–xvi.

[21] *Summa Theologica*, II–II, xxiv, 8, c.

[22] *Summa Theologica*, II–II, 4, c, 3.

[23] For a general discussion, largely based on internal evidence, see H. R. Patch, 'Chaucer and the Common People,' *JEGP*, XXIX (1930), 376–384.

6

An Interpretation of Chaucer's Knight's Tale

WILLIAM FROST

. . . The labours of modern medievalists have clarified
for us much of the intellectual, historical, and literary ma-
terials which went into the creation of the poem Chaucer
put into the mouth of his Knight and dignified as the first
of the Canterbury Tales. Thanks to historical scholarship we
now know not only that its immediate source was in Boccaccio
rather than 'Stace of Thebes and thise bookes olde' (as the
Knight rather vaguely puts it) but also just what Chaucer
imitated from the Italian's *Teseide,* what he left out, and
where he got much of what he added. Arcite's 'maladye of
Heroes' has been diagnosed by Professor Lowes with an
erudition no doubt few fourteenth-century physicians could
have commanded; Chaucer's use of the *Teseide* (in the
Knight's Tale and elsewhere) has been related to his gen-

Reprinted, by permission of author and editor, from *The Review
of English Studies,* XXV (1949), 290–304. Cf. Charles Muscatine,
"Form, Texture, and Meaning in Chaucer's Knight's Tale," *PMLA,*
LXV (1950), 911–29, and *Chaucer and the French Tradition*
(Berkeley: University of California Press, 1957), pp. 175–90.
Unlike Frost, Muscatine holds that the tale is not "the best kind
in which to look for either delicate characterization or the peculiar
fascination of an exciting plot," yet, as the result of stylistic
analysis, concludes, like Frost, that the tale embodies a philosophi-
cal questioning of the noble life.

eral development as a poet by Professor R. A. Pratt; Professor B. A. Wise has traced the inspiration of some passages in the Tale back to 'Stace of Thebes' himself; Professors B. L. Jefferson and H. R. Patch have derived many ideas in the poem from the tradition of Boethius. The mysteries of Chaucerian astrology have been clarified by Professor W. C. Curry; a number of writers have dealt with the conventions of courtly love embodied in the story; and the close relation of the military aspects of the Tale to actual fourteenth-century warfare has been established: indeed, the latest suggestion is that the tournament at the climax of the plot may have been inspired by a real tournament Chaucer probably witnessed in London.[1]

In short, we know something of Chaucer's experiences, library, tastes, opinions, and methods of composition; as well as, by inference, something of the point of view of his earlier audience—we can dimly imagine how it felt to read the Knight's Tale in the 1390s. But on the Tale as a tale—except for widespread comments that it is, generally speaking, a good one—much less has been written and very little agreement been reached. What may be the point of the story is frequently debated, votes having been registered for the Tale as allegory, as a riddle, as a pseudo-epic (marred by omission of too much of Boccaccio's material), and as a piece of realism (marred by an excess of epic machinery). Who should be considered the hero is even questioned, some preferring Palamon, some Arcite, others finding little to choose between them. Among these latter is Professor Root,[2] who feels that the descriptions (of battles, temples, May, &c.), 'with occasional passages of noble reflection,' are the 'flesh and blood' of the poem, 'of which the characters and action are merely the skeleton framework'.[3] 'What is the Knight's Tale', he asks, 'but a splendidly pictured tapestry, full of color and motion?'[4] It is my purpose to attempt, in terms of the Tale itself, an answer to Mr. Root's question.

I

The Knight's Tale develops from three widening con-

centric circles of interest: the merely human interest of the
rivalry between two young heroes, both noble and both in
love, for the hand of a heroine who has no apparent prefer-
ence between them; the ethical interest of a conflict of obli-
gations between romantic love and military comradeship;
and finally the theological interest attaching to the method
by which a just providence fully stabilizes a disintegrating
human situation.

As important as the problems of the plot is the atmosphere
in which they are worked out, the world of the Knight's
Tale. This world, being an amalgam of legendary Athens,
fourteenth-century England, and the never-never land of
chivalric romance, presents to us that curious double relation-
ship to any imaginable real world which most great art—the
Odyssey, Hamlet, Paradise Lost, Faust—seems to attain; that
is, a simultaneous relationship (the delight of readers and
despair of historians) of nearness and distance. Anyone
called 'Theseus, Duke of Athens' must surely be a classical
hero refracted through a medieval lens; so we suppose, only
to discover that there was a living 'Duke of Athens' at the
time Chaucer wrote.[5] But whether classical, realistic, or chiv-
alric, the atmosphere of the Tale has three abiding attributes:
it is predominantly noble, predominantly tragic, and deeply
infused with a sense of significance transcending both hu-
man beings and their material environment. In this essay I
shall consider first the problems of the story, then the general
characteristics of the universe in which the story happens.

II

The problem of who shall win the hand of the fair Emelye,
Duke Theseus's young sister, is intensified throughout the
Knight's Tale by systematic and delicately balanced paral-
lelism in the presentation of the rival heroes, Palamon and
Arcite. At no point is either allowed to take the centre of
the stage or the initiative in setting the plot in motion with-
out the other at once having an equal opportunity. If the
two knights are together they are spoken of as a pair: 'This
Palamon and his felawe Arcite' (1031); if events separate
them the spotlight shifts impartially from one to the other:

> Now wol I stynte of Palamon a lite,
> And lete hym in his prisoun stille dwelle,
> And of Arcita forth I wol you telle. . . . (1334–6)
> . . . And in this blisse lete I now Arcite
> And speke I wole of Palamon a lite. . . . (1449–50)

Moreover, the two knights have much in common: besides being noble, young, and passionately in love, besides being kinsmen, compatriots, and sworn blood-brothers, they are equally valorous:

> There nas no tygre in the vale of Galgopheye
> Whan that hir whelp is stole whan it is lite,
> So crueel on the hunte as is Arcite
> For jelous herte upon this Palamon.
> Ne in Belmarye ther nys so fel leon,
> That hunted is, or for his hunger wood,
> Ne of his praye desireth so the blood,
> As Palamon to sleen his foo Arcite. . . . (2626–33)

If Arcite despairs at being exiled from Athens and the sight of Emelye, Palamon despairs at being still imprisoned and helpless to win her. If Palamon breaks faith with Theseus by escaping from prison, Arcite merits equal punishment for returning to Athens in disguise. At the final tourney, for which each has prepared by prayer and sacrifice to a patron deity, each is seconded by a confederate champion, warlike and exotic: Palamon by 'Lygurge himself, the grete kyng of Trace' (2129), with his white wolfhounds; Arcite by 'the grete Emetrius, the kyng of Inde' (2156), an eagle on his wrist and tame lions and leopards all about him.

So ostensibly impartial is the presentation of the heroes, in fact, that it is no wonder that some Chaucerians—Professor Hulbert, for example[*]—have failed to see any significant distinction between them. The teller of the tale himself never obviously sides with one or the other; to Theseus they are an identical pair of infatuated fools; and even Emelye expresses no preference between 'Palamon, that hath swich love to me' (2314) and 'Arcite, that loveth me so soore' (2315). Finally, as the lines I have been quoting demonstrate, the concurrent stories of the two heroes are narrated in a poetry marked by all manner of rhetorical parallelism.

I am sure myself that the heroes are significantly differ-

entiated from each other, and that a valid preference be-
tween them is implied by the poem; but they are certainly
not individualized in the manner of such rival protagonists
of later storytelling as Richard II and Bolingbroke, or Dobbin
and George Osborne. Much of the beauty of the Knight's
Tale, and of its appropriateness to the man who tells it,
resides in a certain formal regularity of design. Thus the May-
songs of Emelye and Arcite, redolent of youth, freshness,
and spontaneity, come at two crucial points in the plot;
while early May is also the time of the final contest that will
make one hero happy and the other glorious. Thus the Tale
begins with a wedding, a conquest, and a funeral; and ends
with a tournament, a funeral, and a wedding.

III

A conflict between love and comradeship in the hearts
of the two knights is the emotional focus of the story, the
poetry of which develops each of the conflicting elements
as a constituent of the world in which the story takes place.
Comradeship implies war: Palamon and Arcite are first intro-
duced, side by side, 'both in oon armes', on the field of battle.
Chaucer created the military elements of the poem by fusing
his own knowledge of contemporary warfare with a classical
tradition that stretches back through Boccaccio and Statius
to the ancient Greeks. The mixture is rich, allusive, and
concrete:

> The rede statue of Mars, with spere and targe,
> So shyneth in his white baner large,
> That alle the feeldes glyteren up and doun;
> And by his baner born is his penoun
> Of gold ful riche, in which there was ybete
> The Mynotaur, which that he slough in Crete.
> Thus rit this duc, thus rit this conquerour,
> And in his hoost of chivalrie the flour .... (975–82)

These lines are from a description of Theseus, the domi-
nant figure of the poem and, significantly, the man who
unites in his person successes in war and love alike. 'He
conquered al the regne of Femenye' (866), symbolic home-
land of Ypolita, Amazon queen and Theseus's bride. For

neither of the two knights, it finally develops, will such a double triumph be possible; one is to have victory in battle, the other to marry Emelye.

In a drama involving conquest, tourneying, and hand-to-hand combat ankle-deep in blood, comradely loyalty is, of course, a fitting plot-motif; and the outward similarity between Palamon and Arcite enhances the violence of their rupture. They are, moreover, sworn blood-brothers—into Palamon's mouth is put a picture of the relation between them as it has been up to the beginning of the tale and ought, ideally, to continue (1129–40). Since the re-establishment of this normal, desirable, and exemplary relation is to be a part of the denouement, it is noteworthy that immediately after the break between the two knights there occurs a symbolic allusion to one of the most famous instances of fellowship in ancient legend. Scarcely have Palamon and Arcite quarrelled for the first time than Perotheus arrives in Athens and is described as follows:

> A worthy duc that highte Perotheus,
> That felawe was unto duc Theseus
> Syn thilke day that they were children lite. . . .
> So wel they lovede, as olde bookes sayn,
> That whan that oon was deed, soothly to telle,
> His felawe went and soughte hym doun in helle. . . .
> (1191–3, 1198–1200)

And we are reminded of a great myth celebrated in classical poetry—in Horace, for example:

> . . . Theseus leaves Pirithöus in the chain
> The love of comrades cannot take away.[1]

This reference to Theseus' journey to the underworld is, by the way, one classical detail Chaucer *added* to what he took from the *Teseide*.

Romantic love, which drives Palamon and Arcite apart, enters the poem most notably in the praise each lover accords Emelye, the illness and despair each undergoes, and Palamon's prayer in the temple of Venus. Romantic love, however, implying as it does chivalry, courts of love, and the idealization of woman, invests the figure of Theseus also.

Despite his mockery of the lovers the Duke has been, he
says, a 'servant' in his time. He is, moreover, a general who
undertakes a new war to avenge insults done to ladies; an
absolute ruler who allows his punishment of self-acknowl-
edged culprits to be deflected by the merciful intervention of
his wife and sister; a devastator of 'wall and sparre and
rafter' in conquered Thebes, but also an umpire who forbids
fatal bloodshed at the tournament over which he presides.
Thus if the Knight's Tale develops a conflict between an
ethic of battle and an ethic of love, nevertheless in the
figures of Theseus, Ypolita, and Perotheus we are presented
with an emblem of the two kinds of value reconciled and in
accord.

We are also presented, in the minds of Palamon and
Arcite, with two views of the same situation, Palamon being
the spokesman of the greater idealism. The contrast comes
first in the way each regards Emelye. In Boccaccio both saw
her as Venus; in Chaucer Palamon alone, in the following
metaphor charged with religious overtones, makes that iden-
tification:

> Venus, if it be thy wil
> Yow in this gardyn thus to transfigure,
> Bifore me, sorweful, wrecched creature . . . . (1104–6)

Arcite emphatically differs, and seeks to use the difference as
an argument for his own priority; he says to Palamon,

> Thyn is affeccioun of hoolynesse,
> And myn is love, as to creature . . . . (1158–9)

Or, as Dryden translated the lines:

> Thine was devotion to the blest above;
> I saw the woman, and desired her love. . . .
> (*Palamon and Arcite*, i. 319–20)

It is a conflict, not between love and love, but between devo-
tion and desire.

This is the first instance of a significant divergence be-
tween the rivals; a second follows at once in their attitude

toward the law of comradeship. Each, naturally, cites this law as binding on the other; but it is Arcite, not Palamon, who ultimately repudiates it for them both, in the lines:

> And therfore, at the kynges court, my brother,
> Ech man for hymself, ther is noon other. (1181–2)

The third and crucial divergence comes on the morning of the tournament when Arcite prays to Mars for a victory in arms which he thinks will be the means of possessing Emelye, while Palamon prays to Venus for Emelye herself.

Thus to Arcite the situation presents itself throughout as a practical problem of satisfying a desire by pursuit of the logical means to attain it. When he compares himself and Palamon, quarrelling in prison over Emelye, to the two dogs who fought over a bone till both lost it (1177–80) he resembles Theseus at the latter's most pragmatic moment (1798–1812); and on his return to Athens as Philostrate Arcite sets on foot the most elaborate scheme either lover ever conceives of to gain his object. Palamon, on the other hand, though fully as fervent as his rival, includes his passion in a wider conception of Venus-worship; and, far from prizing victory or any other means of success, puts his love for Emelye above life itself (2254–8). In thus extending beyond the grave his love resembles the devoted comradeship of Theseus and Perotheus.

Even the language used about him by the teller of the Tale distinguishes Palamon's experience from that of his comrade: his imprisonment while Arcite is free is spoken of as a 'martyrdom' (1460), and with 'hooly herte' he makes a 'pilgrymage' to the temple of Venus (2214–15).

It seems to me, then, that the outcome of the tale is fully justified by what has gone before—that Palamon wins Emelye because he is worthier of her, in terms of the story, than is Arcite. By this I would not imply either that Arcite is base or that the loser wins nothing; half the interest of the final solution is in the reconciliation between the two knights and the comments of Theseus on Arcite's fate. If it be thought that the evidence on which I have sought to make a distinction between the knights is too slender to support one, then

I can plead in defense that the slightest parts of the poem
are often charged with a significance only apparent in the
light of the whole. When Arcite, for example, on being given
his liberty complains that 'We witen nat what thing we
preyen heere' (1260), his words are full of an irony (because
of his later prayer to Mars) greater than his immediate cir-
cumstances presuppose.

IV

The justice of the solution in relation to the two knights
would be incomplete, however, if that solution were not
brought by justifiable procedure. The course of events is
determined to some extent by the knights themselves, more
largely by Theseus, and ultimately by the various divinities,
especially Saturn, and the supernatural power that they repre-
sent. Of the human figures in the story that of Theseus is
dominant—indeed, so much so as to seem, in comparison to
Palamon, Arcite, and Emelye, almost superhuman. Theseus
is both the guardian of Emelye and the legal possessor of the
persons of the knights from the moment they are brought
before him, more dead than alive, after the battle at Thebes.
Later he releases Arcite, and Palamon escapes; but before
either has had a chance to advance his cause with Emelye
the Duke comes upon them and takes them prisoner again.
At this point the poem implicitly associates him with the
destiny and divine foreknowledge which, according to the
teller of the Tale, lie behind all human events and situations:

> . . . And forth I wole of Theseus yow telle.
> The destinee ministre general,
> That executeth in the world over al
> The purveiaunce that God hath seyn biforn
> So strong it is that, though the world had sworn
> The contrarie of a thing by ye or nay,
> Yet sometyme it shall fallen on a day
> That falleth nat eft withinne a thousand yeer. . . .
> This mene I now by myghty Theseus. . . . (1662 ff.)

Theseus is the executant of destiny. On the morning of the
final tourney he sits in a window of his palace overlooking
the crowd and 'arrayed right as he were a god in trone'

(2529). As a personality he is appropriately impressive: terrifying in action, philosophical in outlook; richly experienced yet detached in point of view; warmly sympathetic to misfortune[8] yet mockingly ironical at the expense of youthful enthusiasm. From the moment when he gives orders that the captured knights be imprisoned to the moment when he arranges the final nuptials of Emelye and Palamon he dominates the plot without ever being a partisan. Thus his pronouncements, and especially his long speech in the final scene, carry peculiar weight.

Destiny proper is represented first by the three divinities to whom the rivals, and Emelye, appeal; then by Saturn, who settles the issue among the divinities; and ultimately by a Divinity—'the sighte above' (1672), 'the Firste Moevere' (2987)—beyond all particular divinities. This ultimate godhead, 'the which is prince and cause of alle thing' (3036), is identified by Theseus with 'Juppiter'; but the conception of him given by Theseus's speech as a whole sets him significantly apart from those other representatives of the classical pantheon who figure in the Knight's Tale. These—Mars, Diana, and the rest—are as much stars as gods;[9] and being stars they are the particular manifestations of Fortune, or Destiny, which is the agent, ultimately, of Providence. In *Paradise Lost* the pagan deities are assimilated to Christian story by their banishment to hell as rebel angels; in the Knight's Tale they still reign in the physical heavens, but reign as deputies of a transcendent sovereign.

V

When the Knight had finished his Tale Chaucer records that it won the general applause of the pilgrims, and the unanimous approval of the gentlefolk among them: 'And namely the gentils everichon' (3113). This last statement we can readily believe; for the Tale is wholeheartedly aristocratic, both in subject-matter and attitude. All the principal figures are of high birth; Arcite, for example, mortified by his disguise as a poor squire, reflects on his lineage in the following lines:

> Alas, ybroght is to confusioun
> The blood roial of Cadme and Amphioun,—
> Of Cadmus, which that was the firste man
> That Thebes built, or first the toun bigan,
> And of the citee first was crouned kyng.
> Of his lynage am I and his ofspryng
> By verray ligne, as of the stok roial. . . . (1545–51)

Theseus represents the full exercise of a sovereignty the material prerogatives of which are made, at several points, very explicit. 'Ful lik a lord' the Duke rides to the lists through a city which is said to be 'Hanged with clooth of gold, and nat with sarge' (2568–9). For the building of the temples besides the 'noble theatre' he has employed all the architects and artisans in the country, regardless of expense: the temple of Mars 'coste largely of gold a fother' (1908). The limitlessness of his wealth is initially apparent when he demands no ransom for his royal prisoners—a circumstance so remarkable in dukes that it is referred to more than once.

Even persons who appear only briefly in the action are of rank: the suppliant Theban women at the beginning of the poem are all duchesses and queens. Even disguised as Philostrate, a mere hewer of wood and bearer of water, Arcite

> . . . was so gentil of condicioun
> That thurghout al the court was his renoun. (1431–2)

The recurrent occasions of life for people of such condition as this are ceremonious, their actions at such times being imbued with the piety of ancient ritual. Arcite, even though he has rejected the code that binds him to his bloodbrother,. insists on returning to Athens, after finding the escaped Palamon, for food and weapons for his rival. The poem as a whole presents in affectionate detail three major ceremonial events: the prayers at the temples, the elaborate formalities of the tournament, and Arcite's funeral. Even the period of mourning for Arcite is apparently of prescribed duration (2967–8).

The action takes place, then, in an idealized aristocratic universe, magnanimous, munificent, and ceremonial. Theseus is the ideal conquering governor, Palamon the ideal lover, Emelye the emblem of vernal innocence. The story ends, too, with its ideal lover at last.

> . . . in all wele
> Lyvynge in blisse, in richnesse, and in heele. . . . (3101–2)

Yet the view of the universe taken by the Tale is a tragic view, and the condition of man presented by the teller is also tragic.

The most direct, simple, and uncompromising expression of this tragic view comes in the words of Egeus, Theseus's father, after the accident to Arcite proves fatal. Egeus (who makes only this single brief appearance in the story) has been taken by some critics for a dotard; however that may be, his speech, of which I will quote the final lines, has central importance:

> This world nys but a thurghfare ful of wo,
> And we been pilgrymes, passynge to and fro.
> Deeth is an ende of every worldly soore. (2847–9)

The sentiment is a commonplace, of course, which could doubtless be matched, if not duplicated, a thousand times in the literature of Chaucer's age and of preceding periods; it nevertheless has power in the Knight's Tale because that poem, although its plot is concerned with success in love and its setting pictures aristocratic splendours, presents on the whole such an abiding and various image of 'every worldly soore'. Man, the teller might be saying, whatever his station in life, is the victim of arbitrary, cruel, and often ironical mischance. The Theban ladies are summarily widowed by civil wars; Thebes sacked by Athens; the knights jailed by Theseus; while noble Arcite slowly and painfully dies of a fall from his horse because, nature having abandoned him, medicine is consequently useless—

> And certainly, ther Natur wol nat wirche,
> Fare wel phisik! go ber the man to chirche! (2759–60)

It is not only the events of the story which provide a rich reference for Palamon's bitter questioning of the 'cruel goddes' in the following lines:

What is mankynde moore unto you holde
Than is the sheep that rouketh in the folde?
For slayn is man right as another beest
And dwelleth eek in prison and arreest,
And hath siknesse and greet adversitee. . . . (1307–11)

As tragically impressive as the events I have mentioned is
the image of the human condition implied by the great de-
scriptions of the temples of Venus, Mars, and Diana (espe-
cially by that of Mars) and by the speech of Saturn detailing
his own influence on mortal affairs. These passages, among
the most admired in Chaucer, are generally treated as set-
pieces, in detachment from context. Actually they are an
organic part of the Tale, for they symbolically extend the
misfortunes and griefs of the central characters and at the
same time provide a background against which these same
misfortunes and griefs will seem less extraordinary. This ex-
tension supports the view of human life taken by Egeus and
Palamon in the lines I have just quoted, and by Arcite and
Theseus in lines I shall presently discuss.

The picture of the temple of Venus refers, it is true, to
both the delights and the sorrows she causes; but it begins
and ends with the sorrows—'ful pitous to biholde'—and it
emphasizes the follies of lovers: 'the folye of kyng Salo-
mon. . . . The riche Cresus, kaytyf in servage' (1942, 1946).
The temple of Diana, which represents innocence and a kind
of divine beneficence and is associated with Emelye, is de-
scribed more naïvely as a collection of wonders merely; but
even here the most vivid pictures are of the hounds devour-
ing Actaeon 'for that they knewe hym naught' (2068), and
of a woman in the throes of a difficult childbirth. The images
inspired by Mars and Saturn give an inclusive and uncom-
promising panorama of existence as a moral hell and a cosmic
chaos. The sow devours the baby 'right in the cradel' (2019);
the man-eating wolf rends his victim at the foot of Mars's
statue, to the glory of the god; the glance of Saturn is 'the
fader of pestilence' (2469); images of manslaughter, arson,
suicide, treason, murder, and rapine make up the decora-
tions of Mars's temple.

This last edifice is built like a dungeon, as the following lines show:

> The dore was al of adamant eterne,
> Yclenched overthwart and endelong
> With iren tough; and for to make it strong,
> Every pyler, the temple to sustene,
> Was tonne greet, of iren bright and shene . . . (1990–4)

Imprisonment is a symbol of great importance to the poem; it is significant that Arcite's long-desired release from captivity leads first to exile and then despair, then to a strenuous life of practical expedients crowned by illusive victory and sudden death. His epitaph is spoken by Theseus (the original imprisoner of the knights) in these words:

> . . . goode Arcite, of chivalrie the flour,
> Departed is with duetee and honour
> Out of this foule prisoun of this lyf. . . . (3059–61)

For Arcite release from prison has been no more than escape into a larger prison, until the final release of death. 'What is this world?' asks the dying knight, whom devices and expedients can help no longer—

> What is this world? What asketh men to have?
> Now with his love, now in his colde grave
> Allone, withouten any compaignye? (2777–9)

But although the picture of 'this world' implied by the Mars and Saturn passages is chaotic and hideous enough, such a view of human existence is by no means the total effect by the Knight's Tale. To begin with, the very presence of the gods, whether astrological or theological, gives a degree of order and significance to the lives of mortals. A trio of divinities accounts for the misery of Palamon: as Palamon puts it,

> . . . I moot been in prisoun thurgh Saturne,
> And eek thurgh Juno, jalous and eek wood,
> That hath destroyed wel ny al the blood
> Of Thebes with his waste walles wyde;
> And Venus sleeth me on that oother syde
> For jalousie and fere of hym Arcite. (1328–33)

And a conflict of divinities accounts for the death of Pala-
mon's rival. Nothing exists in this human world but has its
source, significance, and guidance from above—a kind of
guidance symbolized most concretely by the traditional de-
vice of Mercurie's appearance to advise Arcite to go to
Athens. Thus the very vicissitudes of life fall into an ultimate
pattern decipherable by wisdom and philosophy; even the
destructive divinities are still divine.

More important still, beyond these destructive divinities
governs the Firste Moevere of Theseus's final elegy. This
speech is the climax of the poem. Here Theseus sets forth in
general terms what the particulars of the story have been
leading to. Human decay and corruption (the accident to
Arcite, the violence and pestilence symbolized by Mars and
Saturn, the follies in which Venus has a share) proceed
under the laws of an ultimate Providence, which has fixed a
term to the existence of finite things. Man's proper wisdom is
not to cry out against the 'faire cheyne of love' which binds
the universe, but nobly to accept his destiny—to 'take it weel
. . . that to us alle is due' (3043–4). Hence the importance
of Arcite: his nobility, his education, his tragedy. His death
was not meaningless to him since it empowered him to re-
assert his proper relation tc Palamon and to do his friend
the service he might have done at the beginning. As Theseus
says,

> . . . And certeinly a man hath moost honour
> To dyen in his excellence and flour,
> When he is siker of his goode name;
> Thanne hath he doon his freend, ne hym, no shame.
>   (3047–50)

And after Arcite's funeral, the decent period of mourning,
and Theseus's elegy, stability can be established by the
harmonious union of Emelye and Palamon, who incidentally
represent the formerly warring countries, Thebes and Athens.

VI

Such a tale is clearly suited to the Knight of Chaucer's
prologue who tells it, a man of high rank, wide travel, and

ingenuous loyalty to the ideas of his class and age. The lessons of the Tale, if such they may be called, imply a pious and logical mind in the instructor, a deep acceptance of Christian faith and chivalric standards, and an heroic disposition to face the vicissitudes and disasters of a dangerous calling. That they had been faced in fact we have been assured by the prologue:

> At Alisaundre he was whan it was wonne.
> Ful ofte tyme he hadde the bord bigonne
> Aboven alle nacions in Pruce;
> In Lettow hadde he reysed and in Ruce,
> No Cristen man so ofte of his degree.
> In Gernade at the seege eek hadde he be
> Of Algezir, and riden in Belmarye,
> At Lyeys was he and at Satalye,
> Whan they were wonne; and in the Grete See
> At many a noble armee hadde he be. (51–60)

To present the mind and heart of this Knight is an important function of the Tale. Though hardly a dramatic monologue in the Shakespearian or Browningesque sense of the term, the Tale is nevertheless a dramatic utterance both externally (in the light of its setting) and internally. Scarcely has the Knight finished his story of Palamon and Arcite, and won the applause of all the pilgrims (especially of the gentlefolk), than the drunken Miller is pushing forward, interrupting the Host's attempted introduction of the Monk as second narrator, and insisting loudly on *his* tale instead. The Miller's Tale (as everyone knows) is perhaps the most elaborate improper story in English literature—the most elaborate and in many ways the grossest. It represents an artistic antithesis to the Knight's Tale, being also a tale of the rivalry of two suitors for a young woman. But whereas Palamon and Arcite worshipped the maiden Emelye with an introspective ardour that seemed almost its own reward, Nicholas and Absolon pursue the lickerish Alisoun for the simple object of cuckoldry just (to use Chaucer's simile) as a cat pursues a mouse. Instead of the international and even cosmological background of the Knight's Tale, the scene of the Miller's Tale is small-town, domestic, and bourgeois. Its plot embodies a kind of crude justice meted out by circumstances

both to successful and to attempted adultery. The manners of
chivalry are burlesqued in the figure of the genteel parish-
clerk-and-barber Absolon; while Christianity enters the story
as a ready means of duping an illiterate and credulous hus-
band. The contrast of the Knight's Tale could hardly be
more complete. It is as if the Miller, growing more and more
restive in the moral stratosphere as the leisurely Knight's
Tale winds to its ceremonious and philosophical conclusion,
were to keep silent after the Knight's final words about the
young couple:

> For now is Palamon in alle wele,
> Lyvynge in blisse, in richeesse, and in heele,
> And Emelye hym loveth so tendrely,
> And he hire serveth al so gentilly,
> That nevere was ther no word hem bitwene
> Of jalousie or any oother teene. . . . (3101–6)

What a picture of married life! The Miller will show that
there is another side to *that* story!—

> By armes, and by blood and bones,
> I kan a noble tale for the nones,
> With which I wol now quite the Knyghtes tale (3124–6)

says the Miller.

The Miller's Tale, then, is the principal external means
by which the Knight's Tale is made dramatic and given a
certain artistic distance both from the reader and from the
poet of the *Canterbury Tales*. There are also internal and
ironical means of accomplishing the same object, and they
are fully employed. I refer, of course, to such occasions as
when Theseus remarks that the lover who loses Emelye may
as well 'go pipen in an yvy leef' (1838); or when the women
of Athens (with all the sensibilities of modern cinema
addicts) lament the death of Arcite because, as they put it, he
had 'gold ynough, and Emelye' (2836); or when the species
of trees that make up Arcite's funeral pyre are listed with
no more ceremony of adjective than it is now customary to
give the names in a telephone directory. The very ingenuous-
ness of the Knight as a commentator on his own story may

sometimes give rise to the pleasantest irony: the reader must smile at the speaker, while his heart warms to him. I shall close this essay with one example of such irony, an example which illustrates also the pitfalls into which even a learned Chaucerian may occasionally slip.

The pathetic death of Arcite is a matter of intense grief to his comrade-in-arms and his intended bride. 'Shrighte Emelye, and howleth Palamon' (2817); and Theseus carries away the prostrate heroine. At this point the Knight who tells the story embarks on a generalization, in the following terms:

> What helpeth it to tarien forth the day
> To tellen how she weep bothe eve and morwe?
> For in swich cas wommen have swich sorwe,
> Whan that hir housbondes ben from hem ago,
> That for the moore part they sorwen so,
> Or ellis fallen in swich maladye,
> That at the laste certeinly they dye. (2820–6)

'Coming from the author of the Wife of Bath,' remarks H. B. Hinckley in his *Notes on Chaucer*,[10] 'these words can only be construed as satire, or as insincerity. Was it such a passage as this—a passage which is certainly out of place— that prompted Matthew Arnold's celebrated saying that Chaucer lacked "high seriousness"?'

The Knight, however, is neither insincere, satirical, nor the author of the Wife of Bath; and it is probably a measure of our present distance from the Victorian critics that the irony of Chaucer, his constant perception of personal and spiritual incompatibilties in a complex humanity; is the very quality that gives him, in our eyes, his seriousness as a poet and a critic of life.

Notes

[1] See the notes to the Tale in *The Complete Works of Chaucer* (ed. F. N. Robinson, Cambridge, Mass., 1933), pp. 770 ff. [1957 ed., pp. 669f.] (for Lowes, Wise, Patch, and Curry); also B. L. Jefferson, *Chaucer and . . . Boethius* (Princeton, 1917); Johnstone Parr, 'The Date and Revision of Chaucer's *Knight's Tale*', *P.M.L.A.*, LX (1945), 307–24; and R. A. Pratt, 'Chaucer's Use of the *Teseida*', *P.M.L.A.*, LXII (1947), 598–621, especially 613–20.

[2] See R. K. Root, *Poetry of Chaucer* (Cambridge, Mass., 1922), pp. 163–73. Mr. Root discriminates between the temperaments of

the two knights, but concludes that 'the reader of the tale . . . is unable to decide on which he would wish the ultimate success to light' (p. 170).

³ Ibid., p. 172.

⁴ Ibid., p. 37.

⁵ See H. R. Patch, 'Chauceriana', *Englische Studien*, LXV (1930–31), 354 n.; cited by Robinson in a note on l. 860.

⁶ J. R. Hulbert, 'What was Chaucer's Aim in the Knight's Tale?', S.P., XXVI (1929), 375 ff.

⁷ *Odes*, iv. 7. The translation is Housman's (*Collected Poems*, New York, 1940, p. 164).

⁸ I take his imprisonment of the two knights without asking ransom to be simply part of the *donnée* of the story as it came to Chaucer—and not, without further explanation of motive than the poet gives us, an implication that Theseus lacks chivalry.

⁹ See W. C. Curry, *Chaucer and the Medieval Sciences* (Oxford, 1926), chapter vi.

¹⁰ Northampton, Mass., 1907, p. 113.

7

Characterization in *The Miller's Tale*

PAUL E. BEICHNER, C.S.C.

NOT too infrequently within recent years the mature
reader of Chaucer has been told in effect not to

Tourne over the leef and chese another tale,[1]

but to plunge into the fabliaux, where he will find not only
some of Chaucer's most hilarious humor and cleverest man-
agement of plot but also some of his best portraits and char-
acter delineations. In leading the way, scholars have not
neglected the first low story of *The Canterbury Tales*: they
have studied the analogues to *The Miller's Tale* and have
speculated about possible sources and indebtedness for vari-
ous elements; they have pointed out the dramatic irony of
the situations of the intricate plot; and they have called at-
tention to the art of the portraits of the chief characters
and to various human touches in the story. To state the
case in an over-simplified way, some have been chiefly con-

Unpublished paper delivered before the English Department,
University of Notre Dame, Autumn 1948. Printed with the author's
permission. Points treated in the paper receive separate elaboration
and fuller documentation in the author's "Absolon's Hair," *Medi-
aeval Studies*, XII (1950), 222–33, and "Chaucer's Hende Nich-
olas," *ibid.*, XIV (1952), 151–3.

cerned with plot almost divorced from character, and others have devoted their attention to the characters as almost independent of plot. Chaucer, however, did not invent the plot, which would have remained essentially the same even though he had used a different set of actors in his little comedy; on the other hand, he was not describing characters with such a wealth of colorful detail merely for the sake of the resulting portraits. Chaucer was, it would seem, consciously creating people with whose characters the action of a borrowed plot would not be inconsistent—in other words, through character he was motivating as much as possible a fabliau whose action originally had little or nothing to do with character. The result is a robust, organic literary piece instead of just a vulgar story upon which several fine portraits were wasted. To indicate the way Chaucer accomplished such motivation, this paper will consider, first, Absolon's character in its relation to the role of the duped suitor and in its effect upon Alisoun, and second, Nicholas's character by way of contrast with Absolon's.

In most analogues to *The Miller's Tale* Absolon's part is taken by a smith,[2] since the plot requires easy access to a hot colter or something similar for the branding. If the smith appeared in this role in the story as it came to Chaucer in a lost fabliau or in an oral version, or even if the story contained another character who had to go to the smith for the colter, the poet must have considered the use of a smith as the rejected and duped lover. The plot would be a shade more plausible and economical. But at the same time Chaucer would have felt it necessary to give him the physique of a smith and rather crude sensibilities: he would have to be a stout fellow, big of brawn and bones, one strong enough to heave doors from their hinges even though he need not batter them down with his head. A smith would be dangerously like the Miller himself who tells the story, and it would not have been appropriate for the Miller to allow the duped lover in any way to resemble himself. In any event Chaucer gave us Absolon. In this parish clerk, who at odd times was a barber, Professor Lowes saw a typical small-town dandy.[3] Professor Shelly emphasized the point that he 'is in no wise clerkly' but much like the young squires of *The Canterbury Tales* in their love of fine clothes, song, dance, and gallantry.[4] G. G. Coulton has made it easier to understand Absolon by the light he throws not so much on the ecclesiastical position as on the social and economic position of a clerk in minor orders, who might take either the road to major orders and become a priest or the road to marriage and remain a parish clerk or earn his livelihood by work as a scribe, an accountant, or a performer of odd jobs of the white-collar variety.[5] But it is important for a full appreciation of *The Miller's Tale* to realize that in making Absolon quite the opposite of the Miller, Chaucer was creating a character for whom no punishment could be more severe or appropriate and no cure more effective than to be rejected by Alisoun in her very unladylike fashion. Absolon indeed is more ladylike than Alisoun. He is too ladylike, and therein lies much of the humor when his downfall occurs. From the very first lines of the portrait, Chaucer began to paint such a man.

> Now was ther of that chirche a parissh clerk,
> The which that was ycleped Absolon.
> Crul was his heer, and as the gold it shoon,
> And strouted as a fanne large and brode;
> Ful streight and evene lay his joly shode.[6]

The clerk was not called Absolon through coincidence. Chaucer had in mind, of course, Absalom, the son of David, who was the most beautiful man in Israel, and whose hair was exceedingly luxuriant. In II Kings 14:25–26, we read:

But in all Israel there was not a man so comely and so exceedingly beautiful as Absalom: from the sole of his foot to the crown of his head there was no blemish in him. And when he polled his hair (now he was polled once a year, because his hair was burdensome to him) he weighed the hair of his head at two hundred sicles, according to the common weight.

Biblical commentators of the Middle Ages are more concerned with Absalom's treason than with his hair. Those few, however, who do comment on this text say that the hair signifies *excess*. Hugo of St. Victor writes: 'The appetite of the flesh fosters and produces hair because it fosters excesses in thought: this hair weighs heavy upon the mind so long as *the earthly habitation presseth down the mind that museth on many things'* [Wisdom 9:15].[7] To Adam Scotus the hair of Absalom signifies excess of the flesh, concupiscence of the eyes, and the pride of life: 'Woe to you, O perfidious Absalom, weighed down by your hair—that is, by carnal excess, concupiscence of the eyes, and pride of life!'[8] (Absolon of *The Miller's Tale,* with his excess of hair and excessive combing of it, of course is very much under the influence of all three vicious inclinations.) Peter Comestor in his *Historia scholastica* refers to Josephus as his authority for saying that Absalom's hair was so abundant that it would have been difficult for it to be cut every nine days. Then he adds that the hair which was cut once a year weighed two hundred shekels, and that perhaps this was the weight of the shearing, or perhaps for this price women purchased the hair to adorn their own.[9] Peter Riga states it thus in the *Aurora* or *Biblia versificata:*

> Aurea cesaries in uertice uertitur; anno
> Tonsa semel, siclis digna meretur emi.[10]

The commentators have thus made Absalom unattractive not only because of his treason but also because of his hair.

The full length portrait of Absalom by Peter Riga deserves special consideration, however, because Chaucer probably read it;[11] and even though this reading would have occurred quite early in his literary career and he might not advert to it in writing *The Miller's Tale,* yet his conception of the Biblical character may have been influenced by it. Taking his cue evidently from the Vulgate—'a vestigio pedis usque ad verticem non erat in eo ulla macula'—Peter Riga makes a full and elegant inventory description of Absalom's perfections from crown to toe in an *effictio* which conforms to the rules and models of the 'arts of poetry' and handbooks of rhetoric of the late twelfth and early thirteenth centuries,[12] although this is the method of presenting feminine beauty. Absalom is far more beautiful indeed than the other sons of David. Nature showered him with so many of her gifts that she is in want thereafter, while he is a phoenix without equal. Not one blemish did she leave in him; beauty cloaked him from head to foot. Crown, forehead, eyes, nose, teeth, mouth, cheeks, chin, neck, hands, breast, feet—all are beautiful without spot. Each item of this inventory is then described in at least one couplet, beginning at the crown with the golden hair worthy to be purchased with shekels. Then the forehead, whiter than the swan or the untrodden snow; then on down the face, until on arriving at the chin one is relieved to find that Absalom had a beard beginning to bloom even if it was the only thing that indicated that he was a man:

> Mentum nascenti florens lanugine, sexum
> Femineum dampnans, indicate esse uirum.[13]

Then in like manner, member by member, to the feet. A comparison of the complete description of Absalom with the model description of Helen in the *Ars versificatoria* of Matthew of Vendôme makes that beard a precious thing indeed, and this judgment is confirmed when one reads the *Poetria nova* of Geoffrey of Vinsauf on how to portray feminine beauty.[14]

Peter Riga knew that he had cast Absalom in the mold marked 'feminine,' for when he came to expand the 'Gospel' in his second edition of the *Aurora,* he used the description of Absalom again, *mutatis mutandis,* as the chief part of his portrait of the Blessed Virgin Mary. Nor did John Gower, the friend of Chaucer, let Riga's portrait of Absalom go unnoticed. In the third chapter of the fifth book of *Vox clamantis,* Gower describes 'a beautiful woman, the desire for whom very frequently deprives the ensnared hearts of soldiers of their powers of good judgment.'[15] Eight lines which Gower borrowed from the *Aurora,* six of them from the portrait of Absalom, are firmly embedded in the description; he was doing exactly what Peter Riga had done two hundred years earlier in the second and third editions—applying to a woman what had originally been written to describe a man. . . .

It is right to conclude, therefore, that although Absalom of the Old Testament was considered a paragon of beauty, to some medieval minds at least, it was a beauty more feminine than masculine. The Miller and the poet behind the Miller

would have their audiences gain their first impression of the
parish clerk by associating him with the Biblical character; by
giving him the name Absolon and by making his hair golden
and ridiculously conspicuous (if not so abundant as Ab-
salom's), they would subtly suggest that the gay young clerk
was effeminate. As the description proceeds, the first impres-
sion is deepened, not removed. Any indications of nobility of
appearance, physical strength, or even strength of character
are purposely omitted. A comparison of Absolon with Mirth of
The Romaunt of the Rose will illustrate the point. Both are
similar in their love of fun and dancing; indeed, Absolon is
described as 'joly' or 'gay' almost as often as Nicholas receives
the epithet 'hende'.[16] Both Mirth and Absolon have conven-
tional gray eyes and ruddy complexions, and their taste in
clothes makes them as close as brothers. Thus Absolon,

> With Poules wyndow corven on his shoos,[17]

is as well shod as Mirth,

> With shoon decoped, and with laas.[18]

And Absolon's kirtle of light blue, of which

> Ful faire and thikke been the poyntes set,[19]

is, in the circumstances, quite as extravagant and capricious as
the robe of Mirth:

> Wrought was his robe in straunge gise,
> And al toslytered for queyntise
> In many a place, lowe and hie.[20]

And both are remarkably agile as befits dancers; but here all
similarity ends, for Absolon lacks the saving features of Mirth:

> Full fair was Myrthe, ful long and high. . . .
> His shuldris of a large brede,
> And smalish in the girdilstede.
> He semed lyk a portreiture,
> So noble he was of his stature,
> So fair, so joly, and so fetys,
> With lymes wrought at poynt devys,
> Delyver, smert, and of gret myght.[21]

Furthermore, Chaucer has furnished Absolon with a set of genteel accomplishments which would be totally unimpressive to a young lady of Alisoun's spirit: skill as a barber—

> Wel koude he laten blood and clippe and shave,

even though he may not have practiced dentistry; proficiency as a drafter of deeds and quitclaims; the playing of two musical instruments, singing in a high voice, and tripping twenty dance steps after the school of Oxford: familiarity with taverns and merry barmaids; and agility and mastery in playing Herod in the pageants.[22] The gay white surplice which he wore at parish functions affected Alisoun no more than did his fenestrate shoes or his well-combed hair. And as he flitted around

> . . . with a sencer on the haliday,
> Sensynge the wyves of the parisshe faste,
> And many a lovely look on hem he caste,
> And namely on this carpenteris wyf,[23]

she might have thought (to paraphrase the Host's evaluation of the Monk's storytelling):

> Swich sensynge is nat worth a boterflye;
> Youre werk anoyeth al this compaignye.

Whether Absolon woos by many serenades or many presents, Alisoun finds him boring.

Not only was Absolon to some degree effeminate, but to tell the truth (as Chaucer does), he was somewhat squeamish of vulgar conduct and fastidious of speech. Alisoun's rejection of him would be sufficiently motivated by the first trait, whereas her manner of accomplishing it is the ironic retribution he deserves for his squeamishness and fastidiousness. But is not this method inconsistent with the character of a young lady? Chaucer thought it would not be, if he made her a country-bred girl, a little impudent as well as impish and skittish. And so with as much care as enthusiasm, he portrayed her in a series of comparisons boldly drawn from the countryside.[24] She is as graceful and slender as a weasel (and apparently as hard to catch), with apron as white as morning

milk, and plucked brows as black as a sloe; she is more
pleasant to behold than the new pear tree and softer than the
wool of a wether; her song is as loud and lively as that of a
swallow sitting on a barn (Absolon quavers like the nightin-
gale); she is as playful as a kid or calf and as skittish as a
colt; but her mouth is as sweet as bragot, or mead, or a
hoard of apples laid in hay—and so on. The intrinsic merit of
the portrait has deservedly made the passage a favorite of
reader and critic alike, but its brilliance should not blind one
to its organic function in the whole—by associating Alisoun
with things of the country, to render the unseemly manner
of her rejection of Absolon plausible. Alisoun and Absolon, the
one country-bred and the other citified, are foils for each
other.

The poor scholar of Oxford, 'hende' Nicholas, dwelling with
the carpenter and his young wife, is the character Chaucer
created to fit the part of the accepted suitor and the object
of the branding. Nicholas and his room are described briefly
yet in sufficient detail to make him thoroughly individual:
though a student of the arts he is more interested in astrology
than in his studies and has acquired a local reputation as a
weather prophet which serves him to good purpose in de-
ceiving the carpenter; and he is a lover, sly and secret, al-
though externally as meek as a maid. But one key to unlock
the character and action of Nicholas, I believe, is the word
hende, which Chaucer uses as an epithet eleven times[25]—often
enough indeed to call attention to it, since he is not accus-
tomed to use epithets. In the sense of 'pleasant in dealing with
others; courteous, gracious; kind, gentle, "nice"' the word
hende, according to the *N.E.D.*, is 'a conventional epithet of
praise, very frequent in Middle English poetry.' This is, no
no doubt, the first meaning which Chaucer attaches to the
word. But as the poet repeats *hende* while the story unfolds,
other meanings become appropriate to Nicholas at the same
time; and it would seem that Chaucer chose *hende* as char-
acteristic of Nicholas rather than *curteys* or something similar,
because it does have several meanings which would occur to
the audience as the tale is told. Things happen because
Nicholas is 'hende'.

The first meaning which the *N.E.D.* gives for *hend* or *hende* is 'near, at hand,' but it points out that in this sense the word is used in Middle English only as a predicative and is hardly distinguishable from an adverb. Everyone, however, would have been familiar with this meaning because of its occurrence in such a phrase as 'fer and hende.' Nicholas, being a boarder in Alisoun's house, is 'hende'—always near. This placing of the seducer in the household of the married couple, which apparently is original with Chaucer, is a good stroke. It gives Nicholas an advantage over Absolon in proximity to the lady of their fancy—an advantage which is forcefully stated as follows:

> Ful sooth is this proverbe, it is no lye,
> Men seyn right thus, "Alwey the nye slye
> Maketh the ferre leeve to be looth."
> For though that Absolon be wood or wrooth,
> By cause that he fer was from hire sight,
> This nye Nicholas stood in his light.[26]

This living in such close proximity to Alisoun overpowers Nicholas; he must act. Proximity also makes it practically impossible for Alisoun to avoid 'this nye' Nicholas. . . . And finally, the situation of the jealous old husband and the lover living under the same roof affords Chaucer many opportunities to display dramatic irony.[27]

Not only is Nicholas always at hand but he is also 'hende' in the sense of 'ready or skilful with the hand, dexterous.' Indeed, he is very dexterous with his hands, as four lines of Alisoun's protest in action and word are sufficient to show:

> And she sproong as a colt dooth in the trave. . . .
> "Why lat be," quod she, "lat be, Nicholas,
> Or I wol crie 'out, harrow' and 'allas'!
> Do wey youre handes, for youre courteisye!"[28]

Professor Shelly writes: 'In love, as his actions show, he is master of the attack direct, and his technique is that of the country, not of the court.'[29] But neither is Alisoun's technique of resistance that of the court. The simile of the colt in the trave—'at a forge' according to the gloss in *MS Harley 7333* for this line—is one of the most brilliant action similes Chaucer ever wrote. From the truncated definition of *trave* in the glossaries of Chaucer texts many a careless reader might conclude that the poet is speaking of a colt in the shafts of a cart; but with the definition of the *N.E.D.* in mind—'A frame or enclosure of bars in which a restive horse is placed to be shod'—one can easily picture the leaping and kicking, the twisting and turning of a colt being shod for the first time, and one can imagine the vigor and the futility of Alisoun's resistance to the superior strength of Nicholas. Moreover, the simile is appropriate because Chaucer has already said of Alisoun that

> Wynsynge she was, as is a joly colt; [30]

and he will have use for a smith and forge before the story is over.

Upon the threat of Alisoun to call for help, however, Nicholas immediately becomes 'hende' in the usual meaning of the epithet—'pleasant, gentle, courteous':

> This Nicholas gan mercy for to crye,
> And spak so fair, and profred him so faste,
> That she hir love hym graunted atte laste. [31]

Nothing remains now except for Nicholas to contrive an assignation so that the husband will be never the wiser. Because he is 'hende' in still another sense—'expert, skilful, clever'—Nicholas plans the whole flood episode in great detail as a means to his end. He does not depend merely upon his reputation as a student of astrology and a forecaster of the weather to convince the carpenter of the imminence of a flood worse than that of Noe, but he prepares an elaborate setting for his prediction by remaining locked in his room for two days before the carpenter with deep concern shakes him from his feigned trance and revives the glibness of his tongue with his share of a large quart of mighty ale. Then his prophecy and his plan for the salvation of the carpenter, Alisoun, and himself come pouring out. Such contriving is worthy of the brain of the Pandarus who planned the dinner party of Trojan royalty at the house of Deiphebus so that Troilus might have an opportunity to speak for a short time with Criseyde without arousing suspicion of their love. The *N.E.D.* gives still another meaning for *hende*—'pleasing to the sight, comely, fair, "nice." ' Since Chaucer does not describe the appearance of 'hende' Nicholas, perhaps one is also expected to infer from the epithet that he is pleasing to the sight. At least Alisoun finds neither his person nor his plans repugnant.

The climax of *The Miller's Tale* takes place when Nicholas is 'hende' once too often. Bent on avenging Alisoun's insult to his dignity, Absolon returns from the smithy of Gerveys with a hot colter. By this time, however, 'hende' Nicholas has risen and is *at hand,* and being *clever* he thinks he will improve upon the coarse trick performed by Alisoun. He does 'amenden al the jape,' not in the way he had anticipated, but by bringing about crude and effective poetic justice.

Thus, by making him "hende' in one sense or another, Chaucer has motivated each incident of the plot involving Nicholas; and similarly, he has made the action involving Alisoun and Absolon flow from the fact that she is an earthy country girl and he is an effeminate fastidious dandy. The poet has created such perfect characters for the various roles in the little farce that he has made it appear that the plot was created for them and not that they were created for the sake of the fabliau plot. This high organic unity makes *The Miller's Tale* a masterpiece of its genre.[22]

Notes

[1] *Canterbury Tales,* I (A), 3177.

[2] See Stith Thompson, 'The Miller's Tale,' in *Sources and Analogues of Chaucer's 'Canterbury Tales',* edited by W. F. Bryan and Germaine Dempster (Chicago, 1941), pp. 106–123.

[3] John Livingston Lowes, *Geoffrey Chaucer and the Development of His Genius* (Boston, 1934), p. 220.

[4] Percy Van Dyke Shelly, *The Living Chaucer* (Philadelphia, 1940), pp. 245–246.

[5] G. G. Coulton, *Medieval Panorama* (Cambridge, 1938), chapter XII, especially pp. 146–147.

[6] *C.T.,* I (A), 3312–3316.

[7] *Miscellanea,* lib. IV, tit. xxxii, *De caesarie Absalonis.* (Migne, *P.L.,* 177, col. 714 A.)

[8] *De triplici genere contemplationis,* pars II, § iv. (Migne, *P.L.,* 198, col. 816 A.)

[9] *Historia scholastica, Lib. II Regum,* cap xiv. (Migne, P.L., 198, col. 1336 C.)

[10] *Aurora,* 'II Kings,' ll. 49–50. The thirty-six line description of Absolon from the *Aurora,* along with a free translation of it into Old French verse, is printed in my article 'The Old French Verse *Bible* of Macé de la Charité, a Translation of the *Aurora,*' *Speculum,* XXII (1947), 233–234.

[11] Chaucer mentions the *Aurora* in *The Book of the Duchess,* (ll. 1160–1169). For a complete discussion of the passage, see Karl Young, 'Chaucer and Peter Riga,' *Speculum,* XII (1937), 299–303. Even though it cannot be demonstrated that Chaucer read more in the *Aurora* than the passage referred to, nevertheless the popularity of the work and Gower's reading, rereading, and unrestrained borrowing from it make Chaucer's reading of a whole manuscript extremely likely.

[12] Most of the important 'arts of poetry' are later than the *Aurora,* but Peter Riga, in both practice and theory, was already in the current of the rhetorical Latin poetry which they teach. For his practice, see the short poems in the first book of his *Floridus aspectus;* for his contribution to the theory, see his treatise on rhetorical figures, the *Colores verborum,* which forms the second book of the *Floridus.* Probably he wrote the grammatical work from which Alexander of Villa Dei borrowed the matter for the section 'De preteritis et supinis' in his *Doctinale* (cf. Max Manitius, *Geschichte der lateinischen Literatur des Mittelalters,* III [Munich, 1931], 829–830).

[13] *Aurora,* 'II Kings,' ll. 63-4.

[14] *Ars versificatoria,* I, cap. 56, and *Poetria nova,* ll. 562–599 (Edmond Faral, *Les arts poétiques du XIIe et du XIIIe siècle* [Paris, 1924], pp. 129–130 and 214–215). Geoffrey says in the *Poetria nova* that if you wish to create feminine beauty fully you do it thus: 'If you wish to give a full impression of a woman's beauty, let Nature's compasses draw the outline of the head; let the color of gold gleam in the hair; let lillies bloom in the eminences of the brow.' having given thirty-five lines of such instruction, he concludes: 'And thus let radiance descend from top of head to tip of foot, and let every detail be polished, even to the toenails.'

[15] *Vox clamantis,* lib. V, cap. iii, the heading. (*The Complete Works of John Gower,* ed. by G. C. Macaulay, Vol. IV, *The Latin Works* [Oxford, 1902], p. 203.)

[16] This Absolon, that jolif was and gay. *C.T.,* I (A), 3339
This parissh clerk, this joly Absolon. 3348
And forth he gooth, jolif and amorous. 3355
Fro day to day this joly Absolon. 3371
He kembeth his lokkes brode, and made hym gay. 3374
This Absolon ful joly was and light. 3671
Up rist this joly lovere Absolon,
And hym arraieth gay, at poynt-devys. 3688–3689
Chaucer is emphasizing Absolon's prettiness and showy clothes quite as much as his merry disposition.

[17] *C.T.,* I (A), 3318.

[18] *The Romaunt of the Rose,* 843.

[19] *C.T.*, I (A), 3322.

[20] *R.R.*, 839–841.

[21] *R.R.*, 817, 825–831.

[22] *C.T.*, I (A), 3326–3336; 3383–3384. Although orthodox physicians looked down on barbers, the three branches of whose trade consisted of hairdressing, surgery, and dentistry, I have found no evidence that other people did so. However, in the absence of a barber, it appears that women performed at least some of his tasks. Winifred Wulff in the introduction to *Rosa Anglica seu Rosa Medicinae Johannis Anglici*, Irish Texts Society, Vol. XXV (London, [1923] 1929), p. XVIII, quotes from a medieval tract on the qualifications and duties of a surgeon: 'And although we leave these things (bloodletting, scarification, cautery, sanguisugs) to barbers and women in (our) pride and unworthiness, (yet) they are the work of the chirurgeon because Galen and Rhazes performed these operations with their own hands, as is clear in their own books.'

With the boasting, the ranting, and the raging 'in the pagond and in the strete' often required of Herod in the pageants, Absolon could hardly have chosen a worse part to impress Alisoun favorably. Chaucer, knowing that a young lady does not care to have her lover play the fool in public, assigns to Absolon a role which is at least dubious. .

[23] *C.T.*, I (A), 3340–3343.

[24] *C.T.*, I (A), 3233–3270. Lowes (*Geoffrey Chaucer*, pp. 218–219) called attention to the fact that while Chaucer followed the conventional inventory *method* of depicting feminine beauty, he drew his similes not from books but from the English country-side. Shelly said explicitly (*The Living Chaucer*, p. 244) that Alisoun 'is a country girl, it seems, and of Oxfordshire.' Line 3380, 'And, for she was of towne, he profred meede,' refers not to Alisoun's place of origin but rather to her present social station as a lady of town or to the fact that she is in a position to spend gifts of money for nice things for herself.

[25] *C.T.*, I (A), 3199, 3272, 3386, 3397, 3401, 3462, 3487, 3526, 3742, 3832, 3856 ('The Reeve's Prologue').

[26] *C.T.*, I (A), 3391–3396.

[27] See Germaine Dempster, *Dramatic Irony in Chaucer*, pp. 36–38.

[28] *C.T.*, I (A), 3282, 3285–3287.

[29] Shelly, *The Living Chaucer*, p. 245.

[30] *C.T.*, I (A), 3263.

[31] *C.T.*, I (A), 3288–3290.

[32] In a splendidly suggestive essay which was originally to be included in this volume, E. T. Donaldson independently explored the 'Idiom of Popular Poetry in the *Miller's Tale* (in *English Institute Essays—1950*, pp. 116-40), offering still another approach to the function of language in the larger structure of this tale. [Ed.]

8

Chaucer's Discussion of Marriage [1]

GEORGE LYMAN KITTREDGE

WE are prone to read and study the *Canterbury Tales* as if
each tale were an isolated unit and to pay scant attention to
what we call the connecting links,—those bits of lively narra-
tive and dialogue that bind the whole together. Yet Chaucer's
plan is clear enough. Structurally regarded, the *Canterbury
Tales* is a kind of Human Comedy. From this point of view,
the Pilgrims are the *dramatis personae*, and their stories are
only speeches that are somewhat longer than common, en-
tertaining in and for themselves (to be sure), but primarily
significant, in each case, because they illustrate the speaker's
character and opinions, or show the relations of the travelers
to one another in the progressive action of the Pilgrimage. In
other words, we ought not merely to consider the general ap-
propriateness of each tale to the character of the teller: we
should also inquire whether the tale is not determined to some
extent, by the circumstances,—by the situation at the moment,
by something that another Pilgrim has said or done, by the
turn of a discussion already under way.

Now and then, to be sure, the point is too obvious to be

Reprinted, by permission, from *Modern Philology*, IX (1911–12),
435–67. See bibliographical note, below, n. 1.

overlooked, as in the squabble between the Summoner and the Friar and that between the Reeve and the Miller, in the Shipman's intervening to check the Parson, and in the way in which the gentles head off the Pardoner when he is about to tell a ribald anecdote. But despite these inescapable instances, the general principle is too often blinked or ignored. Yet its temperate application should clear up a number of things which are traditionally regarded as difficulties, or as examples of heedlessness on Chaucer's part.[3]

Without attempting to deny or abridge the right to study and criticize each tale in and for itself,—as legend, romance, *exemplum*, fabliau, or what-not,—and without extenuating the results that this method has achieved, let us consider certain tales in their relation to Chaucer's structural plan,—with reference, that is to say, to the Pilgrims who tell them and to the Pilgrimage to which their telling is accidental. We may begin with the story of Griselda.

This is a plain and straightforward piece of edification, and nobody has ever questioned its appropriateness to the Clerk, who, as he says himself, has traveled in Italy and has heard it from the lips of the laureate Petrarch. The Clerk's 'speech,' according to the General Prologue, was 'sowning in moral vertu,' so that this story is precisely the kind of thing which we should expect from his lips. True, we moderns sometimes feel shocked or offended at what we style the immorality of Griselda's unvarying submission. But this feeling is no ground of objection to the appropriateness of the tale to the Clerk. The Middle Ages delighted (as children still delight) in stories that exemplify a single human quality, like valor, or tyranny, or fortitude. In such cases, the settled rule (for which neither Chaucer nor the Clerk was responsible) was to show to what lengths that quality may conceivably go. Hence, in tales of this kind, there can be no question of conflict between duties, no problem as to the point at which excess of goodness becomes evil. It is, then, absurd to censure a four-teenth-century Clerk for telling (or Chaucer for making him tell) a story which exemplifies in this hyperbolical way the virtue of fortitude under affliction. Whether Griselda could have put an end to her woes, or ought to have put an end to them, by refusing to obey her husband's commands is *parum ad rem*. We are to look at her trials as inevitable, and to pity her accordingly, and wonder at her endurance. If we refuse to accept the tale in this spirit, we are ourselves the losers. We miss the pathos because we are aridly intent on discussing an ethical question that has no status in this particular court, however pertinent it may be in the general forum of morals.

Furthermore, in thus focusing attention on the morality or immorality of Griselda's submissiveness, we overlook what the Clerk takes pains to make as clear as possible,—the real lesson that the story is meant to convey,—and thus we do grave injustice to that austere but amiable moralist. The Clerk, a student of 'Aristotle and his philosophye,' knew as well as any of us that every virtue may be conceived as a mean between two extremes. Even the Canon's Yeoman, an ignorant man, was aware of this principle:

> 'That that is overdoon, it wol nat preve
> Aright, as clerkes seyn,—it is a vyce.' (G. 645–6)

Chaucer had too firm a grasp on his *dramatis personae* to allow the Clerk to leave the true purpose of his parable undefined. 'This story is not told,' says the Clerk in substance, 'to exhort wives to imitate Griselda's humility, for *that* would be beyond the capacity of human nature. It is told in order that every man or woman, in whatever condition of life, may learn fortitude in adversity. For, since a woman once exhibited such endurance under trials inflicted on her by a mortal man, *a fortiori* ought *we* to accept patiently whatever tribulation God may send us. For God is not like Griselda's husband. He does not wantonly experiment with us, out of inhuman scientific curiosity. God *tests* us, as it is reasonable that our Maker should test his handiwork, but he does not *tempt* us. He allows us to be beaten with sharp scourges of adversity, not, like the Marquis Walter, to see if we can stand it, for he knoweth our frame, he remembereth that we are dust: all *his* affliction is for our better grace. Let us live, therefore, in manly endurance of the visitations of Providence.'

And then, at verse 1163, comes that matchless passage in

which the Clerk (having explained the *universal* application of his parable,—having provided with scrupulous care against any misinterpretation of its serious purport) turns with gravely satiric courtesy to the Wife of Bath and makes the particular application of the story to her 'life' and 'all her sect.'

Here one may appreciate the vital importance of considering the *Canterbury Tales* as a connected Human Comedy,—of taking into account the Pilgrims in their relations to one another in the great drama to which the several narratives are structurally incidental. For it is precisely at this point that Professor Skeat notes a difficulty. 'From this point to the end,' he remarks, 'is the work of a later period, and in Chaucer's best manner, though unsuited *to the coy Clerk.*' This is as much as to say that, in the remaining stanzas of the Clerk's Tale and in the Envoy, Chaucer has violated dramatic propriety. And, indeed, many readers have detected in these concluding portions Chaucer's own personal revulsion of feeling against the tale that he had suffered the Clerk to tell.

Now the supposed difficulty vanishes as soon as we study vss. 1163–1212, not as an isolated phenomenon, but in their relation to the great drama of the Canterbury Pilgrimage. It disappears when we consider the lines in what we may call their dramatic context, that is (to be specific), when we inquire what there was in the situation to prompt the Clerk, after emphasizing the serious and universal moral of Criselda's story, to give his tale a special and peculiar application by annexing an ironical tribute to the Wife of Bath, her life, her 'sect,' and her principles. To answer this question we must go back to the Wife of Bath's Prologue.

The Wife of Bath's Prologue begins a Group in the *Canterbury Tales,* or, as one may say, a new act in the drama. It is not connected with anything that precedes. Let us trace the action from this point down to the moment when the Clerk turns upon the Wife with his satirical compliments.

The Wife has expounded her views at great length and with all imaginable zest. Virginity, which the Church glorifies, is not required of us. Our bodies are given us to use. Let saints be continent if they will. She has no wish to emulate them. Nor does she accept the doctrine that a widow or a widower

must not marry again. Where is bigamy forbidden in the
Bible, or octogamy either? She has warmed both hands before
the fire of life, and she exults in her recollection of her fleshly
delights.

True, she is willing to admit, for convention's sake, that
chastity is the ideal state. But it is not *her* ideal. On the con-
trary, her admission is only for appearances. In her heart she
despises virginity. Her contempt for it is thinly veiled, or
rather, not veiled at all. Her discourse is marked by frank and
almost obstreperous animalism. Her whole attitude is that of
scornful, though good-humored, repudiation of what the
Church teaches in that regard.

Nor is the Wife content with this single heresy. She main-
tains also that wives should rule their husbands, and she en-
forces this doctrine by an account of her own life, and further
illustrates it by her tale of the knight of King Arthur who
learned that

> Wommen desiren to have sovereyntee
> As wel over hir housbond as hir love,
> And for to been in maistrie him above, (D. 1038–40)

and who accepted the lesson as sound doctrine. Then, at the
end of her discourse, she sums up in no uncertain words:

> And Iesu Crist us sende
> Housbandes meke, yonge, and fresshe abedde,
> And grace to overbyde hem that we wedde;
> And eek I preye Iesu shorte her lyves
> That wol nat be governed by her wyves. (D. 1258–62)

Now the Wife of Bath is not *bombinans in vacuo*. She ad-
dresses her heresies not to *us* or to the world at large, but to
her fellow-pilgrims. Chaucer has made this point perfectly
clear. The words of the Wife were of a kind to provoke com-
ment,—and we have the comment. The Pardoner interrupts her
with praise of her noble preaching:

> 'Now, dame,' quod he, 'by God and by seint Iohn,
> Ye been a noble prechour in this cas!' (D. 164–5)

The adjective is not accidental. The Pardoner was a judge of
good preaching: the General Prologue describes him as 'a

noble ecclesiaste' and he shows his ability in his own sermon on Covetousness. Furthermore, it is the Friar's comment on the Wife's preamble that provokes the offensive words of the Summoner, and that becomes thereby the occasion for the two tales that immediately follow in the series. It is manifest, then, that Chaucer meant us to imagine the *dramatis personae* as taking a lively interest in whatever the Wife says. This being so, we ought to inquire what effect her Prologue and Tale would have upon the Clerk.

Of course the Clerk was scandalized. He was unworldly and an ascetic,—he 'looked holwe and therto sobrely.' Moral virtue was his special study. He had embraced the celibate life. He was grave, devout, and unflinchingly orthodox. And now he was confronted by the lust of the flesh and the pride of life in the person of a woman who flouted chastity and exulted that she had 'had her world as in her time.' Nor was this all. The woman was an heresiarch, or at best a schismatic. She set up, and aimed to establish, a new and dangerous sect,[3] whose principle was that the wife should rule the husband. The Clerk kept silence for the moment. Indeed, he had no chance to utter his sentiments, unless he interrupted,— something not to be expected of his quiet ('coy') and sober temperament. But it is not to be imagined that his thoughts were idle. He could be trusted to speak to the purpose whenever his opportunity should come.

Now the substance of the Wife's false doctrines was not the only thing that must have roused the Clerk to protesting answer. The very manner of her discourse was a direct challenge to him.[4] She had garnished her sermon with scraps of Holy Writ and rags and tatters of erudition, caught up, we may infer, from her last husband. Thus she had put herself into open competition with the guild of scholars and theologians, to which the Clerk belonged. Further, with her eye manifestly upon this sedate philosopher, she had taken pains to gird at him and his fellows. At first she pretends to be modest and apologetic,—'so that the clerkes be nat with me wrothe,'—but later she abandons all pretense and makes an open attack:

'For trusteth wel, it is an impossible
That any clerk wol speken good of wyves,
But if it be of holy seintes lyves,
Ne of noon other womman never the mo. . . . (D. 688–91)

The clerk, whan he is old, and may noght do
Of Venus werkes worth his olde sho,
Than sit he doun, and writ in his dotage
That wommen can nat kepe his mariage.' (D. 707–10)

And there was more still that the Wife made our Clerk en-
dure. Her fifth husband was, like him, a 'clerk of Oxenford'—
surely this is no accidental coincidence on Chaucer's part. He
had abandoned his studies ('had left scole'), and had given
up all thought of taking priest's orders. The Wife narrates,
with uncommon zest, how she intrigued with him, and cajoled
him, and married him (though he was twenty and she was
forty), and how finally she made him utterly subservient to
her will,—how she got 'by maistrye al the soveraynetee.' This
was gall and wormwood to our Clerk. The Wife not only
trampled on his principles in her theory and practice, but she
pointed her attack by describing how she had subdued to her
heretical sect a clerk of Oxenford, an alumnus of our Clerk's
own university. The Wife's discourse is not malicious. She is
too jovial to be ill-natured, and she protests that she speaks
in jest. But it none the less embodies a rude personal assault
upon the Clerk, whose quiet mien and habitual reticence made
him seem a safe person to attack. She had done her best to
make the Clerk ridiculous. He saw it; the company saw it.
He kept silent, biding his time.

All this is not speculation. It is nothing but straightforward
interpretation of the text in the light of the circumstances and
the situation. We can reject it only by insisting on the manifest
absurdity (shown to be such in every headlink and endlink)
that Chaucer did not visualize the Pilgrims whom he had been
at such pains to describe in the Prologue, and that he never
regarded them as associating, as looking at each other and
thinking of each other, as becoming better and better ac-
quainted as they jogged along the Canterbury road.

Chaucer might have given the Clerk a chance to reply to
the Wife immediately. But he was too good an artist. The

drama of the Pilgrimage is too natural and unforced in its development under the master's hand to admit of anything so frigidly schematic. The very liveliness with which he conceived his individual *dramatis personae* forbade. The Pilgrims were interested in the Wife's harangue, but it was for the talkative members of the company to thrust themselves forward. The Pardoner had already interrupted her with humorous comments before she was fully under way and had exhorted her to continue her account of the 'praktike' of marriage. The Friar, we may be confident, was on good terms with her before she began; she was one of those 'worthy wommen of the toun' whom he especially cultivated. He, too, could not refrain from comment:

> The Frere lough, whan he had herd al this:
> 'Now, dame,' quod he, 'so have I ioye or blis,
> This is a long preamble of a tale,' (D. 829–31)

The Summoner reproved him, in words that show not only his professional enmity but also the amusement that the Pilgrims in general were deriving from the Wife's disclosures. They quarreled, and each threatened to tell a story at the other's expense. Then the Host intervened roughly, calling for silence and bidding the Wife go ahead with her story. She assented, but not without a word of good-humored, though ironical, deference to the Friar:

> 'Al redy, sir,' quod she, 'right as yow lest,
> If I have license of this worthy Frere.' (D. 854–5)

And, at the very beginning of her tale, she took humorous vengeance for his interruption in a characteristic bit of satire at the expense of 'limitours and other holy freres.' This passage, we note, has nothing whatever to do with her tale. It is a side-remark in which she is talking at the Friar, precisely as she has talked at the Clerk in her prologue.

The quarrel between the Summoner and the Friar was in abeyance until the Wife finished her tale. They let her end her story and proclaim her moral in peace,—the same heretical doctrine that we have already noted, that the wife should be

the head of the house. Then the Friar spoke, and his words
are very much to our present purpose. He adverts in sig-
nificant terms both to the subject and to the manner of the
Wife's discourse,—a discourse, we should observe, that was
in effect a doctrinal sermon illustrated (as the fashion of
preachers was) by a pertinent *exemplum*:

> 'Ye have here touched, al-so moot I thee,
> In scole-matere great difficultee.' (D. 1271-2)

She has handled a hard subject that properly belongs to
scholars. She has quoted authorities, too, like a clerk. Such
things, he says, are best left to ecclesiastics:

> 'But, dame, here as we ryden by the weye,
> Us nedeth nat to speken but of game,
> And lete auctoritees, on Goddes name,
> To preching and to scole eek of clergye.' (D. 1274-7)

This, to be sure, is but a device to 'conveyen his matere,'—to
lead up to his proposal to 'telle a game' about a summoner.
But it serves to recall our minds to the Wife's usurpation of
clerkly functions. If we think of the Clerk at all at this point
(and assuredly Chaucer had not forgotten him), we must feel
that here is another prompting (undesigned though it be on
the Friar's part) to take up the subject which the Wife has
(in the Clerk's eyes) so shockingly maltreated.

Then follows the comic interlude of the Friar and the
Summoner, in the course of which we may perhaps lose sight
of the serious subject which the Wife had set abroach,—the
status of husband and wife in the marriage relation. But
Chaucer did not lose sight of it. It was part of his design that
the Host should call on the Clerk for the first story of the next
day.

This is the opportunity for which the Clerk has been wait-
ing. He has not said a word in reply to the Wife's heresies or
to her personal attack on him and his order. Seemingly she
has triumphed. The subject has apparently been dismissed
with the Friar's words about leaving such matters to sermons
and to school debates. The Host, indeed, has no idea that the
Clerk proposes to revive the discussion; he does not even

think of the Wife in calling upon the representative of that order which has fared so ill at her hands.

> 'Sir clerk of Oxenford,' our hoste sayde,
> 'Ye ryde as coy and stille as doth a mayde
> Were newe spoused, sitting at the bord;
> This day ne herd I of your tonge a word.
> I trowe ye studie about som sophyme.' (E. 1–5)

Even here there is a suggestion (casual, to be sure, and, so far as the Host is concerned, quite unintentional) of *marriage*, the subject which is occupying the Clerk's mind. For the Host is mistaken. The Clerk's abstraction is only apparent. He is not pondering syllogisms; he is biding his time.

'Tell us a tale,' the unconscious Host goes on, 'but don't preach us a Lenten sermon—tell us som mery thing of aventures.' 'Gladly,' replies the demure scholar. 'I will tell you a story that a worthy *clerk* once told me at Padua—Francis Petrarch, God rest his soul!'

At this word *clerk,* pronounced with grave and inscrutable emphasis, the Wife of Bath must have pricked up her ears. But she has no inkling of what is in store, nor is the Clerk in any hurry to enlighten her. He opens with tantalizing deliberation, and it is not until he has spoken more than sixty lines that he mentions marriage. 'The Marquis Walter,' says the Clerk, 'lived only for the present and lived for pleasure only'—

> 'As for to hauke and hunte on every syde,—
> Wel ny al othere cures leet he slyde;
> And eek he nolde, and that was worst of alle,
> Wedde no wyf, for noght that may bifalle.' (E. 81–4)

These words may or may not have appeared significant to the company at large. To the Wife of Bath, at all events, they must have sounded interesting. And when, in a few moments, the Clerk made Walter's subjects speak of 'soveraynetee,' the least alert of the Pilgrims can hardly have missed the point:

> 'Boweth your nekke under that blisful yok
> Of soveraynetee, noght of servyse,
> Which that men clepeth spousaille or wedlock.' (E. 113–15)

'Sovereignty' had been the Wife's own word:

> 'And whan that I hadde geten unto me
> By maistrie al the soveraynetee'; (D. 817–18)

> 'Wommen desyren to have soveryntee
> As wel over hir housband as hir love,
> And for to been in maistrie him above.' (D. 1038–40)

Clearly the Clerk is catching up the subject proposed by the Wife. The discussion is under way again.

Yet despite the cheerful view that Walter's subjects take of the marriage yoke, it is by no means yet clear to the Wife of Bath and the other Pilgrims what the Clerk is driving at. For he soon makes Walter declare that 'liberty is seldom found in marriage,' and that if he weds a wife, he must exchange freedom for servitude. Indeed, it is not until vss. 351–57 are reached that Walter reveals himself as a man who is determined to rule his wife absolutely. From that point to the end there is no room for doubt in any Pilgrim's mind: *the Clerk is answering the Wife of Bath;* he is telling of a woman whose principles in marriage were the antithesis of hers; he is reasserting the orthodox view in opposition to the heresy which she had expounded with such zest and with so many flings and jeers at the clerkly profession and character.

What is the tale of Griselda? Several things, no doubt—an old *märchen*, an *exemplum*, a *novella*, what you will. Our present concern, however, is primarily with the question what it seemed to be to the Canterbury Pilgrims, told as it was by an individual Clerk of Oxford at a particular moment and under the special circumstances. The answer is plain. To them it was a retort (indirect, impersonal, masterly) to the Wife of Bath's heretical doctrine that the woman should be the head of the man. It told them of a wife who had no such views,— who promised ungrudging obedience and kept her vow. The Wife of Bath had railed at her husbands and badgered them and cajoled them: Griselda never lost her patience or her serenity. On its face, then, the tale appeared to the Pilgrims to be a dignified and scholarly narrative, derived from a great Italian clerk who was dead, and now utilized by their fellow-pilgrim, the Clerk of Oxford, to demolish the heretical struc-

ture so boisterously reared by the Wife of Bath in her prologue
and her tale.

But Chaucer's Clerk was a logician—'unto logik hadde he
longe ygo.' He knew perfectly well that the real moral of his
story was not that which his hearers would gather. He was
aware that Griselda was no model for literal imitation by
ordinary womankind. If so taken, his tale proved too much; it
reduced his argument *ad absurdum*. If he let it go at that, he
was playing into his opponent's hands. Besides, he was a
conscientious man. He could not misrepresent the lesson which
Petrarch had meant to teach and had so clearly expressed,—the
lesson of submissive fortitude under tribulation sent by God.
Hence he does not fail to explain this moral fully and in un-
mistakable terms, and to refer distinctly to Petrarch as
authority for it:

> And herkeneth what this auctor seith therefore.

> This is seyd, nat for that wyves sholde
> Folwen Griselde as in humilitee,
> For it were importable, though they wolde;
> But that for every wight, in his degree,
> Sholde be constant in adversitee
> As was Grisilde; therfor Petrark wryteth
> This storie, which with heigh style he endyteth.

> For, sith a womman was so pacient
> Un-to a mortal man, wel more us oghte
> Receyven al in gree that God us sent;
> For greet skile is, he preve that he wroghte.
> But he ne tempteth no man that he boghte,
> As seith sent Iame, if ye his pistel rede;
> He preveth folk al day, it is no drede,

> And suffreth us, as for our exercyse,
> With sharpe scourges of adversitee
> Ful often to be bete in sondry wyse;
> Nat for to knowe our wil, for certes he,
> Er we were born, knew al our freletee;
> And for our beste is al his governaunce:
> Lat us than live in vertuous suffrance. (E. 1141–64)

Yet the Clerk has no idea of failing to make his point
against the Wife of Bath. And so, when the tale is finished and
the proper Petrarchan moral has been duly elaborated, he
turns to the Wife (whom he has thus far sedulously refrained

from addressing) and distinctly applies the material to the purpose of an ironical answer, of crushing force, to her whole heresy. There is nothing inappropriate to his character in this procedure. Quite the contrary. Clerks were always satirizing women—the Wife had said so herself—and this particular Clerk had, of course, no scruples against using the powerful weapon of irony in the service of religion and 'moral vertu.' In this instance, the satire is peculiarly poignant for two reasons: first, because it comes with all the suddenness of a complete change of tone (from high seriousness to biting irony, and from the impersonal to the personal); and secondly, because in the tale which he has told, the Clerk had incidentally refuted a false statement of the Wife's, to the effect that

> 'It is an impossible
> That any clerk wol speke good of wyves,
> But if it be of holy seintes lyves,
> No of noon other womman never the mo.' (D. 688–91)

Clerks *can* 'speak well' of women (as our Clerk has shown), and when women deserve it; and he now proceeds to show that they can likewise speak well (with biting irony) of women who do *not* deserve it—such women as the Wife of Bath and all her sect of domestic revolutionists.

It now appears that the form and spirit of the conclusion and the Envoy are not only appropriate to clerks in general, but peculiarly and exquisitely appropriate to this particular clerk under these particular circumstances and with this particular task in hand,—the duty of defending the orthodox view of the relations between husband and wife against the heretical opinions of the Wife of Bath: 'One word in conclusion, gentlemen. There are few Griseldas now-a-days. Most women will break before they will bend. Our companion, the Wife of Bath, is an example, as she has told us herself. Therefore, though I cannot sing, I will recite a song in honor, not of Griselda (as you might perhaps expect), but of the Wife of Bath, of the sect of which she aspires to be a doctor, and of the life which she exemplifies in practice—

'For the wyves love of Bathe,
Whos lif and al hir secte God mayntene
In high maistrye, and elles were it scathe.' (E. 1170–2)

Her *way of life*—she had set it forth with incomparable zest.
Her *sect*—she was an heresiarch or at least a schismatic. The
terms are not accidental: they are chosen with all the dis-
crimination that befits a scholar and a rhetorician. They refer
us back (as definitely as the words 'Wife of Bath' themselves)
to that prologue in which the Wife had stood forth as an
opponent of the orthodox view of subordination in marriage,
as the upholder of an heretical doctrine, and as the exultant
practicer of what she preached.

And then comes the Clerk's Envoy, the song that he recites
in honor of the Wife and all her sect, with its polished lines,
its ingenious rhyming, and its utter felicity of scholarly dic-
tion. Nothing could be more in character. To whom in all the
world could such a masterpiece of rhetoric be appropriate if
not to the Clerk of Oxenford? It is a mock encomium, a sus-
tained ironical commendation of what the Wife has taught.

'O noble wives, let no clerk ever have occasion to write
such a story of you as Petrarch once told me about Griselda.
Follow your great leader, the Wife of Bath. Rule your hus-
bands, as she did; rail at them, as she did; make them
jealous, as she did; exert yourselves to get lovers, as she did.
And all this you must do whether you are fair or foul. Do this,
I say, and you will fulfil the precepts that she has set forth
and achieve the great end which she has proclaimed as the
object of marriage: that is, *you will make your husbands mis-
erable, as she did!*'

'Be ay of chere as light as leef on linde,
And let him care and wepe and wringe and waille!'
(E. 1211–12)

And the Merchant (hitherto silent, but not from inatten-
tion) catches up the closing words in a gust of bitter passion:

'Weping and wayling, care and other sorwe
I know ynough on even and amorwe.'
Quod the Merchant, 'and so don othere mo
That wedded ben.' (E. 1213–16)

The Clerk's Envoy, then, is not only appropriate to his character and to the situation: it has also a marked dynamic value. For it is this ironical tribute to the Wife of Bath and her dogmas that, with complete dramatic inevitability, calls out the Merchant's *cri de coeur*. The Merchant has no thought of telling a tale at this moment. He is a stately and imposing person in his degree, by no means prone (so the Prologue informs us) to expose any holes there may be in his coat. But he is suffering a kind of emotional crisis. The poignant irony of the Clerk, following hard upon the moving story of a patient and devoted wife, is too much for him. He has just passed through his honeymoon (but two months wed!) and he has sought a respite from his thraldom under color of a pilgrimage to St. Thomas.

> 'I have a wyf, the worste that may bel' (E. 1218)

She would be an overmatch for the devil himself. He need not specify her evil traits: she is bad in every respect.

> 'There is a long and large difference
> Bitwix Grisildis grete pacience
> And of my wyfe the passing crueltee.' (E. 1223-5)

The Host, as ever, is on the alert. He scents a good story:

> 'Sin ye so muchel knowen of that art,
> Ful hertely I pray yow telle us part.' (E. 1241-2)

The Merchant agrees, as in duty bound, for all the Pilgrims take care never to oppose the Host, lest he exact the heavy forfeit established as the penalty for rebellion. But he declines to relate his own experiences, thus leaving us to infer, if we choose,—for nowhere is Chaucer's artistic reticence more effective,—that his bride has proved false to him, like the wife of the worthy Knight of Lombardy.

And so the discussion of marriage is once more in full swing. The Wife of Bath, without intending it, has opened a debate in which the Pilgrims have become so absorbed that they will not leave it till the subject is 'bolted to the bran.'

The Merchant's Tale presents very noteworthy features, and has been much canvassed, though never (it seems) with due attention to its plain significance in the Human Comedy of the Canterbury Tales. In substance, it is nothing but a tale of bawdry, one of the most familiar of its class. There is nothing novel about it except its setting, but that is sufficiently remarkable. Compare the tale with any other version of the Pear-Tree Story,—their name is legion,—and its true significance comes out in striking fashion. The simple fabliau devised by its first author merely to make those laugh whose lungs are tickle o' the sere, is so expanded and overlaid with savage satire that it becomes a complete disquisition of marriage from the only point of view which is possible for the disenchanted Merchant. Thus considered, the cynicism of the Merchant's Tale is seen to be in no way surprising, and (to answer another kind of comment which this piece has evoked) in no sense expressive of Chaucer's own sentiments, or even of Chaucer's momentary mood. The cynicism is the Merchant's. It is no more Chaucer's than Iago's cynicism about love is Shakespeare's.

In a word, the tale is the perfect expression of the Merchant's angry disgust at his own evil fate and at his folly in bringing that fate upon himself. Thus, its very lack of restraint —the savagery of the whole, which has revolted so many readers—is dramatically inevitable. The Merchant has schooled himself to his debts and his troubles. He is professionally adept at putting a good face on matters, as every clever business man must be. But when once the barrier is broken, reticence is at an end. His disappointment is too fresh, his disillusion has been too abrupt, for him to measure his words. He speaks in a frenzy of contempt and hatred. The hatred is for women; the contempt is for himself and all other fools who will not take warning by example. For we should not forget that the satire is aimed at January rather than at May. That egotistical old dotard is less excusable than his young wife, and meets with less mercy at the Merchant's hands.

That the Merchant begins with an encomium on marriage which is one of the most amazing instances of sustained irony in all literature, is not to be wondered at. In the first place, he is ironical because the Clerk has been ironical. Here the connection is remarkably close. The Merchant has fairly snatched the words out of the Clerk's mouth ('And lat him care and wepe and wringe and waille'—'Weping and wayling, care and other sorwe'), and his mock encomium on the wedded state is a sequel to the Clerk's mock encomium on the Wife of Bath's life and all her sect. The spirit is different, but that is quite proper. For the Clerk's satire is the irony of a logician and a moral philosopher, the irony of the intellect and the ethical sense: the Merchant's is the irony of a mere man, it is the irony of passion and personal experience. The Clerk is a theorist,—he looks at the subject from a point of philosophical detachment. The Merchant is an egotist,—he feels himself to be the dupe whose folly he depicts. We may infer, if we like, that he was a man in middle age and that he had married a young wife

There is plenty of evidence that the Merchant has been an attentive listener. One detects, for instance, a certain similarity between January and the Marquis Walter (different as they are) in that they have both shown themselves disinclined to marriage. Then again, the assertion that a wife is never weary of attending a sick husband—

> 'She nis nat wery him to love and serve,
> Thogh that he lye bedrede til he sterve'— (E. 1291-2)

must have reminded the Pilgrims of poor Thomas, in the Summoner's Tale, whose wife's complaints to her spiritual visitor had precipitated so tremendous a sermon.[5] But such things are trifles compared with the attention which the Merchant devotes to the Wife of Bath.

So far, in this act of Chaucer's Human Comedy, we have found that the Wife of Bath is, in a very real sense, the dominant figure. She has dictated the theme and inspired or instigated the actors; and she has always been at or near the center of the stage. It was a quarrel over her prologue that elicited the tale of the Friar and that of the Summoner.

It was she who caused the Clerk to tell of Griselda—and the Clerk satirizes her in his Envoy. 'The art' of which the Host begs the Merchant to tell is *her* art, the art of marriage on which she has discoursed so learnedly. That the Merchant, therefore, should allude to her, quote her words, and finally mention her in plain terms is precisely what was to be expected.

The order and method of these approaches on the Merchant's part are exquisitely natural and dramatic. First there are touches, more or less palpable, when he describes the harmony of wedded life in terms so different from the Wife's account of what her husbands had to endure. Then—after a little—comes a plain enough allusion (put into January's mouth) to the Wife's character, to her frequent marriages, and to her inclination to marry again, old as she is:

> 'And eek thise olde widwes, God it wot,
> They conne so muchel craft on Wades boot,
> So muchel broken harm, whan that hem leste,
> That with hem sholde I never live in restel
> For sondry scoles maken sotil clerkis:
> Wommen of many scoles half a clerk is.' (E. 1423–8)

Surely the Wife of Bath was a woman of many schools, and her emulation of clerkly discussion had already been commented on by the Pardoner and the Friar. Next, the Merchant lets Justinus quote some of the Wife's very words—though without naming her: 'God may apply the trials of marriage, my dear January, to your salvation. Your wife may make you go straight to heaven without passing through purgatory.'

> 'Paraunter she may be your purgatorie!
> She may be Goddes mene, and Goddes whippe;
> Than shal your soule up to hevene skippe
> Swifter than doth an arwe out of the bowe.' (E. 1670–3)

This is merely an adaptation of the Wife of Bath's own language in speaking of her fourth husband:

'By God, in erthe I was his purgatorie,
For which I hope his soule be in glorie.' (D. 489–90)

Compare also another phrase of hers, which Justinus echoes:
'Myself have been the whippe.'⁸ And finally, when all the
Pilgrims are quite prepared for such a thing, there is a frank
citation of the Wife of Bath by name, with a reference to her
exposition of marriage:

'My tale is doon:—for my wit is thinne.
Beth nat agast herof, my brother dere.
But lat us waden out of this matere:
The Wyf of Bathe, if ye han understonde,
Of marriage, which we have on honde,
Declared hath ful wel in litel space.
Fareth now wel, God have yow in his grace.' (E. 1682–8)

Are the italicized lines a part of the speech of Justinus, or
are they interpolated by the Merchant, in his own person, in
order to shorten Justinus' harangue? Here is Professor Skeat's
comment: 'These four parenthetical lines interrupt the story
rather awkwardly. They obviously belong to the narrator,
the Merchant, as it is out of the question that Justinus had
heard of the Wife of Bath. Perhaps it is an oversight.' Now
it makes no difference whether we assign these lines to
Justinus or to the Merchant, for Justinus, as we have seen,
has immediately before quoted the Wife's very words, and
he may as well mention her as repeat her language. Either
way, the lines are exquisitely in place. *Chaucer* is not speak-
ing, and there is no violation of dramatic propriety on *his*
part. It is not Chaucer who is telling the story. It is the
Merchant. And the Merchant is telling it as a part of the dis-
cussion which the Wife has started. It is dramatically proper,
then, that the Merchant should quote the Wife of Bath and
that he should refer to her. And it is equally proper, from
the dramatic point of view, for Chaucer to let the Merchant
make Justinus mention the Wife. In that case it is the Mer-
chant—not *Chaucer*—who chooses to have one of his char-
acters fall out of his part for a moment and make a 'local
allusion.' Chaucer is responsible for making the *Merchant*

speak in character; the Merchant, in his turn, is responsible for *Justinus*. That the Merchant should put into the mouth of Justinus a remark that Justinus could never have made is, then, not a slip on Chaucer's part. On the contrary, it is a first-rate dramatic touch, for it is precisely what the Merchant might well have done under the circumstances.

Nor should we forget the exquisitely comical discussion between Pluto and Proserpina which the Merchant has introduced near the end of his story. This dialogue is a flagrant violation of dramatic propriety—not on Chaucer's part, however, but on the Merchant's. And therein consists a portion of its merit. For the Merchant is so eager to make his point that he rises superior to all artistic rules. He is bent, not on giving utterance to a masterpiece of narrative construction, but on enforcing his lesson in every possible way. And Chaucer is equally bent on making him do it. Hence the Queen of the Lower World is brought in, discoursing in terms that befit the Wife of Bath (the presiding genius of this part of the *Canterbury Tales*), and echoing some of her very doctrines.[7] . . . And note that Pluto (who is as fond of citing authorities as the Wife's last husband) yields the palm of the discussion to Proserpine. . . . This, too, was the experience of the Wife's husbands. . . . The tone and manner of the whole debate between Pluto and his queen are wildly absurd if regarded from the point of view of gods and goddesses, but in that very incongruity resides their dramatic propriety. What we have is not Pluto and Proserpine arguing with each other, but the Wife of Bath and one of her husbands attired for the nonce by the cynical Merchant in the external resemblance of King Pluto and his dame.

The end of the Merchant's Tale does not bring the Marriage Chapter of the *Canterbury Tales* to a conclusion. As the Merchant had commented on the Clerk's Tale by speaking of his own wife, thus continuing the subject which the Wife had begun, so the Host comments on the Merchant's story by making a similar application:

> 'Ey, Goddes mercy,' seyde our Hoste tho,
> 'Now such a wyf I pray God kepe me fro!' (E. 2419–20)

'See how women deceive us poor men, as the Merchant has shown us. However, *my* wife is true as any steel; but she is a shrew, and has plenty of other faults.' And just as the Merchant had referred expressly to the Wife of Bath, so also does the Host refer to her expressly: 'But I must not talk of these things. If I should, it would be told to her by some of this company. I need not say by whom, 'sin wommen connen outen swich chaffare!' Of course the Host points this remark by looking at the Wife of Bath. There are but three women in the company. Neither the highborn and dainty Prioress nor the pious nun who accompanies her is likely to gossip with Harry Baily's spouse. It is the Wife, a woman of the Hostess's own rank and temper, who will tattle when the party returns to the Tabard. And so we find the Wife of Bath still in the foreground, as she has been, in one way or another, for several thousand lines.

But now the Host thinks his companions have surely had enough of marriage. It is time they heard something of love, and with this in view he turns abruptly to the Squire, whom all the Pilgrims have come to know as 'a lovyer and a lusty bachiller.'

> 'Squier, com neer, if it your wille be,
> And sey somewhat of *love;* for certes ye
> Connen theron as muche as any man.' (F. 1–3)

The significance of the emphasis on *love*, which is inevitable if the address to the Squire is read (as it should be) continuously with the Host's comments on marriage, is by no means accidental.

There is no psychology about the Squire's Tale—no moral or social or matrimonial theorizing. It is pure romance, in the mediaeval sense. The Host understood the charm of variety. He did not mean to let the discussion drain itself to the dregs.

But Chaucer's plan in this Act is not yet finished. There is still something lacking to a full discussion of the relations between husband and wife. We have had the wife who dominates her husband; the husband who dominates his wife; the young wife who befools her dotard January; the chaste wife who is a scold and stirs up strife. Each of these illustrates a different kind of marriage,—but there is left untouched, sofar, the ideal relation, that in which love continues and neither party to the contract strives for the mastery. Let this be set forth, and the series of views of wedded life begun by the Wife of Bath will be rounded off; the Marriage Act of the Human Comedy will be concluded. The Pilgrims may not be thinking of this; but there is at least *one* of them (as the sequel shows) who has the idea in his head. And who is he? The only pilgrims who have not yet already told their tales are the yeoman, two priests, the five tradesmen (haberdasher, carpenter, weaver, dyer, and tapicer), the parson, the plowman, the manciple, and the franklin. Of all these there is but one to whom a tale illustrating the ideal would not be inappropriate—the Franklin. To him, then, must Chaucer assign it, or leave the debate unfinished.

At this point, the dramatic action and interplay of characters are beyond all praise. The Franklin is not brought forward in formal fashion to address the company. His summons is incidental to the dialogue. No sooner has the Squire ended his chivalric romance, than the Franklin begins to compliment him:

> 'In feyth, squier, thou hast thee well yquit
> And gentilly. . . .' (F. 673–4)

'You have acquitted yourself well and *like a gentleman!*' *Gentilesse,* then, is what has most impressed the Franklin in the tale that he has just heard. And the reason for his enthusiasm soon appears. He is, as we know, a rich freeholder, often sheriff in his county. Socially, he is not quite within the pale of the gentry, but he is the kind of man that may hope to found a family, the kind of man from whose ranks the English nobility has been constantly recruited. And that such is his ambition comes out naïvely and with a certain pathos in what he goes on to say: 'I wish my son were like you. . . . It is the contrast between the

Squire and his own son, in whom his hopes are centered, that has led the Franklin's thoughts to *gentilesse,* a subject which is ever in his mind.

But the Host interrupts him rudely: 'Straw for your gentilesse! It is your turn to entertain the company':

'Telle on thy tale withouten wordes mo!' (F. 702)

The Franklin is, of course, very polite in his reply to this rough and unexpected command. Like the others, he is on his guard against opposing the Host and incurring the forfeit. . . .

Here, then, as in the case of the Merchant, the Host has taken advantage of a spontaneous remark on some Pilgrim's part to demand a story. Yet the details of the action are quite different. On the previous occasion, the Merchant is requested to go on with an account of his marriage, since he has already begun to talk about it; and, though he declines to speak further of his own troubles, he does continue to discuss and illustrate wedlock from his own point of view. In the present instance, on the contrary, the Host repudiates the topic of *gentilesse,* about which the Franklin is discoursing to the Squire. He bids him drop the subject and tell a story. The Franklin pretends to be compliant, but after all, he has his own way. Indeed, he takes delicate vengeance on the Host by telling a tale which thrice exemplifies *gentilesse*—on the part of a knight, a squire, and a clerk. Thus he finishes his interrupted compliment to the Squire, and incidentally honors two other Pilgrims who have seemed to him to possess the quality that he values so highly. He proves, too, both that *gentilesse* is an entertaining topic and that it is not (as the Host has roughly intimated) a theme which he, the Franklin, is ill-equipped to handle.

For the Franklin's Tale is a gentleman's story, and he tells it like a gentleman. It is derived, he tells us, from 'thise olde *gentil* Britons.' Dorigen lauds Arveragus' *gentilesse* toward her in refusing to insist on soveraynetee in marriage. Aurelius is deeply impressed by the knight's *gentilesse* in allowing the lady to keep her word, and emulates it by

releasing her. . . . And finally, the clerk releases Aurelius,
from the same motive of generous emulation. . . .

Thus it appears that the dramatic impulse to the telling
of the Franklin's Tale is to be found in the relations among
the Pilgrims and in the effect that they have upon each
other,—in other words, in the circumstances, the situation,
and the interplay of character.

It has sometimes been thought that the story, either in
subject or in style, is too fine for the Franklin to tell. But this
objection Chaucer foresaw and forestalled. The question is
not whether this tale, thus told, would be appropriate to a
typical or 'average' fourteenth-century franklin. The question
is whether it is appropriate to this particular Franklin, under
these particular circumstances, and at this particular juncture.
And to this question there can be but one answer. Chaucer's
Franklin is an individual, not a mere type-specimen. He is
rich, ambitious socially, and profoundly interested in the
matter of *gentilesse* for personal and family reasons. He is
trying to bring up his son as a gentleman, and his position
as 'St. Julian in his country' has brought him into intimate
association with first-rate models. He has, under the special
circumstances, every motive to tell a gentleman's story and
tell it like a gentleman. He is speaking under the immediate
influence of his admiration for the Squire and of his sense
of the inferiority of his own son. If we choose to conceive
the Franklin as a mediaeval Squire Western and then to
allege that he could not possibly have told such a story, we
are making the difficulty for ourselves. We are considering—
not Chaucer's Franklin (whose character is to be inferred
not merely from the description in the General Prologue
but from all the other evidence that the poet provides)—not
Chaucer's Franklin, but somebody quite different, somebody
for whom Chaucer has no kind of responsibility.

In considering the immediate occasion of the Franklin's
Tale, we have lost sight for a moment of the Wife of Bath.
But she was not absent from the mind of the Franklin. The
proper subject of his tale, as we have seen, is *gentilesse*.
Now that (as well as marriage) was a subject on which the

Wife of Bath had descanted at some length. Her views are contained in the famous harangue delivered by the lady to her husband on the wedding night: 'But for ye speken of swich gentilesse,' etc. Many readers have perceived that this portentous curtain-lecture clogs the story, and some have perhaps wished it away, good as it is in itself. For it certainly seems to be out of place on the lips of the *fée*. But its insertion is (as usual in such cases) exquisitely appropriate to the teller of the tale, the Wife of Bath, who cannot help dilating on subjects which interest her, and who has had the advantage of learned society in the person of her fifth husband. Perhaps no *fée* would have talked thus to her knightly bridegroom on such an occasion; but it is quite in character for the Wife of Bath to use the *fée* (or anybody else) as a mouthpiece for her own ideas, as the Merchant had used Proserpine to point his satire. Thus the references to Dante, Valerius, Seneca, Boethius, and Juvenal—so deliciously absurd on the lips of a *fée* of King Arthur's time—are perfectly in place when we remember who it is that is reporting the monologue. The Wife was a citer of authorities—she makes the *fée* cite authorities. How comical this is the Wife did not know, but Chaucer knew, and if we think he did not, it is our own fault for not observing how dramatic in spirit is the *Canterbury Tales*.

A considerable passage in the curtain-lecture is given to the proposition that 'swich gentilesse as is descended out of old richesse' is of no value: 'Swich arrogance is not worth an hen.' These sentiments the Franklin echoes:

> 'Fy on possessioun
> But if a man be vertuous withal!' (F. 686–7)

But, whether or not the Wife's digression on *gentilesse* is lingering in the Franklin's mind (as I am sure it is), one thing is perfectly clear: the Franklin's utterances on marriage are spoken under the influence of the discussion which the Wife has precipitated. In other words, though everybody else imagines that the subject has been finally dismissed by the Host when he calls on the Squire for a tale of *love*, it has no more been dismissed in fact than when the Friar attempted to dismiss it at the beginning of his tale. For the Franklin has views, and he means to set them forth. He possesses, as he thinks, the true solution of the whole difficult problem. And that solution he embodies in his tale of *gentilesse*.

The introductory part of the Franklin's Tale sets forth a theory of the marriage relation quite different from anything that has so far emerged in the debate. And this theory the Franklin arrives at by taking into consideration both *love* (which, as we remember, was the subject that the Host had bidden the Squire treat of) and *gentilesse* (which is to be the subject of his own story).

Arveragus had of course been obedient to his lady during the period of courtship, for obedience was well understood to be the duty of a lover. Finally, she consented to marry him—

> To take him for hir housbonde and hir lord,
> Of swich lordshipe as men han over her wyves. (F. 742–3)

Marriage, then, according to the orthodox doctrine (as held by Walter and Griselda) was to change Arveragus from the lady's servant to her master. But Arveragus was an enlightened and chivalric gentleman, and he promised the lady he would never assert his marital authority, but would content himself with the mere name of sovereignty, continuing to be her servant and lover as before. This he did because he thought it would ensure the happiness of their wedded life. . . .

But, just as Arveragus was no disciple of the Marquis Walter, so Dorigen was not a member of the sect of the Wife of Bath. She promised her husband obedience and fidelity in return for his *gentilesse* in renouncing his sovereign rights. . . . This, then, is the Franklin's solution of the whole puzzle of matrimony, and it is a solution that depends upon love and *gentilesse* on both sides. But he is not content to leave the matter in this purely objective condition. He is determined that there shall be no misapprehension in the mind of any Pilgrim as to his purpose. He wishes to make it perfectly clear that he is definitely and formally offering this theory as the only satisfactory basis of happy married life. And he accordingly comments on the relations between the married lovers with fulness, and with manifest reference to certain things that the previous debaters have said.

The arrangement, he tells the Pilgrims, resulted in 'quiet and rest' for both Arveragus and Dorigen. And, he adds, it is the only arrangement which will ever enable two persons to live together in love and amity. Friends must 'obey each other if they wish to hold company long.' . . . Hence it was that this wise knight promised his wife 'suffraunce' and that she promised him never to abuse his goodness. . . . The result, the Franklin adds, was all that could be desired. The knight lived 'in blisse and in solas.' And then the Franklin adds an encomium on the happiness of true marriage:

> 'Who coulde telle, but he had wedded be,
> The joye, the ese, and the prosperitee
> That is bitwixe an housbonde and his wyf?' (F. 803–5)

This encomium echoes the language of the Merchant:

> 'A wyf! a Seinte Marie! *benedicite!*
> How mighte a man han any adversitee
> That hath a wyf? Certes, I can nat seye!
> The blisse which that is bitwixe hem tweye
> Ther may no tonge telle or herte thinke.' (E. 1337–41)

The Franklin's praise of marriage is sincere; the Merchant's had been savagely ironical. The Franklin, we observe, is answering the Merchant, and he answers him in the most effective way—by repeating his very words.

And just as in the Merchant's Tale we noted that the Merchant has enormously expanded the simple fabliau that he had to tell, inserting all manner of observations on marriage which are found in no other version of the Pear-Tree story, so also we find that the Franklin's exposition of the ideal marriage relation (including the pact between Arveragus and Dorigen) is all his own, occurring in none of the versions that precede Chaucer. These facts are of the very last significance. No argument is necessary to enforce their meaning.

It is hardly worth while to indicate the close connection between this and that detail of the Franklin's exposition and certain points that have come out in the discussion as conducted by his predecessors in the debate. His repudiation of the Wife of Bath's doctrine that men should be 'governed by their wives' is express, as well as his rejection of the opposite theory. Neither party should lose his liberty; neither the husband nor the wife should be a thrall. Patience (which clerks celebrate as a high virtue) should be mutual, not, as in the Clerk's Tale, all on one side. The husband is to be both servant and lord—servant in love and lord in marriage. Such servitude is true lordship. Here there is a manifest allusion to the words of Walter's subjects in the Clerk's Tale:

> That blisful yok
> Of sovereynetee, noght of servyse; (E. 113–14)

as well as to Walter's rejoinder:

> 'I me reioysed of my libertee,
> That selde tyme is founde in mariage;
> Ther I was free, I moot been in servage.'(E. 145–7)

It was the regular theory of the Middle Ages that the highest type of chivalric love was incompatible with marriage, since marriage brings in mastery, and mastery and love cannot abide together. This view the Franklin boldly challenges. Love *can* be consistent with marriage, he declares. Indeed, without love (and perfect *gentle* love) marriage is sure to be a failure. The difficulty about mastery vanishes when mutual love and forbearance are made the guiding principles of the relation between husband and wife.

The soundness of the Franklin's theory, he declares, is proved by his tale. For the marriage of Arveragus and Dorigen was a brilliant success. . . . Thus the whole debate has been brought to a satisfactory conclusion, and the Marriage Act of the Human Comedy ends with the conclusion of the Franklin's Tale.

Those readers who are eager to know what Chaucer thought about marriage may feel reasonably content with

the inference that may be drawn from his procedure. The
Marriage Group of Tales begins with the Wife of Bath's
Prologue and ends with the Franklin's Tale. There is no con-
nection between the Wife's Prologue and the group of stories
that precedes: there is no connection between the Frank-
lin's Tale and the group that follows. Within the Marriage
Group, on the contrary, there is close connection throughout.
That act is a finished act. It begins and ends an elaborate
debate. We need not hesitate, therefore, to accept the solu-
tion which the Franklin offers as that which Geoffrey Chau-
cer the man accepted for his own part. Certainly it is a solu-
tion that does him infinite credit. A better has never been
devised or imagined.

Notes

[1] [Kittredge's pioneer article on the Marriage Group has never
been superseded, though it has been flatly challenged, as by H. B.
Hinckley, "The Debate on Marriage in the *Canterbury Tales*,"
PMLA, XXXII (1917), 292–305, and later by C. P. Lyons, "The
Marriage Debate in the *Canterbury Tales*," *ELH*, II (1935), 252–
62. W. W. Lawrence, "The Marriage Group in the *Canterbury
Tales*," *MP*, XI (1912–13), 247–58, argues that the group must be
extended to include the *Tale of Melibee* and the *Nun's Priest's
Tale;* he is supported by John S. Kenyon, "Further Notes on the
Marriage Group in the *Canterbury Tales*," *JEGP*, XV (1916),
282–88. Marie Neville, "The Function of the *Squire's Tale* in the
Canterbury Scheme," *JEGP*, L (1951), 167–79, examines the
bridging function of this tale within the Marriage Group, while
Albert N. Silverman, "Sex and Money in Chaucer's *Shipman's
Tale*," *PQ*, XXXII (1935), 329–36, proposes that the commer-
cialization of marriage underlying the *Shipman's Tale* adds variety
to the marriage debate. The genesis of the Marriage Group and
the significance of textual changes made by Chaucer in the com-
ponent tales are discussed, to mention but two among several
important articles, by Carleton Brown, "The Evolution of the Can-
terbury 'Marriage Group,'" *PMLA*, XLVIII (1933), 1041–59, and
Germaine Dempster, "A Period in the Development of the *Canter-
bury Tales* Marriage Group and of Blocks B² and C," *PMLA*,
LXVIII (1953), 1142–59. Despite objections and qualifications,
however, Kittredge's article remains "both witty in itself and the
cause of wit in other men," as James Sledd observes (see next
article in anthology).—Ed.]

[2] Since the *Canterbury Tales* is an unfinished work, the drama
of the Pilgrimage is of course more or less fragmentary, and, fur-
thermore, some of the stories (being of old material, utilized for
the nonce) have not been quite accurately fitted to their setting.

Such defects, however, need not trouble us. They are patent enough whenever they occur, and we can easily allow for them. Indeed, the disturbance they cause is more apparent than real. Thus the fact that the Second Nun speaks of herself as a "son of Eve" does not affect our argument. The contradiction would eventually have been removed by a stroke of Chaucer's pen, and its presence in no wise prevents the Legend of St. Cecilia from being exquisitely appropriate to the actual teller.

[Evidence that *secte* means not a religious sect, as Kittredge takes it, but *sex*, is offered by Helge Kökeritz, "The Wyf of Bathe and 'al hir secte,' " *PQ*, XXVI (1947), 147–51. W. W. Lawrence, *Chaucer and the* Canterbury Tales (New York: Columbia University Press, 1950), p. 141, n. 24, disagrees with Kökeritz.—Ed.]

⁴ We may note that the tale which Chaucer first gave to the Wife, as it seems, but afterwards transferred to the Shipman, had also a personal application. It was aimed more or less directly at the Monk, and its application was enforced by the Host's exhortation to the company: "Draweth no monkes more unto your in" (B. 1632). And it contained also a roving shot at the Merchant. Compare the General Prologue (A. 280–2) with the words of the Merchant in the *Shipman's Tale* (B. 1416–24).

⁵ D. 1823ff.

⁶ D. 175.

⁷ Cf. D. 226–33 with E. 2265–75.

9

The *Clerk's Tale:* The Monsters and the Critics

"Deffie Theofraste, and herke me."

JAMES SLEDD

In the study of the *Clerk's Tale*, the chief problems
have been taken to be the morality and probability of char-
acters and action. The Marquis Walter marries the peasant
girl Griselda, after first exacting from her a promise of com-
plete obedience. Griselda becomes the perfect wife and lady,
but Walter determines to test her patience and obedience
and proceeds to do so most severely. He takes her two chil-
dren from her in their infancy, ostensibly to murder them,
actually to have them tenderly but secretly reared. Griselda
surrenders the children, patiently and obediently. After some
years, Walter pretends that he will put away his wife and
take another, and sends Griselda back to her peasant's cot-
tage. Patiently and obediently, she goes, but she is not left
in peace for long. Walter summons her again to the palace,
to receive his new wife and the wedding guests. Griselda
is all patience and obedience, ready and skilful to do her
master's will. As a final test, she is publicly called upon to
praise the bride, and when her patience and obedience bend
but do not break, the Marquis drops his pretenses and takes
her again into his loving arms. The pretended bride is Gri-

Reprinted, by permission of author and publisher, from *Modern
Philology*, LI (1953–4), 73–82. Copyright, 1953, bv the University
of Chicago.

selda's long-lost daughter, the bride's brother her little son; and they all live happily ever after.

From the beginning, as Petrarch, who was one of Chaucer's sources, directly tells us, and as Chaucer makes equally clear in his somewhat different way, two very different effects have been produced by this sad story. Some readers have been moved to compassion and wonder, others to contempt and disbelief; and for some generations now, the contemptuous and the skeptical have outnumbered the compassionate admirers. The fact remains that Boccaccio, Petrarch, Chaucer and dozens of others have found the story worth telling, and that countless readers have found it worth reading. Walter and Griselda, either or both, may be desperately wicked, and their actions improbable or impossible; but Chaucer's telling of their story cannot be abruptly dismissed as an unfortunate episode in an otherwise commendable poetic career. I think one can say without undue solemnity that the *Clerk's Tale* deserves and demands consideration, not as a monument to a departed taste, but as a tale whose admittedly limited values still can be perceived, though perhaps not deeply felt; and it is part of my thesis in this moderately solemn paper that in the present century the tale has suffered because outstanding scholars have too hastily condemned it.

The first of the representative studies to which I shall refer was both witty in itself and the cause of wit in other men: Kittredge's famous article entitled "Chaucer's Discussion of Marriage," which appeared some forty years ago. To the more moderate statements in that article, most students have given full assent, whether they have been interested in the tales as tales or as dramatic speeches; and a certain exaggeration of the dramatic aspects is due simply to the fact that Kittredge was writing to redress a balance. In Kittredge's view, the study and criticism of "each tale in and for itself" was perfectly proper, though much had been lost because the tales were read *only* as isolated units. He was at his most persuasive in showing the extent of that loss. As a result, Chaucerians have since rather generally accepted even his extreme statement that structurally, the tales which the pilgrims tell "are only speeches that are somewhat longer than common, entertaining in and for themselves (to be sure), but primarily significant, in each case, because they illustrate the speaker's character and opinions, or show the relations of the travelers to one another in the progressive action of the Pilgrimage." Here Kittredge claims a good deal more than one need claim in order to maintain the theory of a Marriage Group, as various scholars have maintained it, before and after 1912; for one can do full justice to the dramatic element in the *Tales* without slighting them as narratives.

The consequences of the Kittredge version of the theory, even when allowance is made for rhetorical overstatements, are rather striking. For him, one of the finished acts of "Chaucer's Human Comedy . . . begins with the Wife of Bath's Prologue and ends with the Tale of the Franklin," thus including the *Clerk's Tale* as its fourth large unit. The "subject" of this finished act "is Marriage, which is discussed from several points of view, as the most important problem in organized society. The solution of the problem brings the act to an end" when the Franklin summarizes the whole debate and presents his and Chaucer's doctrine of forbearance and equality in Christian marriage—"a definitive conclusion which we are to accept as a perfect rule of faith and practice."[1] In short, the Marriage Group is not only dramatic; it is a problem play. Presumably, then, one's ultimate judgment on the Group will be rhetorical or moral or sociological; but since Chaucer presents his doctrine of marriage dramatically, and since the speeches in the drama are tales which the speakers use for their own rhetorical purposes, this ultimate judgment would rest on an intricate series of earlier judgments, rhetorical, moral, sociological, and poetic as well. The student who accepts a Marriage Group must develop elaborate critical machinery in order to deal with it, in its parts and as a whole; but such subtlety has not marked discussions of the *Clerk's Tale*.

The hidden complexity of Kittredge's theory is no objection to it, though one might wish that so simple a doctrine of marriage had not demanded so much maneuvering for its expression; but the consequences of his exaggeration of his basic contention are more serious. Despite some eminently sound remarks on the *Clerk's Tale* as a tale, Kittredge in his article leaves the impression that he could not quite stomach that monster Walter and his monstrous wife. The story as story is treated as infinitely less important than the story as a dramatic speech expressing one of the opposed views of marriage, so that followers of Kittredge have every inducement to discuss the drama and every excuse for ignoring the tale. That is a dangerous predicament, as Professor Malone has showed,[2] for it follows either that Chaucer shared the taste of his age—a perverted taste—or that he deliberately told a bad story in order to make a good drama. Even more unfortunately, the drama itself becomes hard to defend, since the neglect of the story forces gay conjecture, the discovery, if not the invention, of something to take the story's place. A moderate statement of the theory of a Marriage Group imposes no necessity for such conjecture; but unless one states his theory with circumspection, he will find himself neglecting the tales which Chaucer did write, inventing dramatic episodes which Chaucer did not write, and yet exposing Chaucer, when all is said, as a botcher who could not make his own intentions clear. For a solution, therefore, of the problems of morality and probability in the *Clerk's Tale*, considered as a tale, the student cannot go to Kittredge, whose tactics are really to submerge the narrative problems in the problems of the drama.

Like so much else of the best Chaucerian scholarship, the next two studies which I shall consider were partly inspired by a remark of Kittredge. I mean Professor Griffith's book on the origin of the Griselda story, and the article by Mr. W. A. Cate on the same topic.[3] For Griffith and Cate, the assumption of the standards of realistic fiction makes possible the initial assertion that the story is peculiar, contradictory, and irrational. Readers have not always been affected in this way, for the frankly marvelous has not always been in disrepute; but Mr. Griffith's Griselda and Mr. Cate's Griselda is no longer the saintly heroine of a piteous, marvelous, and gracious tale. She and her story have undergone a sea-change into something illogical, incoherent, and incomprehensible, and not all the praise which Griffith and Cate give to various tellers of the story can hide their conviction that there is something radically wrong with it.

Beginning, then, with this conviction, they seek an explanation of the improbabilities which Boccaccio, Petrarch, and Chaucer all tolerated; and essentially, Griffith and Cate agree in the explanation which they find. Griffith, said Cate, "is . . . entirely correct in his belief that the Griselda novella represents a literary treatment of a highly rationalized subgroup . . . the 'Patience Group' of Cupid and Psyche folktales . . ., and . . . Gualtieri's domineering, illogical, and ill-motivated actions are caused by—and are an expression of—his otherworld nature." Griselda is the moral wife of an other-world lover, and only when this fact is understood can the problems of her story be resolved.

No one could question this statement of the origin of the Griselda story. One *can* ask exactly what follows from it, and what does not. It has not been made clear to me that the story is so thoroughly improbable as Griffith and Cate seem to believe, or that to understand Chaucer's version one must keep looking over one's shoulder at a folk tale of which Chaucer knew nothing. The misconception which I am getting at only creeps round the edges of the studies by Griffith and Cate, but in some of the reviews of their work it stands out in clear daylight, as naked as Walter's bride. In the words of one review, "There is no doubt that Griffith's theory does succeed in explaining much in Boccaccio's and Chaucer's stories that has hitherto seemed peculiar and even repulsive." Transferring the epithets, I would call this judgment peculiar, repulsive, and unfair to an excellent book, in which some admirable things are said about Boccaccio's story. The judgment is unfair because, by claiming too much, it brings suspicion on a genuine accomplishment, and it is repulsive because its consequences are bad criticism and hence bad history. A knowledge of literary origins may sharpen our appreciation of narrative success and show us the causes of narrative failure, but it is a means to interpretation, not a substitute for it; and until the literary versions of the Griselda story have been interpreted independently and in their own terms, we cannot even compare them accurately with the folk tale from which they sprang. Griselda and Walter are the grandchildren of monsters; their own condition must be determined by a separate inquiry.

The fourth and last study which I shall examine tells us much more about the *Clerk's Tale* itself than any of the other three, from which it differs in its scope and in its purpose. In his notable book, *The Literary Relationship of Chaucer's "Clerkes Tale,"*⁴ Professor Severs set himself an ambitious task: "to determine precisely the poet's sources for his tale of Griseldis; to establish satisfactory texts of the sources; and to examine the poet's treatment of them." I shall say nothing of his careful study of the manuscripts and texts of Chaucer's immediate sources, Petrarch's Latin and an anonymous version in French prose. In fact, I am concerned only with Severs' first and fourth chapters, much less than one-half of a work whose solid merit has been generally recognized. In these chapters, perhaps because Chaucer followed his sources closely and "made no changes in the sequence of events which he found" there, Severs accepts, without structural analysis of the story, the conclusion of Griffith and Cate. "There are present," he says, "in the tale of Griselda certain vestigial relics of the pre-literary form—elements which, either illogical or impertinent in the literary versions, become fully comprehensible only when we realize that they are traces of the primitive folk tale." This conclusion he supports by a rather terrifying list of illogicalities and impertinences, in which it is taken for granted that what was originally magical in the Griselda story "has become monstrous."⁵

A difficulty arises when it turns out that Chaucer, in Severs' account, did nothing to make the story less absurd. On the other hand, his "chief contribution seems to have been a heightening and intensification of the contrasts" which the story offered, so that Walter becomes "more unfeeling" and Griselda "more submissive." "The essential qualities of character and setting" were thus "brought into more vivid contrast," and "the successive situations [were] developed into a more effective, more arresting plot." It is hard to see how an already absurd plot could be made more effective by heightening its absurdity, but the key to the argument, if I follow it at all, seems to lie partly in Severs' method and partly in the term "contrast." Since Chaucer did not change "the sequence of events," Severs compares the *Clerk's Tale* with its sources, not structurally, but passage by passage, phrase by phrase. If isolated passages in Chaucer seem somehow better than the corresponding passages in his sources, and if the diction of his English poetry seems somehow more effective than the diction of the French and Latin prose on which it was based, then one is tempted to conclude that Chaucer achieved an "almost magical transformation." The only theoretical basis which I can imagine for such reasoning would be a concept of a good narrative poem as a series of episodes strung together in defiance of probability, but full of vivid contrasts and described in "vivid, connotative terms" and I am driven to conclude, with all respect, that it is some such notion which Severs asks us to entertain.

What now emerges from this brief survey of scholarship? Chiefly the fact that the problems of morality and probability which the *Clerk's Tale* poses have been treated, in the best and most representative studies, as insoluble within the tale. Kittredge would submerge them in the problems of the Marriage Group; Griffith and Cate would display their origin in the Cupid and Psyche tales; Severs would recognize them and display their origin still more fully, but tacitly dismiss them as inessential. If the *Clerk's Tale* merits the amount of attention which has already been devoted to it, surely it deserves more direct treatment of these central issues.

The moral question is not just one question, but two at least. In one of its forms, it is the question why alleged cruelty and criminal stupidity are represented either without proper abhorrence, or even with the praise that should be reserved for virtue; we are asked, it is said, to tolerate an intolerable tyrant, and to admire a dolt. In another form, the moral question is whether the *Clerk's Tale* offers us *sentence* or *solas*, whether it is a sermon or a story or both together; our answer here will affect the standards of judgment which we apply to the tale. Its early tellers, Petrarch and Chaucer included, have of course invited a moral judgment. The adventures of Patient Grizel have been variously used to teach submission to the will of God, or female virtue as a means to get rich husbands,[6] and no one would deny the currency, in medieval and modern times, of the belief that poetry is an accessory to moral philosophy. On the other hand, there is abundant evidence, from Petrarch's first two readers onward, that the story was valued "in and for itself," and if one grants the possibility of less limited readings, one may justly maintain that a simple narrative analysis is at least an indispensable first step. I shall therefore say little, and that little in my conclusion, about the second form of the moral question, and proceed at once to the first, which Lounsbury raises somewhat crudely, but typically and with his usual vigor.

According to Lounsbury, the events of the Griselda story, "while susceptible of poetic treatment, are in no way consonant with the truth of life," and its "central idea . . . is . . . too revolting . . . for any skill in description to make it palatable. Griselda does not even exhibit the degree of sensibility which exists in the females of the brute creation. Her patience outrages every instinct of maternity, and the respect which men pay to that quality in woman," so that "the modern man, and still more the modern woman, . . . is much disposed to give it the name of weak-spirited, and even despicable."[7] She is a ninny, Walter a brute, and the conduct of both as preposterous as it is unreal.

If one makes the necessary assumptions, all this, and more, is undoubtedly true. It is not only Griselda's children, whose sex life will be ruined by their childhood experiences, that one has to worry about. There is also, to take but one example, the reputation of the Pope, whose counterfeit letters are made the excuse for the pretended divorce. Once it is assumed that the fictions of the fourteenth century may be equated with realities half a millennium later, and that every medieval story must have a "central idea" acceptable to the "modern woman," the irrelevant inferences which a tolerably

agile mind can draw are unlimited; the *Clerk's Tale* can be
made to look as silly as the assumptions on which the moralist
condemns it.

Lounsbury himself was unwilling to go so far, and his
own qualifications take much of the sting out of his charges,
which indeed are very simply answered. If a storyteller is
to get under way at all, he must take for granted some prin-
ciples of moral judgment, principles which he might be quite
unwilling to accept or advocate in real life or which he
might hope to transform and transcend in the very work in
which initially he assumed them. For the purposes of the
Clerk's Tale, wifely obedience to husband, lord, and bene-
factor is explicitly set up as a good, and in accordance
with the medieval tradition of exalting a single virtue in its
essence, other signs of Griselda's goodness are not much
needed. In fact, more highly detailed and less objective repre-
sentation, as surely as ill-judged humor, might have wrecked
this secular saint's legend, in which extreme cruelty and
extreme long-suffering had to be pictured without arousing
disgust for brutality or contempt for the absurd. Medieval
readers were less troubled by Griselda's obedience than we
are, as anyone can see who looks into their treatises on
female duty; but my argument is not that in any world of
reality, medieval or modern, Griselda would be looked upon
with favor. When one brings the world of fiction and the
world of reality too abruptly into contact, both worlds are
distorted; the Clerk's "Envoy" makes capital of the distor-
tion. Instead, my argument is that Griselda is represented as
supremely good, by signs which medieval readers of her
story could not take *except* as signs of goodness, and we
have no more right to take them as signs of badness than
we have to mistranslate Middle English. Griselda's super-
human endurance arouses wonder, her unmerited sufferings
provoke compassion; to the production of this effect, the judg-
ment that she is good is an essential preliminary; but the
presuppositions of a poem are not to be confused with the
text of a sermon. We need not write a history of medieval
taste, therefore, to discover the narrative values of the *Clerk's
Tale*, which other means make clear enough; and though

the remoteness of the tale's presuppositions may prevent us from realizing those values fully, our difficulty will be lessened if we remember that Chaucer does not invite us, but ultimately forbids us, to apply the rules of his fictional world outside his fiction.

What values *other* than narrative values we may discover is a question which can best be dealt with, as I have suggested, when the narrative has been more fully explored; the pious reflections of Petrarch and others may grow naturally out of the story, but the story cannot be evolved from the pious reflections. What I shall say of the repeated objection to its improbability is hardly more novel than the objection itself, and I shall not be foolish enough to claim that in the *Clerk's Tale* all problems are happily solved. A number of defects, as the folklorists have well shown, were inherent in the material; for to the extent that Walter and Griselda are represented as human and subject to the known limitations of fourteenth-century humanity, the original motivation of the folk tale must somehow be replaced. What the folklorists have not shown so well is the method by which and the extent to which that replacement was accomplished in the literary versions, where at least a partially successful effort was made to transform the generally improbable into the specifically probable. The difficulty of the task now seems disproportionate to the modest reward which the best solution offered. To destroy the extremes in the Griselda story would be to destroy its effect, but a wrong treatment could make those same extremes either ludicrous or sickening. The behavior of Walter and Griselda had to be prepared for by the quiet establishment of initial premises from which that behavior might follow, and their actions had then to be narrated with the kind and amount of detail which would make them moving, not revolting or grotesque. Thus the first two parts of the *Clerk's Tale* present the characters of Walter and Griselda and relate them one to the other in such a way that when later the element of the marvelous is introduced, we are receptive to it. The marvelous is then frankly depicted as marvelous, with reassuring remarks thrown in by the narrator at peculiarly difficult points, so that, having accepted the first two parts of the story, we are brought, not unwillingly, to accept what follows. Chaucer proceeds, as Severs has indicated, to make all he can of some situations; but he does not push Walter's cruelty beyond the limits of humanity, and Griselda's rather stylized grief is neither agonizing nor insipid. In this way, when the folk tale has passed under three pairs of skilful hands, it has been transformed as successfully as it could be; its monsters remain rare birds, but no longer monstrous.

Part I of the tale, to be specific, is devoted entirely to Walter; he must be the best possible man who could be capable of so cruelly testing his wife. He is represented, therefore, as young, strong, courteous, honorable, and intelligent, a capable ruler who could make himself both loved and feared by his subjects and who could be moved by considerations of the common good; but he is not without less admirable qualities, notably self-indulgence and devotion to his present pleasure. In his exchange of speeches with his subjects when they entreat him to marry and promise to provide him with a noble bride, he is the traditional skeptic, fearful that in marriage he will lose his liberty; and he grounds his insistence that he will choose his own wife on blunt distrust of heredity as well as on faith in God. His fear of marriage motivates his later demand upon Griselda for a premarital oath of complete obedience, and his distrust of heredity prepares for his choice of a peasant. In Part II it will appear that he has already decided, if ever he should marry, to marry Griselda, whose goodness he has had the sense to recognize; but with typical self-will and secretiveness, he conceals this decision until the day of the wedding. To his subjects, he says nothing of his choice; but he charges them, on their lives, that they will reverence whatever wife he takes, and he demands a vow that against his choice they will never complain. If he can demand and get such obedience from his chief subjects, it is hardly improbable that he will demand and get it from the poorest peasants; and if he marries a peasant, his attendant lords will certainly expect behavior which will try their patience.

No such complexities are needed in the characterization

of Griselda. She is poor, but beautiful and good, and she draws her strength not only from hardship and her long self-sacrifice in caring for her father. Even before her introduction into the story is signalized by the announcement of her excellent virtue, we are carefully reminded that God can send His grace into the very stalls of oxen; and since marriage has been suggested to Walter and accepted by him for the common good, we know that Griselda will be enabled, in so important a matter, to keep her oath of obedience to her benefactor, lord, and husband. By the introduction of Christian assumptions, the initial framework of largely secular values and probabilities is thus gradually extended. If the prototype of Walter had superhuman power in the folk tale, the Griselda of Chaucer's version enjoys the grace of God; and at her marriage, the power of divinely favored virtue is immediately manifested. Griselda is transformed from the good and beautiful peasant girl to the still more lovely, virtuous, and capable lady, the perfect mistress of her household, and noted for her skill in public affairs. The story may now proceed with the old marvels of the folk tale; but they have been placed on a new foundation, and they have been rendered available (it might be further argued) as the bearers of a new significance.

With Part III, the testing begins, and from this point, as I have said, the marvelous is frankly but not carelessly accepted. The narrator assumes a disarming role, with his direct condemnation of Walter's cruelty but his simple assertion that such things can be; for

> wedded men ne knowe no mesure,
> Whan that they fynde a pacient creature.

Chaucer can hardly be blamed, it might be said in passing, if his attempt to expand the limits of human nature by poetic fiat has misled some of his readers to defend him by asserting that the world of the *Clerk's Tale* is the real world and that there have, too, been men like Walter and women like Griselda. Wiser readers have noted that Griselda's strength, in the world which Chaucer and the others created for her, is made believable by repeated scriptural echoes that remind us of its source. These echoes are heard, for example, in Griselda's farewell to her daughter and in her words to Walter at their separation:

> "Naked out of my fadres hous," quod she,
> "I cam, and naked moot I turne agayn."

God's grace, our knowledge of Walter's secret pity and repentance, and the narrator's broad hints that all may yet be well, combine to take the edge off Griselda's sufferings and to assure us that Walter is not so ruthless as she might believe; and as the carefully ordered tests grow more severe, the reassurances become more obvious. Griselda is tested first by the loss of her daughter and then of her more precious man-child, only less dear to her than her tormentor: but the scene in which the boy is taken from her is deliberately left undeveloped; we are promptly told, quite bluntly, that "al fil for the beste"; and if Griselda thinks her children dead, we know that they are safely cared for. More concentrated suffering is imposed on Griselda by her dismissal, by the summons to welcome her successor, and last by the order to praise the second bride; yet we really cannot worry too much about the children, or Griselda, or the Pope himself, for even before the dismissal, the grand restoration is already being prepared. Whatever other merits the *Clerk's Tale* may have, it does not operate through variety or surprise. Chaucer takes every opportunity for pathos, but comfortable pathos; and he hurries over those parts of the story, such as the twelve long years of Griselda's separation from her children, which any but a summary and objective treatment would make too painful. Gross sentimentality would indeed be a more likely charge against the *Clerk's Tale* than that of improbability, which takes a last blow from Walter's words at the reconciliation: "'This is ynogh, Grisilde myn,' quod he," precisely as he had received her promise of obedience before the marriage; and the repetition of the line seems to suggest again that the story is all of a piece.

It is far from a perfect tale, as I would be the last to deny. If sentimentality is one likely charge against it, plain dulness is another, for interesting complications—Grisilde answerde and seyde, "Stynt thy clappe!"—interesting complications cannot be expected from a story how the marvelous patience of a pious wife converts a husband from cruel suspicion to the ultimate conviction that she is really what she seems. Through it all, Griselda must remain immutable, and Walter's activity consists solely in teasing her and wondering how she stands it. Chaucer does his best to make Griselda a convincingly human embodiment of patience and Christian humility, and he makes the most of her big situations without allowing them to become grotesquely painful, but I do not wish that the *Clerk's Tale* were longer.

I will, however, risk one word more in its defense. Dulness and sentimentality are perhaps harsh terms for a tale which rather neatly evades the blunt opposition of mere sermon to mere story, and the Clerk's is such a tale. Whatever one thinks about the categories of the didactic and the mimetic or about the idea of medieval poetry as one vast composite denunciation of cupidity, the simple narrative analysis which I have attempted must somewhere be made; yet the Clerk's *moralitee* is too obvious to be ignored, and need not be received with embarrassed silence. Briefly and tentatively, I should say that what is put into the story in one form is extracted from it in another, and that this is the answer to the second of my "moral questions." Standards of conduct are assumed in order that the story may have its proper effect of compassionate wonder; they are raised to a higher level when the story is given its moral application. Similarly, divine grace and the transcendent goodness of Griselda, which help to make her ultimate triumph probable, are made the bases of the argument for Christian submission to the will of God. In this way, the effectiveness of the story becomes the source of power in the exemplum, and the presuppositions of the poem, though distinct from the text of the sermon, are integrated with it.

The discovery, if not the invention, of a higher integration stretches the limits of moderate solemnity. It has been suggested that Chaucer himself had some reservations about his story, and one might guess that his attitude toward it was somewhat mixed. At any rate, he was willing to risk the experiment, in the "Envoy," of clashing his world of fiction against reality. The experiment worked. He still gets his laugh, and by laughing himself he managed to keep the best of both worlds. Perhaps the lesson for us, if I may be allowed a moral and an envoy of my own, is that our critical methods have sometimes been too simple even for the *Clerk's Tale*. It is a fairly straightforward, middling kind of yarn, but oversimple assumptions have led to its unjust condemnation as flatly bad; and these thoughtless assumptions, for example the confusion of fiction with reality, may cause more serious misjudgments of better pieces.

I will take a single instance. If the pilgrimage is dated April, 1387, then the Squire, who was twenty years old, was conceived in July, 1366. At that time the Knight was in the Middle East. I once drew the consequences of these facts and submitted my parody to a learned journal. The editors returned it, not because it wasn't funny, as perhaps it wasn't, but because it was, they said, too "speculative."

I would have called it an illegitimate inference.

Notes

[1] *Chaucer and His Poetry* (Cambridge, Mass., 1915), pp. 185, 209 f. [See pp. 157–8 above.]

[2] Kemp Malone, *Chapters on Chaucer* (Baltimore, 1951), pp. 210 ff., 222 ff.

[3] D. D. Griffith, *The Origin of the Griselda Story* (Seattle, 1931); W. A. Cate, "The Problem of the Origin of the Griselda Story," *SP*, XXIX (1932), 389–405.

[4] J. Burke Severs, *The Literary Relationships of Chaucer's* "*Clerkes Tale*" (New Haven, 1942).

[5] Since this assumption is almost universally made, I take a convenient phrasing of it from Nevill Coghill, *The Poet Chaucer* (London, 1949), p. 140.

[6] Cf. the *Clerk's Tale*, ll. 1142–62, and the titlepage of the 1619 quarto, "The ancient, true and admirable History of Patient Grisel." It is there proclaimed that "maidens, by her example, in their good behaviour may marrie rich husbands." A lesson much like that of Kittredge's Marriage Group is taught by Maria Edgeworth's excruciating *Modern Griselda*, from which we learn that a husband and his wife will be happiest if neither seeks power over the other; but most readers will prefer the eighteenth-century moral, "how more than ordinary obedient, Wives ought to be that bring no Portions."

[7] Thomas R. Lounsbury, *Studies in Chaucer* (New York, 1892), III, 340 ff.

10

Chaucer's *Merchant's Tale*

J. S. P. TATLOCK

For unrelieved acidity the *Merchant's tale* is approached nowhere in Chaucer's works, and rarely anywhere else; it is one of the most surprising pieces of unlovely virtuosity in all literature. Without a trace of warm-hearted tolerance or genial humor, expansive realism or even broadly smiling animalism, it is ruled by concentrated intelligence and unpitying analysis. Its dexterity may be diverting to the reader, but that is not the teller's mood. His utmost is to cast a lowering smile. There is little of the external; none of that description of people's looks or dress which is so brilliant in others of the bawdy tales, little of interior or outdoor scenes; even January's garden is vaguely dismissed—the author of the *Romance of the rose* could not do it justice, nor Priapus himself (suggestive deity). Though the tale contains greater obscenity than any other of the *Canterbury tales*, . . . all this sounds as if due to the kind of savagery which makes one bite on a sore tooth; it serves as an insolently deliberate counterirritant to the cruel feeling, and is neither easily humorous nor rawly animal. The

Reprinted, by permission of Doctor Hugh Tatlock and of the University of Chicago Press, from *Modern Philology*, XXXIII (1935–6), 367–81. Cf. G. G. Sedgewick, "The Structure of the *Merchant's Tale*," *UTQ*, XVII (1948), 337–45.

basal refinement of the speaker is shown by disclaimers and apologies at the coarsest points.[1] One might feel half-ashamed of so greatly enjoying so merciless a tale, and might balk at prolonged analysis, if this did not end, as we shall see, in cheerfully detaching us from the prevailing mood.

Though no direct source is known, the essentials of the same fantastic plot are in more than a half-dozen tales from the fourteenth and fifteenth centuries, in Italian, High and Low German, Latin, French, English; no one of them enough nearer to Chaucer than the others to pass as the sole origin, unless (as noted by Varnhagen and Koch) that in the Italian *Novellino,* of the fourteenth century or earlier. The plot may well have been learned by word of mouth, even in more versions than one. But should anyone ask who taught the poet how to invest it with form and words, there is no answer.

Chaucer's attentive skill appears most of all in the characterization. This is less subtle than in some of the tales, and is outlined in bold, black strokes. While such little as exists in other versions of this story is chiefly of the woman, it is on the husband (much as Kittredge and Root intimate) that the teller expends most of his unloving care. January's advanced age, so far as we can see, is among the fresh additions to the story. While persons of far more than his sixty years were not at all uncommon in the Middle Ages, and while the mortality in excess of that of today was doubtless mostly in the early years of life, it is probable, since the strifes and strains of adult life began then from five to ten years earlier than now, that January was meant to seem a really old man. But here, considering the mood of the poem, was a difficulty. An old man whose young wife plays him false has always, it is true, been regarded as fair game for ridicule, and is so treated in the *Miller's tale;* but not a loving old man who has become blind, unless by the very hard-hearted. Therefore the sour narrator heads off any possible sympathy for January by a full-length portrait beginning in the fourth line of the poem. That we must needs despise what should be pitiful fixes the mood. All his life he has been a lecher, described in rather gross terms, and the narrator professes uncertainty whether his belated desire for matrimony is due to religious motives or to dotage

(1253). Indeed, were this a historical and not an imaginary narrative, one might well suspect that his success with his light-o'-loves had departed, and that his exhibit of repentance and his sudden enthusiasm about marriage were a briefly buoyant escape from humiliation and despair. Senile lechery seems to anybody repulsive, ridiculous at best. It is characteristic of him that his description of various kinds of women is in terms of things to eat, that it is when he is in bed that he thinks over his candidates for bride, and that he weds a woman of no rank whose chief points are her youth and alluring figure; although interest in receiving a dowry was quite frank in the Middle Ages, he submits instead to giving a strict marriage settlement, and this in spite of the skilful negotiations of his marriage brokers. He cannot get over the idea that sex is always humorous; he practices the sensual stare, identifies virtue and innocence with ignorance, evidently aspires to the thrill of training his bride to be knowing in Venus' school, can hardly repress his impatience, and finds intense pleasure in insincere sentimental compassion over what is in store for her. His folly is even less spared than his self-indulgence. He is so determined that the facts about women, men, and life shall be as he wishes them to be that his toadies find it safe to lay it on with a trowel.[2] He seems to be one of the unfortunate inheritors of prosperity and adulation who believe that after a lifetime on the wrong path they can easily find and enjoy the right one. The point of momentary pathos where he would obtain the pears for May and cannot—"Allas, allas, that I am blynd!"—is instantly spoiled by his ridiculous posture, crouching with the tree in his arms, that he may prevent any lover from following, and that from his back she may climb up to her lover who is already there above (2339–49). His folly is due to his egotism, and it is on this that the most unerring delicate strokes are spent. Though he is superficially well bred, in the two scenes where he consults his friends as to his marriage the asking of advice is shown, perhaps for the first time in literature, as motived unconsciously but entirely by the itch to talk about one's own affairs. With portentous solemnity he announces his intentions, laps up Placebo's fulsome speech, can hardly sit through Justinus' counsel of caution and moder-

ation, but at once turns again to Placebo. When he has settled
on May, he thinks every other man's wit so bad that there can
be no more to say, and when he next meets them he drops
the veil and requests that none shall oppose him. The decision
of the conferences naturally is that he shall marry whom and
when he pleases. His egotism will not even die with him, for
he is one of those spouses who desire for a young mate a life-
long widowhood. At the end he is deluded no more by May's
presence of mind than by his own vanity which recoils from
an unwelcome truth.

With so repulsive and fatuous a husband there was danger
that a certain amount of sympathy would be turned to the
faithless wife, the sort of danger Chaucer also anticipated in
other poems. This was averted by making May not worse than
January but hardly a person at all. No one can pity a lay-
figure. She is scarcely described, rarely speaks, and before the
end has not a thought or a feeling except the most obvious.
Whatever traits she has are learned of only by inference, and
neither deserve nor invite sympathy. We infer inevitably
that she is mercenary, and are so informed by hints; she is
hypocritical enough to be a reasonably good actress in playing
the game with simpering blandness, as she sits "with so
benyngne a chiere," meeker than Queen Esther; that she ac-
cepts her lot with cold scorn is implied in other hints—God
knew what she thought when she saw her most filthy bargain
caroling in his shirt, and whether she thought his lovemaking
paradise or hell, and later in one breath she tearfully protests
her fidelity and signs to Damian; that she is sensual with
normal stimulus is shown by her instant response to Damian
after only four days of marriage. All possibility of glamor in
the *amour* is destroyed by the fact that the place she needless-
ly selects for reading their first love letter is a privy, and that
she tears it up and throws it therein—another infallible indica-
tion of the mood intended by the poet. Whatever this tale is,
it is not a love story. "Fresh" and "benign" are the two words
constantly used of her; that so blooming a girl can be so un-
scrupulous is the bitterest stroke of all. She plays on the not
wholly infirm January's belated but sincere desire for an heir
by the silly pretense that her longing for the little green pears

in early June is the longing of pregnancy. Her tears, like her excuses, are ready on tap. She recalls such a portrayal of soulless sensuality as the figure of Astarte in John Sargent's mural in the Boston Public Library.

Damian is even more of a paper doll. Possibly Chaucer disliked to consort intimately even in imagination with sneaking people; he had much to learn from some writers of today. Further, the personality of January, which, together with the situation, is Chaucer's main interest, stands out the better against an unfigured background; the technique here is not expansion but concentration. However little guilt attached, in the view of fashionable readers and writers in the later Middle Ages, to the young woman who entered on a *mariage de convenance* and took a lover, still less attached to him. But for Damian any interest or sympathy is impossible. He goes through the motions expected in fashionable literature from a youth newly in love; he covets May at once, takes to his bed, writes verses, as to the consummation of his desires merely does as he is bid, and after the exposure leaves the exculpation to May. The timidity and lack of enterprise are here in plenty which seem to have been so attractive to the masterful dame of the later Middle Ages, at least to read about. We infer that he is good-looking and well bred, but that is all. The male type which Chaucer elaborated with so much sympathy in Troilus, and with tolerant amusement in Aurelius, could not be treated with more negligent indifference than here. His tricks of a dandy and his pleasantness to everyone read like a parody on Chaucer's earlier account of the ennobling effect on Troilus of his happy love. In the garden he is in the ludicrous posture of squatting under a bush to wait in safety from January's jealous hands and ears; as with January and persons in other tales, so here, Chaucer heightens moral degradation by degrading physically. If in the *Franklin's tale* Chaucer had outgrown what is sometimes called the "conventions of courtly love," in the *Merchant's* he arrantly turned against them. Much water had flowed under the bridge since he wrote the *Troilus;* compared with these two tales, it reads like the work of a much younger and more inexperienced though comprehensive and potent spirit.

The only other human personalities in the tale are January's two friends, Placebo and Justinus. The former is merely the "yes-man," who flatters in order to serve his own ends, who perceives his patron's desires and gives corresponding advice, and affects indignation at the honest man who tells the truth. His name, of course, was then a familiar and clever joke; the first word of an antiphon in the vespers of the dead, "*Placebo Domino in regione viventium*," it lent itself to a sour pleasantry, repeated by Chaucer's Parson and by the friar in the *Sumner's tale*. The extraordinary speech in which, before his patron and all, he glories in his methods and motives in flattering (1491–1505) must be taken merely as an example of a not rare medieval literary usage—the confession. Just as the soliloquy, hardly practiced in real life by sane people, was used by the Elizabethan playwright as a dramatic means of conveying essential and completely trustworthy information to the audience, so was the public confession used by medieval dramatic narrators. To say nothing of Jean de Meun and William Dunbar, Chaucer himself uses it with the Wife of Bath and the Canon's Yeoman, with the Pardoner and the Sumner's friar. We are by no means called upon to believe that all of these would in actual life have said all which they say. This self-exhibition of a flatterer is merely another specimen of the teller's slashing bitterness which sweeps far beyond the protagonists. Nothing defines the teller's feeling better than the fact that the sole human being in the poem to whom he gives his own power of attorney is the other friend, Justinus, the world-worn disillusioned who has not lost his internal peace, who has learned resignation by expecting little, and gives the wisest advice he thinks has any chance of being accepted. The best of his gibes from his own experience is that among the privileges of matrimony are its abundant opportunities for the virtue of penitence (1665–67). The most sympathetic line in the whole poem introduces his final reply to January:

> Justinus, which that hated his folye.

The only other composed and placid note in the poem is not among men at all. January and May have their divine counterparts in Pluto and Proserpina. It was doubtless Chaucer's unerring tact and taste which led him to substitute this pair for the Lord God and St. Peter (as in the *Novellino*), or Jove and Mercury or Venus (who figure elsewhere). It was fitting in so gray a tale to choose not the bright Olympians but the dusky gods of Hades. It is true that, to preserve a modern tone, he calls them king and queen of *fairye*, following the practice of such popularizers of the classic as the early English lay and ballad of Orfeo, but Chaucer knew better. Proserpina is the tart feminist who to win equality with man will use the most feminine of methods, and by all means has the last word. The deceitful and the unfair in the feminine is indeed eternal; heaven does not redress the balance of earth. This same solidarity of women in unfairness to men had been hit off by Justinus in his account of her women friends' championship of his own wife, whom he himself can merely patiently endure (1550). Pluto, though he knows it hopeless, gives January his chance, but to restore bodily sight is bootless when the eyes of the mind are darkened. He is the man of power who tolerates with amusement and possibly a dash of admiration his wife's irrational and immoral tactics, because he values peace more than trivial victory. This is the only part of the poem where the sarcasms approach good nature.

The alterations made by Chaucer in the plot, chiefly the addition of all that precedes the blindness, mostly promote the characterization. January's folly and egotism are exhibited by the conferences with Placebo and Justinus, the details of the legal preliminaries to the marriage emphasize the bride's mercenary motive; those of the marriage itself give opportunity for irony. Sara and Rebecca, held up in good faith as models in the prayer *Deus qui potestate virtutis* in the nuptial mass, one need not forget show their "wysdom and trouthe" in the book of *Genesis*, the one in meanly driving away a husband's respectable concubine and firstborn son, the other in deceiving a blind husband in behalf of an equally deceitful child. Many additions to incident and speech contribute to dramatic irony (of which Chaucer is one of the masters in English), to the harsh contrast between the realities and January's conscious expectations. Of the dramatic irony he is the

sole victim. The most brilliant case has been recorded before
—a "yong thynge" can be molded like warm wax in the
hands, thinks January; he does not know the next appearance
of warm wax will be in the hands of his own young thing, nor
for what purpose—counterfeiting the garden key. His shaky
confidence in his own masculinity and his compassion for May
prove misplaced; her actual sentiments are in keen contrast
with what he expects in her. As if to enforce further a differ-
ent view of love from that which is so heartfelt in the *Troilus,*
January himself unconsciously plays the part of Pandar to his
own undoing in bringing the lovers together; though like a
tyrant irritated for a moment by Damian's fancied neglect of
him, his temporary elation, the cheap expansive kindliness of
the gratified sensualist praised by his toadies, plays into the
lover's hand. Damian need not fear that May will betray him.
The bodily blindness which smites January, and even the cure
of it, are a mere nothing to his permanent mental blindness.
Until near the end there is no touch of humor without more
than a touch of mordancy; no one who grasps the whole, no
reader except an exceedingly casual one, can think it a piece
of irresponsible amusement. But of the end one might so
think. Here the full intensity of the bitterness seems to have
evaporated, the strain needed to relax, as if one might as well
make the best of things and helplessly laugh; and thus the
complete triumph of May. But there is another justification
for her triumph. The deep-down more than merely worldly
meaning of the whole poem is the inexorable chastisement
for stubborn shutting the eyes to facts, and with this sound if
one-sided philosophy May is the true heroine, well adjusted
to her particular world, which allows the male nothing better
than the gray peace of Justinus and Pluto. Yet the harshness
has hardly abated, and in a half-dozen spots toward the end
is even heightened by a new clashing of emotions, the creep-
ing in of a little truly Chaucerian compassion for January.

Not the least of his satisfactions no doubt the writer found
in the style, which completely fits the cold intelligence of the
whole. Chaucer never wrote more brilliantly. Scarcely any-
where do we find so many of those unified couplets, balanced
and antithetical,[3] the force of which he had learned from the

Latin elegiac distich, the closed couplet of Ovid; which the sixteenth century was to learn again from the same master, and hand on to the seventeenth for developing—overdeveloping. The style, and these couplets, were probably what most attracted the youthful Pope to paraphrase this congenial poem. In Chaucer they are an occasional embellishment, the more forceful not only because used merely when most fitting, but also because with him first appearing in English. In the irony there is one peculiar practice, especially in the grave exordium of the narrator, in which he affects as his own the pious hopes and ridiculous optimisms which swarm in January's mind. Repeatedly the glaze of unreality seems too weak to hold in the powerful feeling beneath. Ironic control is shattered by the direct blow or brazen sneer.' *In meditatione sua exarsit ignis, et locutus est in lingua sua.* One cannot but picture a volcanic crater, the black rough floor burst now and again by a spurt of white-hot lava. Further, the teller's bitterness is so intense that it runs amuck at everything. The clergy, he implies, are no chaster than the laity. With such a married life to follow, religion itself is bemocked in the marriage rite (said to have made all secure enough—with ceremonial), and the benediction of the nuptial bed, and high mass just before Damian's successful wooing, and January expressing his lust in the words of Solomon's Song, then commonly interpreted by the love of Christ for his church—"olde lewed wordes," the narrator calls these words of the Holy Ghost. He even—and this is hard to forgive him—compares January's roar (ridiculous word) on seeing the lovers in the tree to a mother's cry over her dying child. Nothing is sacred. The early part is full of double meanings, and forward allusions which differ from the dramatic irony only in not being directly attributed to the characters.

> And namely whan a man is oold and hoor,
> Thanne is a wyf the fruyt of his tresor;

the best of his treasures, yes, but the mercenary wife was the product of his treasure. A wife's submissiveness and attentions to her infirm husband prove here to be only in appearance. The warnings of Theophrastus, rejected with affected indigna-

tion by the narrator, are fulfilled. A husband cannot be de-
ceived who takes his wife's advice, but can always boldly keep
his head up; it is at the urging of May that they follow
Damian into the garden, and are there disgraced. The scrip-
tural heroines adduced as models were all deceivers of their
men.⁵ Throughout there is no end to this sort of thing. It
seemed like *fayerye* to look at May; at once her later fairy
ally Proserpina comes to mind. The narrator affects apprehen-
siveness lest she may reject and denounce Damian. Chaucer's
"favorite line," the softly Italianate

Pitee renneth soone in gentil herte,

appears in a connection, as has been said, which turns its milk
of human kindness sour; no one can suppose that Chaucer
means sincerely to attribute to May any womanly tender-
heartedness. Most of these further meanings come naturally
to the reader, and, there is no reason to doubt, were intended.
There are no cheap surprises; all is close knit and prepared.
In spite of all this, the narrator is by no means wholly in the
grip of an emotion, but is its master. With all his concentration
he admits slight impersonal touches of imposing decoration,
even gusts of fresh air from the open heavens, especially in
the defining of times and influences by the movements of the
planets;⁶ also in mere glimpses of ritual and stately festivity.
In the combination of Christian language and ceremonial with
pagan mythology—Bacchus as January's butler, Venus with her
nuptial firebrand dancing, Pluto and Proserpina at large in
the garden—there is also something both Italian and delicately
fantastic, as there is (though not so delicately) in the plot.
All this just saves the poet from any accusation of taking his
story too seriously.

He chose an Italian setting. January was born and presum-
ably lives in Pavia, a little south of Milan, the old Lombard
capital which Chaucer is likely enough to have visited in
1378. We find the Italian custom of siesta. Damian has a
characteristic Italian name, most familiar as that of one of two
early martyrs (Cosmos and Damian), Romans in one tradi-
tion, commemorated in the canon of the Roman mass and

even the medieval English; also as that of St. Peter Damian, Italian reformer of the eleventh century. There were sex and even priapean elements in the popular cult of San Damiano in Italy,[1] but it is impossible to say whether Chaucer was aware of them, though we have noticed his mention of Priapus. Justinus, Justyn, obviously is so named because, with him and Placebo, *videbitis quid sit inter justum et impium,— videntur mihi sermones tui boni et justi; justus* corresponding to the "righteous" of the English Bible. Found elsewhere in the later empire, Justinus is the name of various saints, but chiefly in Italy, and Giustino has long been a characteristic and not rare Italian name. There is no reason to believe that Chaucer learned the tale with an Italian locale; nor in his less dignified tales does he habitually consider the original setting in choosing his own. He is prone to place the more homely near home, the most romantic in remote climes, the sophisticated or fantastic sometimes in the more familiar parts of Western Europe; for the *Merchant's,* Lombardy is not inevitable, but is fitting enough. Several matters may have made him think of Italy. The likeliest known source is in the Italian *Novellino* (though localized nowhere). He may have had Boccaccio and one of his peculiar veins in mind. Why did he name the young wife May and the old husband January? May and December have been familiar in modern times as nicknames for such a pair, but I find no sign of them earlier than the sixteenth and seventeenth centuries, nor outside England, and they may well be an altered derivative from the *Merchant's tale* itself. Boccaccio's *Filocolo* is believed to have been familiar to him, and contains the close analogue to the *Franklin's tale* which many believe its source; here, it will be remembered, the task required of the lover is a garden in January blooming as in May. The garden which figures so largely in most versions of the fruit-tree story might well have caused Chaucer's mind to dart back to this May garden in January, and in Italy. Indeed, what frosty old January hopes for is a May garden blooming in himself. Finally, I would recall what I said long ago as to possible reminiscence from Boccaccio's juvenile *Ameto.* This has not been proved, let us say emphatically, but is in no way improbable, and should not be denied. One sometimes reminds himself that when a possible relation cannot be rigidly proved it may be wiser to suspend judgment than to deny it. There seems great likelihood that during Chaucer's visits of probably three or four months in Italy he would read many books which would be too costly to buy and carry back with him to England; this fact, and his remarkably retentive memory for what struck him, may explain certain of the resemblances in his works to Boccaccio's, including the *Decameron*, even after the lapse of years. The husband's old age is in no other version of the story and in no subsidiary source, and, unlike his blindness, is needless in this plot. Nor are the loves of an aged man and a young woman at all common in the vast field of pre-Chaucerian narrative, and so far as I see, if found at all, are mostly barely mentioned. But by no means so in *Ameto*. The most marked resemblance here is in the bedroom scenes and the nymph Agapes' account of her life (not the fruit-tree story, though not dissimilar) and in her rich old bridegroom's physical senility. His early lascivious life, his flatteries to his bride, his bent figure, prickly beard, lean and flabby neck, his endearments, his feebleness, and use of external means to rouse his ardor, and the extremely opposite emotions of groom and bride are alike in the two, though more memorable and repulsive in Boccaccio. A man of observation and imagination might have invented all this, as Boccaccio did—I am far from belittling this fact; yet so many of such recurrences are surprising if mere coincidence. It would not be hard to believe that the savagery of the *Merchant's tale* was a masculine Englishman's retort to the young Italian author's effeminate insincerity and sentimental voluptuousness. Boccaccio was not yet the manful original genius he turned out later. In several ways we may be reminded of William Wycherley three centuries after Chaucer, especially in *The plain dealer*, and his attitude toward his contemporaries.

By this time, if not before, it will be granted that the *Merchant's tale* among Chaucer's works is anything but typical or characteristic. It would be confusing to compare it with works by Juvenal or Swift or Byron or Samuel Butler, or with De Maupassant's *Boule de suif;* but it has more of their spirit than of that of him for whom the epithets so usual as to be almost shopworn are tolerant, charitable, genial. Any pontifical explanation would be far too bold. To attribute the tale to some time of bitterness and disillusion in the poet's own life would be no wiser than Dowden's oversimple explanations of certain of Shakespere's plays. Doubtless Chaucer at times had had in his proper person something of the feeling so vivid in the poem, but there is no reason to ascribe this here to anything but his active imagination. He may have been deceived as Argus was, but, as he says himself of this,

Passe over is an ese, I sey namoore.

Nor is the writing of such a tale for the Merchant called for by anything in the account of him in the general *Prologue*, nor sufficiently by his own prologue. An adequate dramatic introduction is afforded by the account there of his disappointing first two months of marriage, and by hostility to lustful clerics, aged lechers, and women who betray merchant-husbands, excited by the *Wife of Bath's Prologue* and her intended telling of the present *Shipman's tale*. But there is nothing in sight to make inevitable the telling by so composed a personage of so ruthless a story, still less to explain Chaucer's writing it.

The best motive to think of is a purely literary one. Chaucer has no more marked trait of manner than his varieties of tone, pitch, key, mode—each fulfilled with equal ease and adequacy. No one word fits perfectly; what is meant is his own attitude to a poem, his own emotional reaction to its matter, degree of identification of himself with it, and the kind of response which he desired from his readers. It is hard to think of any narrative poet who approaches him in this sign of virtuosity. To confine ourselves to the *Canterbury tales*, the *Knight's tale* is gallant and poetically decorative, but detached; the *Miller's, Reeve's,* and *Sumner's* keen on the surface and light-heartedly animal; the *Shipman's* more refined and worldly, more disillusioned; the *Man of Law's* leisurely, imposing, and aloof, rhetorically rather than poetically decorative; the *Prioress'* heartfelt and maternal; the *Nun's Priest's* full of variety of tempo, and humorous enjoyment; the *Pardoner's* simple yet full of deep insight, and matchless for uncanny mystery; the *Wife of Bath's* subordinating romance to ethical clarity and grasp of personalities; the *Friar's* surface-satire but with darts of discernment; the *Clerk's* slow and sympathetic, subordinating human reality to ideal beauty; the *Squire's* romantic yet lifelike wall-painting; the *Franklin's* an exquisite blend of reality and the ideal, of the marvelous and the homely; the *Second Nun's* entering with imaginative sympathy into an ideal largely bygone even to Chaucer. We need not suppose that he was often consciously on the hunt for an unpracticed mode; rather that his informing instinct ever pushing on—

My besy gost, that thursteth alwey newe—

divined possibilities of fresh expression in each fresh matter. Thus the *Merchant's tale,* like the *Shipman's* in refinement ending in grossness, goes far beyond it in seriousness, disillusionment, imagination, hardly restrained emotion. It expresses not at all Chaucer's everyday personality, and perhaps but little of his experience of life; it is a firm embodiment of a mood in the imagination. No doubt he thoroughly enjoyed his savagery, for the unwontedness and the chance for irony and brilliance; and its level of fantasy keeps the tale from being too far out of character. The more its people alienate us from humanity, the nearer it draws us to their versatile and kindly creator in admiration and fellow-feeling. Therefore the last impression of the *Merchant's tale* is repugnant. Cold makes us aware of warmth, and something purely acrid heightens the worth of his prevailing clemency. Chaucer did not unreflectingly follow a compelling temperament, but was aware of his course.

Notes

[1] Ll. 1810–11, 2350–51, 2362–63.
[2] Ll. 1478–1518, 1916–19, 2066.
[3] This statement is based on an unpublished dissertation by Mrs. M. A. Hill, at Stanford University, 1924, "A study of rhetorical

balance in Chaucer," partly printed in *PMLA*, XLII, 845–61; see also G. P. Shannon, "Grimald's heroic couplet," *ibid.*, XLV, 532–42 (part of another Stanford University dissertation).

[4] Ll. 1265–66, 1268–69, 1317–18, 1655, 1738–39.

[5] Ll. 1269–70, 1288–92 and 1381–82, 1294–1310 and 2172–74, 1356–58 and 2135, 1362–74.

[6] Ll. 1795–99, 1885–87, 1969–70, 2220–24.

[7] G. J. Laing, *Survivals of Roman religion* (New York, 1931), p. 76.

[31] Magheri-Moutier (ed.) XV, 123–25; and see *Anglia*, XXXVII, 100–106. H. M. Cummings (*Indebtedness of Chaucer's works to . . . . Boccaccio* [Cincinnati, 1916] p. 36), in spite of his desire to be judicial and just, does not come to grips with the real point here.

11

The Progress of Chaucer's Pardoner, 1880-1940

G. G. SEDGEWICK

RESEARCH and criticism are pretty generally agreed about
the Short Story to which the Pardoner gave classic shape. Its
'analogues' are now counted in legions, as perhaps they were
in Chaucer's own day. Tyrwhitt spotted an Italian specimen
a hundred and sixty years ago, in 1881 Richard Morris noted
the earliest known form of the tale, parallels have been crop-
ping up everywhere ever since, and no doubt they will con-
tinue to appear as long as there are new stocks of folk-lore
to examine. No one any longer expects to find Chaucer's
precise original. As far back as the 13th century, the story had
filtered from the Orient into the deep well of European
exempla from which all ecclesiasts could draw. We may
choose to fancy that Chaucer himself first heard it from the
mouth of a preacher. At some time, as we now see, some-
body—whether Chaucer or another—enriched the tale by fusing
into it a mysterious personage engaged in the Quest for Death.
Ten Brink long ago believed, and Professor Carleton Brown
now believes, that this figure is the Wandering Jew casting his
shadow over the Three Robbers; but the strange shape of the
Old Churl as evoked by the Pardoner—if shape he might be

Reprinted, by permission, from Modern Language Quarterly, I
(1940), 431–58. Two paragraphs at the beginning of the article
have been omitted.

call'd—has seemed to others even more portentous. Whatever meaning you put upon him, surely in this particular tale he is an emanation of Chaucer's art alone. . . . But praise of the Pardoner's narrative art is not relevant to this study, and indeed it has now become superfluous. In 1886, W. A. Clouston remarked that Chaucer tells the tale 'in a manner that is superior to any other version in prose and verse'—a moderate judgment that no one will question, even after enjoying the glitter of 'The King's Ankus.'

Unhappily, a sense of proportion has too often been lacking in admirers of the prize exemplum—for it was an exemplum, and nothing more, to Chaucer's Pardoner. Sometimes you wish his narrative art had not been so impressive, since then no one could have lifted a 'perfect short story' out of its context or thought of it as an end in itself. Chaucer never meant it to be so taken. Reading it in and out of context are two quite different things. But the 'riotoures thre' seem to hypnotize many readers into overlooking or resenting the fact that Chaucer had other things to do than merely tell a fine story. To Lounsbury, the 'long disquisition in which the Pardoner indulges on the evil effects of drunkenness and gaming' was an 'intrusion of irrelevant learning' which 'breaks the thread of the tale . . . and adds nothing to its effect.' The heresy is still extant. As late as 1935, Mr. Carleton Brown (following the lead of Dr. H. B. Hinckley) felt he had to 'account for' the irrelevant intrusions that Lounsbury reprobated. These troubles will be discussed later. At the moment it is enough to say that they result from misunderstanding of Chaucer's design and may be attributed to the spell cast by the great tale.

Of the 'credibility' of the Pardoner and his revelations, it is safe to say that no responsible critic has really doubted it during the last sixty years. Editors are still bound to warn beginners against the myth of monstrous unlikelihood which Jusserand undertook to dispel in 1880. They must still point out that the Pardoner of Chaucer's fiction is no more strange than the pardoner of historic fact. They must still refer to the convention of the self-confessor in medieval satire which links the Wife of Bath to the Old Woman in the Romaunt of the

Rose and the Pardoner to False Seeming. It is also well to be reminded of the immediate inspiration which the ecclesiast may have got from his moist and corny ale—though I have heard Professor Kittredge say that one drink would hardly account for the result, especially when the Pardoner had a cake for shoeing horn. And, lastly, no one who has listened to intimate autobiography in the smoking-room of a transcontinental train need feel troubled by the Pardoner's abandon. As Ten Brink remarked long ago, the rogue 'unmasks his trade and practices with that shamelessness and bare-faced frankness which the atmosphere of the Canterbury Tales requires.' Jusserand's classic fantasy (which, by the way, must not be taken as literal comment) expands this statement with persuasive eloquence:

On the further bench of the tavern the pardoner remains still seated. There enter Chaucer, the knight, the squire, the friar, the host—old acquaintances. We are by ourselves, no one need be afraid of speaking, the foaming ale renders hearts expansive; here the secret coils of that tortuous soul unfold to view; he gives us the summary of a whole life, the theory of his existence, the key to all his secrets. What matters his frankness?—he knows that it cannot hurt him; the bishop has twenty times brought his practices to light, but the crowd always troops round him. And who knows if his companions—who know if his more enlightened companions, to whom he shows the concealed springs of the automation—will, tomorrow, believe it lifeless.

Later on in this essay, I shall point out how, by skilful manipulation, Chaucer practically leaves his Pardoner with no other choice than to speak exactly as he did.

Various other critical agreements can be reviewed as quickly. The most important of these admits the debt which the whole scheme owes to the medieval sermon. For while Chaucer sees the Pardoner as anything but a parson, he does make him preach a queer sort of exhibition sermon which is undoubtedly a masterpiece in its given setting. It has been, and still is, misunderstood even by some who have a deep and lively interest in the 'medieval mind.' But everybody now understands that somehow or other Chaucer got himself steeped in all the dyes of traditional preaching before he set about creating the Canterbury Tales and several of the pilgrims in it. We have long known his familiarity with the stores of exempla from which he furnished the Pardoner with other material besides the Three Robbers' tale. Brave attempts, not altogether successful, have been made to exhibit several of the Tales, the Pardoner's among them, as more or less 'typical' medieval sermons. And though this 'sermon' is certainly not 'typical,' Chaucer's very departures from the type imply thorough acquaintance with it. A study of the Parson's tale and the Pardoner's use of it will probably satisfy most readers as to Chaucer's knowledge of the sermon stuff. If it does not, they may fall back on Dr. G. R. Owst's impressive studies of medieval preaching' which, extravagant as they are in their general claims of value, do succeed in showing that practically every detail of the Pardoner's practice and utterance can be paralleled in the homilies, the tractates, the sermon manuals, or other records relative to preaching. The 'lost soul' whom Chaucer inflicts on the Pilgrimage fairly reeks of the medieval pulpit: he is a supreme example of the Preaching Fox.

Some of Chaucer's reading was much more secular than sermons, as Professor W. C. Curry has proved to the shocked admiration of scholarship in his essay 'The Secret of Chaucer's Pardoner.'⁷ From a study of the physiognomy literature, Mr. Curry shows that the ecclesiast had the physical characteristics of a type of unfortunate known in those writings as *eunuchus ex nativitate*. But no gentle reader need consult the originals in so far as they concern the Pardoner; for there is no 'secret' of this sort about him. Chaucer himself revealed the 'secret' with sufficient clarity, as Mr. Curry points out, in one bleak line:

I trowe he were a geldyng or a mare

—it does not matter which. And this is what everybody, medieval or modern, would 'trowe' him to be from his appearance and voice alone. The fact remains, however, that Chaucer did draw on the Physiognomies, if for no other purpose than to make his figure 'scientific' or to amuse himself otherwise: he was concerned with 'minute accuracy' in respects of which Jusserand was probably unaware. Certainly, he knew those writings, for he mentions one of them; and the 'typical' traits, there set forth, of the *eunuchus ex nativitate* went, beyond dispute, into the Pardoner's portrait. Contrary to Mr. Curry's assumption, I very much doubt that any of the pilgrims (except Chaucer and the Physician) were familiar, or needed to be, with the Physiognomies; and if I agreed with Mr. Curry, I should regret that he came too late to supervise the reading of the Lady Prioress. But there is no need to minimize what he has added to our knowledge of Chaucer's methods if not to our understanding of the Pardoner.

This is perhaps the point at which to speak of Professor J. M. Manly's suggestion that the Pardoner and other pilgrims were drawn from life models. His 'new light on Chaucer'[8] illumines a good many dark corners and re-illumines many familiar ones; it blends with any clear doctrine about Chaucer ever presented. As for the Pardoner, it has localized him more precisely than ever he was before. During the 1380's and 1390's, his House of Rouncivale, an interest of Chaucer's patron, John of Gaunt, was much in the public eye, and not always favourably. We learn, for example, that real pardoners of that house had been notoriously converting collections to their own use, just as their fellow in fiction boasted of doing. Records of this fact, published by the late Professor Samuel Moore[9] before *New Light* appeared, make it 'difficult to believe' that a contemporary audience would not link the person and goings-on of the Pardoner with some actual rogue. Further, 'his new Italian fashions,' as Mr. Manly calls them, are distinctive features that Mr. Curry's physiognomy books obviously cannot account for. If you pause to think of it, a most striking peculiarity of the portrait, not mentioned in *New Light,* is its combination of pardoner and *eunuchus* in one person. This is certainly not 'typical,' as all records and traditions testify decisively. There are good reasons for thinking that, along with many other elements, Chaucer put traits of some well-known individual or individuals into the Pardoner's complex.

II

Chaucerian research, like admiration of the Pardoner's tale, is sometimes afflicted with a faulty sense of proportion. Eaten up with the zeal of discovery, scholars are tempted to see the philosopher's stone in some very ordinary run of the mine. With every deference to Mr. Curry, for instance, one may again point out that his researches do not reveal the 'secret' of Chaucer's Pardoner, as he seemed to think; further, that an oddly naïve view of the Pardoner's last actions is the reward of his mistake. And with every gratitude to Dr. Owst, one cannot agree with him in regarding the study of medieval sermons as the whole duty of man.

Three examples of the scholar's error should be dealt with faithfully. One is perhaps unimportant and innocent enough; but each of the others has proved to be a considerable nuisance; and all three set their ferment working in a mass of valuable information.

The first, which may be called the Flanders Heresy, is based on a single phrase:

In Flaundres whilom was a compaignye.

Why did Chaucer say 'Flanders'? One attempt to answer this question has taught us much about the troubled relations of England with the Low Countries and, particularly, about the Flemish reputation for avarice and hard drinking. If the matter had been left so, there would be no heresy. Flanders, even if mentioned only once, would do as a perfectly good local habitation for three rioters. But is it not too much to 'wonder . . . if in this tale Chaucer is merely telling an idle story [!] to amuse his distinguished audience or if he through the Pardoner, a professional moralizer [!], is not glancing at his own troublous times when he develops this theme of avarice and projects it for its background upon the history of Flanders'?[20] Perhaps this guess at Chaucer's intention is not altogether serious; for surely the poet would not have left a purpose like that to depend on one word used in a conventional narrative opening. Quite certainly it was not the 'purpose' of the Pardoner—all he wanted to do was to make money. And with equal certainty, Chaucer's eye at the moment was fixed on the Pardoner himself, not on international relations. If such a 'purpose' is once referred to the whole pattern which it is alleged to explain, it is rejected instantly. A direct and simple explanation of the apparently mysterious phrase has long been at hand. Skeat said that it probably came from 'an original which is now lost';[11] and one exemplum of a type which, admittedly, Chaucer must have known begins *In marchia flandrie*. For the time being, until we find the poet's precise originals, and in so far as we are interested in his design, that is sufficient answer to the question.

The more pervasive Sermon Heresy, already hinted at in passing, centres attention on the Pardoner's material—or, more exactly, on a part of it—rather than on the Pardoner himself. To do this is to run the risk of overlooking or mistaking Chaucer's 'purpose,' and so to pervert the direction of the material.

Chaucer had no intention of constructing a medieval sermon, 'typical' or otherwise. He did set out to portray a certain remarkable charlatan of a preacher who, in the course of self-revelation, delivers a 'sermon' as a sample of his trade-tricks. Fussy as that statement is, it is not quite meticulous enough. For the whole homily as actually delivered to simple folk 'dwellyng upon lond' is not set down *verbatim*: part of it is *reported*, in satiric vein, to another kind of audience that is listening not so much to the homily as to the self-revelation. Let us say, merely for the sake of convenience, that the Pardoner fits his rural 'sermon' into an 'address' delivered to the Pilgrims. It is a joy to watch his off-hand ease at the job of conveying an exposition within an exposition. Into the 'prologe' which expounds his method to his present audience is woven a long quotation from a past performance; he slips deftly from indirect to direct report, from enveloping 'address' to 'sermon' proper and back again: so that, when he announces 'my tale I wol bigynne,' he knows he can proceed full steam ahead with his prize exemplum, since 'address' and 'sermon' are now running on the same track. He has promised ('I graunte, ywis') to tell a 'moral tale,' and he will pay the debt in full measure. But with a characteristic difference. He will show how a 'moral tale' sounds when told for an immoral purpose:

> By God, I hope I shal yow telle a thyng
> That shal by reson been at youre likyng.

> For though myself be a ful vicious man,
> A moral tale yet I yow telle kan,
> Which I am wont to preche for to wynne.

The 'moral tale,' that is, belongs to both 'sermon' and 'address' —only it is doubly interesting in the 'address.'

So considered, the 'sermon' takes its proper place as one element in the design. No one minimizes the value of knowing what the homiletic material is or how well Chaucer knew it. But to get lost in it, I repeat, is to lose sight of what Chaucer is doing.

One special variety of this Heresy that is more than negatively dangerous has lately been aired again in Mr. Carleton Brown's admirable edition of the *Pardoner's Tale*. Mr. Brown and others have not troubled themselves about the 'sermon' as 'typical,' but with its lack of coherence. There is no necessary relation, they say, between the 'tavern sins,' set forth and illustrated at length, and the theme of Avarice with its superb exemplum. It will be remembered that Lounsbury also condemned the 'intrusion of irrelevant learning' which 'breaks the thread of the tale.' Besides, as Mr. Brown points out, there is a clumsy transition where the 'riotoures thre' suddenly appear; for previously we have heard only of

> a compaignye
> Of yonge folk that haunteden folye.

From all this discrepancy it is plausibly inferred that Chaucer has put together incongruous materials from different sources and failed to cover up the joints. Dr. Hinckley and Mr. Brown have 'accounted for' the trouble by supposing that part or all of the tale was originally written for the Parson and later shifted to its present place.

Clumsiness in introducing the 'riotoures thre' must be admitted at once. And, probably enough, it does indicate that Chaucer has jumped too suddenly from one kind of exemplum to another. But the clumsiness is slight and unimportant, like the inconsistencies in Shakespeare which everyone notices and promptly forgets. It is reasonable also to suppose (in absence of proof) that Chaucer robbed the Parson to pay the Pardoner. But *why* did he do so? Surely not for the express purpose of committing incongruity! One can hardly be grateful for an 'accounting' that involves Chaucer in a major artistic blunder.

Before ratifying the audit, we had better ask if the material is really incongruous. Logically it is, of course. But the Pardoner never set out to achieve logic in preaching to the ignorant. His object 'is alwey oon and evere was'—money. And as an extractor of fool's cash, his 'sermon' cannot be beaten. Flaunting his relics and no doubt his gaudy cross, he practically blackmails every man and woman (especially woman) of his humble congregations into making an offering. His text, *Radix malorum est cupiditas*, gives him a clear pretext for dilating on all *mala* relevant to his hearers, and so a chance to score a bull's eye on every human target in sight. For the so-called 'tavern vices'—gluttony, drunkenness, swearing, gambling—are, regrettably, vices to which all flesh alike is heir. If the preacher can fasten all the probable sins of his congregation on the three rioters of his story, he can make it appear from their fate that the love of money is somehow the root of all mortal ills and that the way of salvation lies along the purse-strings. He is not setting up a logical argument but an emotional barrage. By dilating on the sins of rioters (and of his hearers) with all the arts of the popular orator, he creates an air of 'heavy fear and sin, the mood of a *Danse Macabre.*' After this 'dilatation' he strikes home with his deadly exemplum on *cupiditas*. And then, following close on the account of the robbers' death, comes an irresistible summary and appeal:

> Thus ended been thise homycides two,
> And eek the false empoysonere also.
>
> O cursed synne of alle cursednesse!
> O traytours homycide, O wikkednesse!
>
> O glotonye, luxurie, and hasardrye!
> Thou blasphemour of Crist with vileynye
> And othes grete, of usage and of pride!
> Allas! mankynde, how may it bitide
> That to thy creatour, which that the wroghte,
> And with his precious herte-blood thee boghte,
> Thou are so fals and so unkynde, allas?

> Now, goode men, God foryeve yow youre trespas,
> And ware yow fro the synne of avarice!
> Myn hooly pardoun may yow alle warice,
> So that ye offre nobles or sterlynges,
> Or elles silver broches, spoones, ringes . . .
> Cometh up, ye wyves, offreth of youre wolle!

This is something more potent than 'logic'—it is demagogic genius. And it 'accounts' for the 'intrusion of irrelevant learning' quite sufficiently.

The sermon heresies have a close but unexpected relative. Several times I have referred to the 'sins of the tavern.' In Chaucer criticism this phrase is associated with Professor Frederick Tupper's well-known essay on 'The Pardoner's Tavern,'[12] in which, with great and learned vivacity, he argued that Chaucer had arranged to have those sins exposed by a preacher who was himself guilty of them. Further, Mr. Tupper insisted that the preacher perform *in a tavern*, while the Pilgrims were seated around him. Such an exposé of the 'tavern sins,' said Mr. Tupper, would play ironically against a background of clinking canakins and laughing tap-wenches.

This view was certainly fresh and provocative in 1914. It added considerably to our knowledge of the 'medieval mind,' and it was one detail of Mr. Tupper's elaborate scheme wherein each pilgrim figured as denouncing his own besetting sin.[13] With general consent the scheme has been 'exploded';[14] and consequently part of Mr. Tupper's argument need not detain us. Evidently, however, the explosion did not quite disrupt the findings of the special essay, for one of them is still accepted in criticism, though it seriously hinders proper understanding of the Pardoner.

Mr. Tupper was certain, I repeat, that the 'tavern vices' were actually exposed *in a tavern*. In fact he dared all and sundry to contradict him and, so far as I am aware, no one has accepted the challenge. But not all readers of the Pardoner's Tale have been so confident. I think Mr. Tupper was mistaken in believing that the pardoner of Jusserand's fantasy —'still seated . . . on the further bench of the tavern'—was meant to be Chaucer's Pardoner in person: to be exact, Jusserand's taverner is a *typical* figure enjoying himself, 'after a well occupied day,' in the company of carefully selected pilgrims. Legouis saw the Pardoner go into the tavern for his drink and come out again: 'il est entré dans la taverne "pour s'aviser d'un sujet honnête tout en buvant," et il en sort décidé à les divertir.'[15] Professor F. N. Robinson is almost but not quite sure; in his view both 'prologe' and tale are 'apparently delivered . . . at the tavern.' 'At least,' Mr. Robinson goes on to say, 'there is no indication that [the Pilgrims] take the road before the Pardoner begins.' There is also, I may interject, no certain indication that they do not. But the editor's final inference is that 'a story which is . . . an attack upon . . . revelry is told in a tavern.'

Now the plain truth is, Chaucer leaves the situation quite ambiguous. At the beginning the Pardoner tells the Host that

> heere at this ale-stake
> I wol bothe drynke, and eten of a cake.

When the gentles protest, he asks for a pause:

> but I moot thynke
> Upon som honest thyng while that I drynke.

Towards the close of his prologue, he remarks,

> Now have I dronke a draughte, of corny ale.

After the tale, when the Knight has quieted things down,

> Anon they kiste, and ryden forth hir weye.

Those four excerpts provide the whole basis on which any guesses about the situation have to rest. In the first and second a distinct pause is indicated. The third may well suggest that the Pardoner has been consuming his ale during the course of the 'prologe'—in which case the Pilgrims may be gathered in front of the booth. The fourth quotation would seem to imply that there was no prolonged hiatus between the kissing and the riding forth. It is at least possible that, after a pause to suit the Pardoner's convenience, the Pilgrims rode on, their entertainer talking to the usual accompaniment of hooves and harness.

But that literal tavern interior of Mr. Tupper's will never do. Only a frivolous person, I suppose, would wonder how the 'tap-wenches' and the proprietor of the ale-stake liked strenuous attacks on their livelihood—especially if delivered on their own premises. And Harry Bailly—he too wanted a drink, but as an innkeeper would he feel justified in being a party to such a disturbance of the peace? Further, it is difficult to enjoy the spectacle of the Lady Prioress standing with the Pardoner at a bar-rail. As for the alleged absurdity of asking the Host to climb down from his horse and kneel on the ground—which is Mr. Tupper's trump-card—*that* is precisely what triumphant impudence might propose, 'Al newe and fressh at every miles ende,' and precisely what the Pardoner saw the Host would never agree to do.

As so very often, a commonplace consideration has been overlooked. If Chaucer had had the slightest interest in providing a 'tavern background,' he would have provided one. Since he did not, we may infer, what should have been obvious from the start, that he was concentrating the whole of his effort on the character and directing his reader's whole attention to the same object. Mr. Tupper's tavern-ironies are irrelevant as well as improbable. Chaucer saw sufficient irony in the spectacle of the Pardoner inveighing against his own sins, perfectly aware that he was doing so. And he provided the required tavern atmosphere in sufficient quantity without any help from the tap-wenches.

The Tavern Heresy, like its fellows, puts stress on the wrong thing—on the sins not on the sinner, on the situation not on the person in it. Certainly Chaucer never meant to do anything of the sort. This time, however, one is grateful to the error for being so attractive and so informing.

III

What follows is mostly 'subjective interpretation' of the Pardoner and his behaviour. A good deal of it has been outlined, in passing, during the course of the review just concluded; and what will now be said is very largely an amalgam of findings which I think have been established by two genera-

tions of criticism. There has to be a good deal of conjecture
in the amalgam, since all 'interpretation' is, in part, funda-
mentally conjectural. This, one may insist, does not make the
process any the less important or indeed the less imperative.
But to say that Chaucer was an artist and usually knew what
he was doing is not too brave an assumption. Consequently,
when you read on one page of a book that the Pardoner's
discourse is a 'work of art' and a few pages farther on that it
is chargeable with some glaring inconsistency or excrescence,
you suspect a lapse in the critic's own mind. Perhaps, if he
had risked a little more 'conjecture,' he would have arrived
at a conclusion more consistent. No doubt Chaucer nodded
like all other artists, but I think he did not often snore. With
that conjecture in mind, I have tried to exhibit the whole
Pardoner Scheme as what I firmly believe it to be—a power-
fully consistent work of art.

It is convenient to study the Pardoner's development in
five stages: (1) his portrait in the General Prologue, (2) his
interruption of the Wife of Bath's discourse, (3) the 'head-
link,' (4) his 'address,' consisting of a prologue, the 'sermon'
proper, and a 'benediction,' (5) the epilogue, consisting of the
Pardoner's 'afterthought,' as I shall call it, his quarrel with
the Host, and the Knight's peace-making. In spite of debate
about the position of (2), I am sure Chaucer must have in-
tended these stages to be considered in that order; and in so
considering them I shall try to remember that artistic divisions
are not water-tight. The whole scheme outlined above must
be studied as in one block.

1. To begin at the very beginning, one should note the
first appearance of the word Pardoner:

> Ther was also a Reve, and a Millere,
> A Somnour, and a Pardoner also,
> A Maunciple, and myself.

With due reservations about 'myself' (how blandly impudent
it is!), that is the Pardoner's gang: the slums of the Pilgrim-
age, tellers of harlotries all of them—except 'myself' and the
one who would have told the worst harlotry if he had been
allowed. Mr. Curry notes that there is no evidence of contact

between the Pardoner and respectable folk. There certainly is not. None of the 'gentils' would touch him with the proverbial pole, and even Harry Bailly's final intimate contact was effected under stern duress.

The only Pilgrim who rides with him is the scabby Summoner, 'his freend and his compeer'—an association that quietly insists on attention. In one of the documents quoted by Dr. Owst,[16] Bishop Grandisson flays *'vos archi-diaconórum officiales, vestrive commissarii et registrarii, saeva cupiditate dampnabiliter excecati,'* who wink at unlawful preaching and encourage it for personal profit. As in the partnership of physician and apothecary,

> ech of hem made oother for to wynne—
> Hir friendshipe nas nat newe to bigynne.

Alongside his 'compeer,' the Pardoner leaps to sight as suddenly as a jinni out of the smoke:

> With hym ther rood a gentil Pardoner . . .
> That streight was comen fro the court of Rome.
> Ful loude he soong "Com hider, love, to me!"
> This Somonour bar to hym a stif burdoun;
> Was nevere trompe of half so greet a soun.

Of the companionship so established, Professor H. R. Patch remarks that it is 'the most violent satire in all of Chaucer's poetry.'[17] He means that these lines thrust without warning into the worst corruption of the medieval church in all its branches; and he is justified in using strong words, though he must be thinking of the corruption rather than of Chaucer's verses. Chaucer plainly means those lines to be arresting. But I should prefer to say 'contradiction' instead of 'satire'; and 'broadly comic' instead of 'violent.' That famous first couplet challenges the ear by a heightened pitch of the same cool impudence which has been noticed before and which is everywhere characteristic of Chaucer. The Pardoner would be quite capable of explaining that he learned his ditty from the Pope and of calling on the Summoner for corroboration. Though that would be the Pardoner's joke, not Chaucer's, the couplet does manage to convey something like its temper in a less 'violent' form. Those two lines announce the theme, so to speak, of a whole tone-poem; and the 'stif burdoun' of the Summoner supports it with a sort of horribly hearty counterpoint.

I have used the word 'contradiction' advisedly. All interpretations of the Pardoner have to play upon the contradictious theme of 'hypocrite' or 'charlatan' suggested in the ironical couplet. At point after point, as the portrait develops, a duplicity lurks in statements or hints that are apparently plain. Does the walletful of pardons come from Rome all hot, or does the Pardoner merely say so? Is he or is he not in minor orders? Does he believe in the efficacy of relics or is he completely cynical about them? To anticipate a later part of the scheme, is he or is he not capable of reverence? There are, of course, not two opinions about his charlatanism. But there is no final making-up of the mind about the Charlatan himself. Did Chaucer 'hate' him, as Mr. Patch believes, or did he not, or did he 'hate' him only sometimes, or was he nothing more than immensely entertained by him? It is usually sentimental to press or even to put questions like these last, but they do arise without offense in the strange case of the Pardoner. That is why I have thought it worth while to spend so much space on four lines. I might allow Mr. Patch to call them 'startling irony.'

No other portrait in the General Prologue prepares for its outcome in so minute a fashion. Evidently, Chaucer must have seen exactly what he was going to do with the Pardoner by the time he felt able to describe him in such detail and with such complete foreshadowing. Notwithstanding the doubts of Koch and one or two others, there is no real difficulty in reconciling the relics named in the Prologue with those the Preacher showed to the rustics; one list merely expands the other in perfectly straightforward fashion. Chaucer was not telling his story to children who forbid the teller to 'vary events by so much as one small devil.' But with extraordinary fidelity, as he proceeds with the plan, he does develop every major and minor theme announced in the Pardoner's portrait: irreverence, lust, shameless exhibitionism, physical impotency, avarice, superb skill as charlatan.

One theme not announced there—his drinking—is supplied by his association with the Summoner.

2. The Pardoner interrupts the Wife's discourse just where he *would* interrupt it as an expert professional—at the conclusion of one of her numerous little homilies. And he does so in his own surprising manner:

> Up stirte the Pardoner, and that anon:
> 'Now, dame, . . .
> Ye been a noble prechour in this cas.'

The 'cas' is the sexual relation, which naturally interests the singer of 'Come hider, love, to me.' He is later to say he will 'have a jolly wenche in every toun,' but at the moment he is more decorous: 'I was aboute to wedde a wyf.' This is jocosity, of course. But in view of his profession and his House of Rouncivale, it is impudent; and in the light of the portrait, dangerously shameless. This, I take it, is the reason why the Wife of Bath broadly hints that his outburst is due to drink. She speaks firmly, but I think with a certain veiled and allusive moderation which you would not expect from her. 'You had best look out,' she says; 'if you get married, you may drink an ale far more bitter. Take heed or some one will make an example of you.' The Pardoner promptly and wisely withdraws, but not without another bit of impudence:

> . . . teche us yonge men of youre praktike.

The incident is unimportant enough in itself, but it conveys a good deal of suggestion. Beside making one of the little diversions which Chaucer likes, it brings the Pardoner actively upon the stage for a moment, touches up some salient points of the portrait, prepares for a later warning that will be more vigorous, and ever so lightly suggests a possible exposure.

Even if this interpretation be rejected, the very nature of the incident would appear to forbid placing it *after* the Pardoner's main performance; in other words, the Pardoner's tale must follow the Wife of Bath's. M. Curry does not

place it so, apparently accepting the Chaucer Society's or-
der without question; and he could bring powerful support[18]
to his aid if he wished to. I have no desire to thicken the
darkness that still envelops the order of the Canterbury
Tales, or indeed to discuss the question at all except in so
far as it affects a study of the Pardoner. But unless Chaucer
has been guilty of a surprising lapse, the interruption simply
cannot follow the tale. In the first place, such an order would
involve the flattest kind of anti-climax: for the Pardoner's
performance as interrupter is excellent as such, but fright-
fully feeble as compared with his efficiency as preacher. The
minor episode, as I have shown, has value considered as
merely, preparatory, but next to none at all considered as
epilogue. Further, *if* it is an epilogue, it shows the Pardoner
up as a complete fool. After the appalling exposé he suffers
at Harry Bailly's hands, he would be the last person, as Mr.
Curry should agree, to 'entremette' himself into a discus-
sion of marriage or of any question involving sex. Once bit-
ten, twice shy. Now if any view of Chaucer's design is more
secure than another, it is that he never imagined the Par-
doner as an idiot—as he would be if he courted a second
exposure. No doubt Chaucer's general plan changed in the
course of development; no doubt he might find that a change
involved a wrong disposition of Rouchestre and Sidyngborne
on the Canterbury road, or some other similar trouble. But,
if he did, he would surely find it better to shuffle two names
than to risk a dramatic fatuity.

3. The Pardoner's 'head-link' is worth more attention than
it has got or can now get. I think there is a not too subtle dig
in Harry Bailly's summons to the new story-teller, 'thou beel
amy, thou Pardoner.' *Beel amy* is a 'common form of address,'
as the editors stingily say; but this is its only occurrence in
Chaucer, and it can be read as conveying a leer from the
Host, whose French is surely rather unexpected. There is
also a hint of return thrust, as well as eager zest, in the
Pardoner's echoing of Harry's dubious saint:

'It shall be doon,' quod he, 'by Seint Ronyon!'

Other things, however, are more significant than these trifles; and one of them can easily be overlooked.

Harry Bailly would not be sensitive to the Pardoner's abomination, but the gentles were. And their swift outcry—

But right anon thise gentils gonne to crye—

has a double importance. On its surface it recalls the portrait of the rascal as he has appeared to the respectable part of the Pilgrimage: too clever to be predictable, physically abnormal, disturbingly contradictory, scoundrelly beyond words, a clear candidate for interdict. Even the Wife of Bath has eyed him darkly. As for the bawdry which the Miller had already uttered in their hearing without much protest, they had expected he would tell 'his cherles tale in his manere,' and they had known the worst he could do before he began. But they were troubled by the Pardoner's duplicity: altogether too visible on the one hand, and on the other a quite unknown quantity. If the inevitable fabliau came from the visible side, no doubt they could stand it; it was the other quarter they feared. *Ignotum pro horrendo.* This, I believe, is a possible reading of the gentles' mind, or of what Chaucer thought would be there.

The most interesting thing about their protest, however, is its dramatic usefulness. As the text plainly states, it wards off a fabliau and demands doctrine:

Nay, lat hym telle us of no ribaudye!
Telle us som moral thyng.

These commands the Pardoner knows he dare not disobey: 'I graunte, ywis.' But at the same time they have confronted him with a galling choice. He knows plenty of moral things, but to tell one *as such* is completely out of his character and habit; and what is more, he knows the Pilgrims know that also. To recite the bare exemplum before *this* audience is to cramp his style intolerably, for the usual effect is not in view. At the moment there can be only one effect that will redound to his glory: since he is known to be a charlatan, he can prove he is the cleverest of his kind from Berwick unto Ware. In short, he must tell a story at once moral and his own. No wonder he pauses for a moment:

> but I moot thynke
> Upon som honest thyng while that I drynke.

But only for a moment. We can easily imagine his rapid thinking as he swallows the ale: 'I have it! The Wife of Bath made a hit with her confessions. Why shouldn't I follow her example and give an exhibition, with running comment, of my technique? They have asked for morality and they shall have it; but it will be morality, with my special difference, from the mouth of a dark horse. There can be no risk. Here and now I am perfectly secure.' Much of this is naked 'assumption,' but it is assumption harmonious with the immediate context and with the general manner of the Canterbury cycle. By the device of the 'protest' Chaucer jockeys his Pardoner into a corner from which he can escape in only one way, and this he takes after pausing but a moment. The charlatan's self-revelation is, therefore, not only 'credible' on other grounds, it is as near to dramatic inevitability as it can be made.

4. He loses no time in getting to work:

> 'Lordynges,' quod he, 'in chirches whan I preche,
> I peyne me to han an hauteyn speche.'

Some important aspects of the 'address' that follows have already been discussed fully enough. Sometimes I think it would be good sport for a scholar like Mr. C. S. Lewis, who can write Middle English verse with unashamed skill, to reconstruct the whole of the 'sermon' which the Pardoner was wont to preach to villagers. The exploit might help to lay the ghost of the 'typical sermon'; for if carried out and read intelligently, it might show why Chaucer did *not* write one. But such a sport may require the services of another Pardoner. Having only Chaucer's to go by, we must never forget the rascal's dilemma and his effort to escape from it. The way out was not to preach a 'typical short story.' What he did was to fuse two elements diametrically opposed: the sermon and narrative which in themselves faced one way, the self-revelation which faced another. Nothing could be plainer than his own statement:

> Thus kan I preche agayn that same vice
> Which that I use, and that is avarice.
> But though myself be gilty in that synne,
> Yet kan I maken oother folk to twynne
> From avarice, and soore to repente.
> But that is nat my principal entente;
> I preche nothyng but for coveitise.

The Pilgrims were thereby privileged to see a truly marvellous spectacle of the devil calling sinners to repentance, actually achieving that result, and getting pay for his 'assoillyng'!

The Pardoner's 'prologe,' like many other things in Chaucer, is carefully constructed to give an air of improvisation. Apparently it rambles, as if the draught of corny ale were working: the speaker seems to be uttering just what comes into his head. With perfect casualness, he suggests a picture of his rural victims; he digresses to give a graphic imitation of himself at work in front of them—

> . . . it is joye to se my bisynesse;

over and over he rings it out, 'as round as gooth a belle,' that he preaches 'nothing but for coveitise.' For this occasion he shortens or merely reports the display of cheap fireworks by which he awes the yokel, and he takes his immediate audience by the more potent fascination of himself. As soon as this is duly exercised, he can carry out the letter of his promise:

> herkneth, lordynges, in conclusion:
> Youre likyng is that I shal telle a tale. . . .
> For though myself be a ful vicious man,
> A moral tale yet I yow telle kan.

He can now tell his great story as if his two audiences, past and present, were one—as they are in interest, but with what difference in feeling!

The difference is important for two reasons: first, because it affects the closing episode, as we shall soon see, and secondly, because the Pardoner's new audience includes, in a sense, all readers of the tale. Chaucer cannot pause, any more than a dramatist ever can, to display the reaction of the gentles and the others. But if a reader will try to imagine the effect the Pardoner produces on the Pilgrims, he will also be analyzing the effect upon himself. There can be no doubt that the Knight, for instance, is listening intently. To him, the speaker may be loathsome, but he is likewise fascinating. As a devout man, the Knight is revolted by this public exposure of the Church's corruption: if Mr. Patch wishes, he feels the effect as 'violently satiric.' And no doubt, he feels a sort of anger as he imagines what damage these foxes do in the vineyard:

> I rekke nevere, whan that they been beryed,
> Though that hir soules goon a-blakeberyed!

To him, therefore, the exemplum will be all the more shocking because of its very power. The moral tale which 'shal by resoun been at youre likyng'—one of the Pardoner's little ironies—is really as vicious as the teller. The contradiction we noted in the Pardoner at the beginning is the core of his performance at the end.

5. There remain the curious and difficult questions raised by the 'benediction' and the closing episode. What is the state of the Pardoner's mind as he ends the story and goes on in his 'afterthought'? What is the exact significance of the quarrel between Host and Pardoner and of the Knight's intervention?

To the first question, Mr. Carleton Brown proposes a 'simpler solution' than ordinary by declining to raise it. The Clerk, he says, ends a serious tale on 'a becoming note of gravity' and then relapses 'into playful banter': so also the Pardoner. It is hard to see what this parallel, in itself very dubious, 'solves'; and I think one need only state it to find it altogether too 'simple.' If subleties really exist, they are not 'solved' by waving them aside. And as I have been trying to show, Chaucer's design in this whole affair is very subtly complicated: it extorts 'interpretation,' however much one may shrink from the process. The Pardoner's benediction or 'closing formula' (often so-called) is a most insistent case in point.

His sermon' is finished:

> And lo, sires, thus I preche.
> And Jhesu Crist, that is oure soules leche,
> So graunte yow his pardoun to receyve,
> For that is best; I wol yow nat deceyve.

Everyone who reads these last three lines finds them moving and strange, and to almost everyone they seem to come in a questionable shape. Lacking Mr. Brown's ability to pass them over, we again ask what impulses lie behind them.

First and most emphatically, they are not the 'closing formula' of the *sermon,* though undoubtedly they have a gravity befitting the superb story and the moving appeal which have just been uttered. But the Pardoner had ended his 'sermon' when he said, 'lo, sires, thus I preche.' He is now speaking to the Pilgrims only, all pretense laid aside, concluding the entertainment which the Host had called on him to furnish, and presumably about to retire to his place alongside the Summoner. At least ten of his fellow-pilgrims conclude their turns with a benediction (in several cases very unedifying); and, of course, medieval narrative generally ends on some such conventional note. Primarily, therefore, the Pardoner is again 'following a tradition.' The point might seem obvious in itself, and it has not gone unnoticed in criticism. But of the two best-known answers to our question, one passes lightly over the obvious and the second neglects it altogether.

In 'The Pardoner's Secret,' Mr. Curry recognizes the element of tradition, yet nevertheless speaks of it as the beginning of a 'masterstroke of deception.'[19] Noting that the Pilgrims may be under his spell, the Pardoner is said to see them as another and fatter flock of victims. Then, to report Mr. Curry, he turns to them suddenly and tells them that this is the way he preaches to *ignorant* people; but *they,* the

Pilgrims, are his friends, and he prays that *they* may receive
Christ's pardon; he would never deceive *them;* consequently
they are to come and kiss the relics.

This version of the benediction is, I believe, quite unten-
able. First, in order to arrive at it, Mr. Curry is compelled to
do queer things with Chaucer's metre. But, what is really
important, he makes the 'sudden turning' come at the wrong
place. He forgets that he has noted the presence of tradi-
tional custom; and his paraphrase obscures the very patent
shift which occurs in the Pardoner's speech and manner at
the *close* of the so-called 'formula.' For at this point, as
plainly as words and verse can indicate it, there is a marked
transition to what I have called the 'afterthought':

. . . For that is best; I wol yow nat deceyve—

so closes the benediction. And then follows something in a
vein unmistakably different:

> *But, sires, o word forgat I in my tale:*
> I have relikes and pardoun in my male.

Correct placing of this shift might have been another warn-
ing to Mr. Curry not to regard either the benediction or the
'afterthought' as deceit. On the contrary, I am very sure, the
one is quite serious and sincere. And as as for the other, I
am just as sure that it is ironic banter. Only an utter fool
would *seriously* ask the Knight and the Monk, not to speak
of the Host, to kneel down or else give money 'at every miles
ende.' Though the Pardoner is defective physically, he has
his wits about him; there is no need to write him down an
ass, as Mr. Curry does on two separate occasions. And, in
Mr. Brown's phrase, 'an experienced salesman' would never
in one breath twit a buyer with being guilty of both sin and
waistline, especially when the buyer is Harry Bailly. The
'afterthought' cannot be rationally read except as a piece
of impudent horseplay.

Of all comments on the benediction the most important
occurs in an essay on 'Chaucer's Pardoner' by Professor
George Lyman Kittredge, published as long ago as 1893, and

substantially repeated in *Chaucer and His Poetry* of 1915.
This famous essay still remains by long odds the most com-
plete and satisfying study of the Pardoner ever made. In
many respects it seems final. But I agree with Mr. Curry in
finding its solution of the final problems unacceptable, though
on very different grounds.

Mr. Kittredge believes that the Pardoner 'ought to have
stopped' at the close of the exemplum; and that he is car-
ried beyond the proper limits by the histrionic excitement
of his preaching. Then (so Mr. Kittredge thinks) realizing
that the appeal for repentance and offering, which follows
the tale, cannot be directed to the pilgrims, he suddenly
cuts it off; and, remembering he once 'preached for Christ's
sake,' he utters a solemn benediction in 'a very paroxysm
of agonized sincerity.' But the mood of revulsion can be only
momentary. In order to cover up his indiscretion he plunges
at once into 'a wild orgy of reckless jesting,' in which he
describes his presence as 'a regular insurance policy' for the
pilgrimage and demands premiums for the same.

This rough summary of two pages from *Chaucer and His
Poetry* falls far short of justice to Mr. Kittredge's persuasive
argument. The original passage and its context cast a spell
very unlike the Pardoner's in intention but nearly equal in
effect. It *may* tell the whole truth; and every time I read it,
I am tempted to throw overboard every conclusion of my own.
But in my cooler moments it appears to me based on a too
narrowly selected portion of the text and on a view of the
whole document that incurs more difficulty than it resolves.

There is a fallacy concealed not only in the summary given
above but in Mr. Kittredge's own pages. His belief that the
Pardoner says too much results from what may be called
retroactive reasoning. For it could never have occurred to
Mr. Kittredge (let alone the ordinary reader) except as a
throw-back from the doctrine of benedictory paroxysm. *If*
this doctrine is to hold, *then* it is necessary to go back and
regard the Pardoner's sermon as too long for his own com-
fort. But for such a view Chaucer himself gives no warrant
in any sign or hint or warning whatsoever. In other words,
he must have set about to fool us readers (not to speak of

the pilgrims) just as thoroughly as the Pardoner fooled the
ignorant folk. And, in that event, we should almost inevitably
be fooled into missing a sight of the paroxysm also. (Actually,
as Mr. Kittredge notes, everybody in the pilgrimage does
miss it.) Such are the implications of his argument, and some-
how we do not like to believe anything so uncomplimentary
to ourselves. Even a writer of detective yarns drops one or
two clues that we could have picked up if we had been
alert enough. No life-line of the sort is discernible in the 667
lines of verse which Chaucer previously devotes to the
Pardoner. Such deception of an audience is not the usual
habit of an artist; and we may therefore be inclined to doubt
if Chaucer intended any such thing.

What hints *did* Chaucer drop about his intention? They
would seem plentiful enough. First we may revert to the end
of the 'prologe':

> A moral tale yet I yow telle kan,
> Which I am wont to preche for to wynne.

Now the 'moral tale' is only one part—admittedly the most
highly coloured—of a whole pattern. But the 'wynning' is
another, equally important in its way. Half-a-dozen times
over, the Pardoner says as much to the pilgrims. No doubt
he *could* have stopped at the point where Death overtook
the Robbers, but then the final strokes of his genius in extor-
tion would have gone unseen. And such a killing as he always
made! One remembers that

> Upon a day he gat hym moore moneye
> Than that the person gat in monthes tweye,

and that he had

> wonne, yeer by yeer,
> An hundred mark sith [he] was pardoner.

Chaucer was exhibiting more than a form of narrative and
homiletic art: he was exhibiting also a charlatan's power
over folk whose souls went blackberrying. How utterly irre-
sistible that power was we have already noted in the terrific

summing-up and call to repentance which follows the grim exemplum. If it is true that portrait, 'prologe,' and all must be read as one block, as I believe they must, it is a mistake to say that Chaucer meant the Pardoner to 'preach' too long.

A second difficulty with Mr. Kittredge's view is by this time familiar. The benediction is neither so 'sudden' nor so 'unexpected,' as he says. As we have seen, it was the end, not of the 'sermon,' but of his performance as under contract to the Host; and the Pardoner is following a convention that any story-teller might be expected to observe. Of this simple but important fact Mr. Kittredge makes no mention. The words of the 'formula' are indeed solemn—no more so, by the way, than the Man of Law's benediction—and they ought to be solemn, in order to harmonize with the tone of what precedes. They are, I shall point out, a thoroughly sincere expression of personal feeling, and in a very real sense they may be called surprising. But the surprise is one that needs no previous hint or sign. At any rate, it bears no necessary mark of paroxysm.

Nor can the 'afterthought' be properly described as 'a wild orgy of reckless jesting.' Undoubtedly a critic is bound to call it that if he commits himself to the paroxysm theory; for if there is a paroxysm, there must, I suppose, be some sort of corresponding reaction. One may be excused, however, for finding Mr. Kittredge's prose paraphrase of the wild orgy rather more surprising than Chaucer's verses, which are no more extravagant than anything said about or by the Pardoner elsewhere. Indeed they are the sort of utterance one expects either from the character depicted in the portrait or after his impudence in interrupting the Wife of Bath and the shamelessness of his own 'prologe.' A man who comes straight from Rome to sing a love-song and boast of his jolly wenches needs no orgiastic stimulus to be capable of anything in the 'afterthought.'

Finally, this theory imposes a forward-looking compulsion on the quarrel between Pardoner and Host. Mr. Kittredge sees nothing but 'rough jocularity' in the Host's reply to the *beel amy*, of whose 'emotional crisis' neither Host nor any

one else can know; and he attributes the Pardoner's speech-
less anger at Harry Bailly to another turn of emotion arising
from that crisis. But the text at this point bears a different
and painfully obvious meaning. One would hate to face the
Host when jocularity steps over the line into mere rough-
ness. As a matter of plain fact—here Mr. Curry and the
Portrait come into their own—Harry Bailly flings the Par-
doner's impotence full in his face, meaning 'no offense' by
it, only 'rough jocularity'! Hamlet had a word for fun like
this: 'No, no, they do but jest, poison in jest, no offence i'
th' world.' A man may be aware that a member of his com-
pany is afflicted with physical defect or deformity; but to
mention the fact, in language however moderate, is a fighting
offense. And the Host's language has never been accused of
moderation. The worst of such 'jocularity' is that it cannot
be answered in words. No previous emotional crisis is needed
to account for the Pardoner's wrathful silence.

The argument just outlined leads me to reject Mr.
Kittredge's interpretation of the episode. The substitute I
propose is far less spectacular, but it does represent an attempt
to read the document in the light of the whole Pardoner-
scheme.

The portrait, it will be recalled, begins with an ironic con-
tradiction and supports this theme by posing a number of
irresoluble ambiguities. The scoundrel pictured there is in-
tensely vivid and at the same time curiously baffling; and the
disturbance he creates is revolting to physical and moral sense
alike. Physically and morally he is charlatanism incarnate.
When he interrupts the Wife of Bath, the general effect of the
portrait is dramatically though vaguely reinforced. It begins
to take on a clear dramatic outline in the Host's leering sum-
mons and the protests of the gentlefolk, and it fills out into
savage clarity in the 'prologe.' The Pardoner's 'address' is a
prolonged working-out of the discord struck at the very begin-
ning. Such, in the view of this study, is a summary of the
process up to the benediction.

According to such a view the Pardoner is in control of him-
self and his speech throughout. No one can deny that he does
what he is told to do, but he does it in his own characteristic

and shocking way. When his stint has been performed—'Lo, sires, thus I preche'—he prepares to take his leave of the stage. What he now says to the Pilgrims is in a way surprising at the moment but not inharmonious, when you come to think of it, with what went before. Of course a benediction is partly a matter of traditional formula. But in it, if ever at any time, a Pardoner may be allowed to say something at once sincere and stripped of shamelessness. 'I have not deceived you,' he says in effect, 'nor will I do so now. The false "assoillyng" I have just exhibited tends to destruction; but there *is* a cure for souls that is truly efficacious. I have proclaimed myself a charlatan, but I would not have you think me a heretic.' In Chaucer's verse this is no paroxysm but a dignified and eloquent farewell. The teller of the Quest for Death knows what dignity is even if he does not put his knowledge into practice very often; and five centuries of listeners have never denied him eloquence. There is 'some good' in the Pardoner, as two English editors say with commendable restraint.[20] Tomorrow, perhaps, he will even be afraid and tremble 'before that formidable power which he said he held in his hands and of which he has made a toy.'[21]

It would have been well for the Pardoner if this eloquent note had been his last. Here, not earlier, is the point at which he overreached himself; and he did so, I believe, because he was tempted where he was weakest. Chaucer, it seems to me, had made up his mind that this lofty rogue should take a fall— not necessarily that Chaucer 'hated' him but because, in slang phrase, he had been asking for trouble. Of all people in the Pilgrimage, the Pardoner most deserves to be thrown: there can be no clearer case for meting out poetic justice. At any rate, the fall was arranged.

I imagine that a hush has fallen over the pilgrims as the Pardoner brings his 'sermon' to a close. No one, not even the Host, has a word to say. True, there is no basis for this assumption in the text except that a shift is plainly indicated there. The preacher evidently *intends* to stop, does stop in fact—and then goes on. He says he 'forgot one thing'—which he had fully developed only a few lines previously—and then continues in vein very different from the preceding. I should

like to suggest, moreover, that a shift from moral revulsion
to wild jesting would also seem to require a second or two
for the readjustment. But frankly, my chief basis for the as-
sumption lies in my own experience in reading the poem. The
tale itself is impressive beyond words; the summary and ap-
peal that follow it are appallingly impressive in another way;
and the solemn benediction crowns it all with a third emphasis.
It is a performance that might well impose silence. The Pil-
grims' reaction, already analyzed in the person of the Knight,
would not differ in kind from that of the ordinary intelligent
reader; probably it would not be feebler. And, except Mr.
Curry, every critic who has stopped to comment, no matter
how he 'interprets' the benediction, notes a shift in tone as the
Pardoner passes on to the 'afterthought.' To my fancy there
is a momentary hush where the change occurs.

The Pardoner, as I see him, looks around at the silent pil-
grimage with perhaps some surprise and certainly deep satis-
faction. Since Harry Bailly has nothing ready to say, he moves
on his own behalf as swiftly as he did on a previous occasion.
It suddenly occurs to him, 'They have been impressed in spite
of themselves! What do they think now of the man forbid? I
will get some fun out of their embarrassment.' The hush has
flattered the preacher's vanity and so leads to his undoing.
Tempted beyond measure, he lets fling at the Pilgrims with
his impudently ironic joke, all guards down. His brother, daun
Russell, could have given him a warning:

> 'Nay,' quod the fox, 'but God yeve hym meschaunce,
> That is so undiscreet of governaunce
> That jangleth whan he sholde holde his pees.'

Unhappily for the Preaching Fox, there is no one at hand
to warn him; and so, in Mr. Curry's pretty pun, he blunders
into reckoning without his Host. To tell the truth, Harry
Bailly has scarcely reckoned with himself. He is ashamed to
have been so impressed; he feels, quite rightly, that the Par-
doner of all people is making a fool of *him;* and he is angry. I
believe the evidence of anger is plain. The Host is indeed
prone to 'rough jocularity,' witness his 'words' to the Cook,
the Franklin, the Physician, Chaucer himself, the Monk, the
Nun's Priest, the Manciple. But his words to the Pardoner

pass the jocular limit. For sheer obscene brutality they have no parallel in the Canterbury Tales—and that is saying a good deal. Then, as the Pardoner is left speechless, he compounds the injury by pointing to his victim's rage.

Even that is not all. The Pilgrims are laughing, relieved to get their own weakness withdrawn to cover, amused at the Host's discomfiture, and more than delighted at the quick deflation of a swollen bubble. It looks to the Knight as if anything might happen, and he therefore steps in to direct the crisis in his usual masterly way. He feels that the Pardoner, thoroughly evil though he is, has provided superb entertainment and has been exposed with a blatancy quite too cruel. He therefore orders the Host to take the initiative in making amends: he says 'ye' to Harry Bailly and 'thee' to the Pardoner. That kiss which they exchange—it will not necessarily be fatal—is a supreme stroke of comic irony. This is the very note which Chaucer struck at the beginning of the Pardoner's portrait in the General Prologue. We are back where we began.

The end should warn us not to inject 'violent satire' into the beginning. Love-song and kiss are widely separated; but they are products of the same temper, which is the temper of Human Comedy and therefore neither violent nor satiric. We begin and end the whole affair with a laugh that need not be either strident or bitter unless we feel inclined to be so in ourselves. Satirists have their own laudable work to do, but Chaucer is not one of them. He cannot be said to 'hate' the Pardoner any more than he 'hates' the Host: Harry Bailly too is 'enveluped in synne' and, as chief offender, he is made to administer the kiss to his *beel amy*. Contrariwise, Chaucer does not 'pity' the Pardoner any more than the Host does: he merely deals with him in a different fashion. Is it possible that words like 'hate' and 'pity' indicate a sentimental wish to make Chaucer a partisan on one's own side?

All this is very far from implying that Chaucer was easily tolerant of evil. That would be silly. Far from tolerating the charlatan, he *presented* him, fully-rounded and without reservation; and the effect is immeasurably more impressive than any satirist can achieve within the limitations of his trade. It was not Chaucer's business to issue warrants against the House of Rouncivale. It *was* his business to *see* one remarkable member of the House and to write down what he saw. Now that the moral issue has been raised, we need only say that Chaucer enables us to sharpen our senses against the scourge and blight of charlatanism. This I know, for with his help I have watched quacks vending medicine and politics and religion in our own day.

Such is one view of the Pardoner as he emerges from a progress through the 'modern mind.'

Notes

[1] *Originals and Analogues of some of Chaucer's Canterbury Tales,* Chaucer Society, Second Series (1886), p. 436.

[2] See H. S. Canby, *Modern Philology,* II (1904), 477–487.

[3] Lounsbury, *Studies in Chaucer,* III, 366. Lounsbury does admit defense on 'the ground of dramatic propriety.' But the admission is obviously half-hearted.

[4] *Notes on Chaucer,* Northampton, Mass., 1907, pp. 157–159.

[5] Ten Brink, *History of English Literature, II* (London, 1893), 170.

[6] *Preaching in Medieval England,* Cambridge, 1926; *Literature and Pulpit in Medieval England,* Cambridge, 1933.

[7] *Journal of English and Germanic Philology,* xviii (1919), 593–606; *Chaucer and the Mediaeval Sciences,* New York and Oxford, 1926, pp. 54–70.

[8] *Some New Light on Chaucer,* Bell (London, 1926[?]), pp. 122–130, pp. 288–290.

[9] *Modern Philology,* xxv (1927), 59–66.

[10] D. M. Norris, *PMLA,* xlviii (1933), 641.

[11] *The Complete Works of Geoffrey Chaucer,* v, 275. Skeat's note goes on to illustrate the abundance of food and drink in Flanders.

[12] *Journal of Eng. and Germ. Phil.,* xiii (1914), 553–565.

[13] See 'Chaucer and the Seven Deadly Sins,' *PMLA,* xxix (1914), 93–128.

[14] See J. L. Lowes, 'Chaucer and the Seven Deadly Sins,' *PMLA,* xxx (1915), 237–371.

[15] *Geoffrey Chaucer,* Paris, 1910, p. 185.

[16] *Preaching in Medieval England,* p. 104 n.

[17] *On Rereading Chaucer,* Harvard Press, 1939, p. 164.

[18] See S. Moore's article, 'The Position of Group C etc.,' *PMLA,* xxx (1915), 116–122; and J. S. P. Tatlock, 'The Canterbury Tales in 1400,' *PMLA,* l (1935), 100–139.

[19] *Chaucer and the Mediaeval Sciences,* p. 67.

[20] Drennan and Wyatt, *The Pardoner's Tale,* Clive, London, 1911, p. 24.

[21] Jusserand, *English Wayfaring Life,* p. 333.

12

Chaucer's Pardoner, The Scriptural Eunuch, and The Pardoner's Tale

ROBERT P. MILLER

A RECENT article in SPECULUM suggested that Chaucer's
Pardoner may best be understood in terms of Augustinian
theology.[1] It is possible that the principles discussed there may
be profitably elaborated. The intent of this paper is to indicate
that the tradition of which St Augustine was perhaps the most
influential expositor provides more than a general climate of
idea: specifically, that Scriptural imagery, utilized by Chaucer
in the portrait and tale of the Pardoner, serves to illuminate
quite precisely the nature of the man and the "moralite" of
his sermon.

We are learning that the mediaeval author sought to build
up the surface or *cortex* of his work in such a way as to indi-
cate some particular *nucleus*, or inner meaning.[2] For this pur-
pose he had at his command two main sources of material:
the Book of Nature or God's Creation—the data of sense per-
ception, and another Book—the Bible—which offered the un-
perceived data of revelation. Both "Books" provided the
opportunity to achieve by study and interpretation a better

Reprinted, by permission of author and editor, from *Speculum*,
XXX (1955), 180–99.

knowledge of their Author. The Old Testament foreshadowed the "New Law" of charity under a series of types or figures, and was consequently to be reinterpreted in this light. Both the Bible and the Book of Nature provided a type of surface reality—a series of signs which, if properly understood, reflected the will and the law of God.

The *compaignye* created by Geoffrey Chaucer for the most famous fourteenth-century literary pilgrimage has been almost microscopically examined by the modern scholar in the effort to arrive at the most satisfactory understanding possible of the text of the *Canterbury Tales*. The characters are so firmly conceived that attempts have been made to identify the actual prototypes whom Chaucer may himself have known; and considerable study has been devoted to the various mediaeval sciences which provided details of psychological or physiognomical characteristics. It is surprising, however, to find scholarly effort directed so intensively upon what the mediaeval author called the *cortex* of his work, without an equally persistent effort to discover what *nucleus* might lie beneath. What we now call realism was of itself only a point of departure in a world where man's sensible experience consistently reflected the presence and nature of his Creator— where reality itself lay beneath the sign. The criterion of ulterior signification is, in fact, a hallmark of literature as a mode of expression. We expect the "cortex" to set forth a "nucleus" which is not denotable by scientific description. The reality of literature in any age may be said to lie beneath the sign, although the complexity of signification may not, perhaps, be as extensive or as arbitrary as that afforded the mediaeval artist by a highly developed system of conventional Scriptural symbolism.

Surface realism, however, even in the Middle Ages, was desirable insofar as it did not obscure the real issue of a particular work; and there is ample justification for historical study of the "realistic" details of mediaeval literature by which its inner sense is communicated to the reader. We have tended, nevertheless, to minimize the importance of the main source of mediaeval symbolic expression: that is, the Bible which, as the Word of God, provided, along with the Book of

God's other works, the means for ulterior knowledge. Even if enigmatic, the words of the Bible could not be doubted, and here too, as with the Book of nature, interpretation demanded insight. With respect to either, the letter killed, while the spirit gave life.

In his analysis of the Pardoner and his "secret" eunuchry, Professor Curry has adequately demonstrated that Chaucer's account is "scientifically correct."[3] But, although he approaches an inner equivalent for the detail he examines, Curry clarifies only the "letter" of this provocative characteristic. It would be strange indeed if Chaucer had intended his characters to be recognizable as particular living individuals, or as scientific phenomena, and nothing more. In this paper I wish first to indicate the literary purpose of the detail of eunuchry used in the description of the Pardoner—the *nucleus* beneath this element of the *cortex*. The detail may be shown to apply, not particularly to an individual *quaestor* of the House of Rouncevale, but to any pilgrim on his earthly pilgrimage. The Pardoner's "secret" may thus hold the secret of his literary existence. It will be my purpose to show how Chaucer, in making his Pardoner a eunuch, intended to expose and to stress the essential nature of this Canterbury pilgrim. It should be understood that this paper does not attempt to establish sources for idea or phraseology, except generally in Biblical context. For the present purpose it has been necessary to limit severely the associations connected with various Scriptural images, and citations of patristic writers have usually been minimized to offer an indicative selection of statements which may be found repeated in different ways elsewhere.

I

The last of all the pilgrims described in the General Prologue, the Pardoner is pictured as riding along singing a duet with that other "noble ecclesiaste," the Summoner. These two compeers, whose business in theory is to increase and multiply the congregation of the faithful in the Church, are ironically singing a popular song of carnal, rather than spiritual, love— of cupidity (to use the conventional mediaeval distinction) rather than of charity. Like January in his garden, the Pardoner tries to put on a gay and new exterior: with his hood folded in his wallet, "Hym thoughte he rood al of the newe jet." Chaucer does not fail to note, however, that, despite his "newe" appearance and the lecherous look in his eye, this man is somewhat less than he seems.

> 684 Swiche glarynge eyen hadde he as an hare . . .
> A voys he hadde as smal as hath a goot.
> No berd hadde he, ne nevere sholde have;
> 690 As smothe it was as it were late shave.
> I trowe he were a geldying or a mare.

The images of the hare, goat and horse—all common symbols of lechery—do not prevent notice that this man is also described as a eunuch. In choosing this descriptive detail Chaucer may have had in mind a concept used in several Biblical texts and dealt with by many patristic commentators. In such terms the rather extraordinary detail of eunuchry may be shown not to be haphazard.

The symbol of the eunuch receives noteworthy Scriptural treatment in three separate texts: Deuteronomy xxiii, 1, Isaiah, lvi, 3–5, and Matthew, xix, 12. They are sometimes considered independently in Biblical commentaries, but more often the texts are referred to each other for clarification and exposition. Thus Rupertus, in a very full consideration of the prohibition of eunuchs under the Old Law, cites all three texts:

'A eunuch . . . shall not enter into the church of the Lord' (Deut. xxxiii, 1). In Isaias we read: 'And let not the eunuch say, Behold, I am a withered tree. For thus says the Lord to eunuchs: If they shall keep my sabbaths, and do my will, and hold fast my covenant, in my house and in my walls I shall give them a place . . .' (Isa. lvi. 3–5). Are, then, the Law and the Prophet contradictory, that the Law should say, 'A eunuch shall not enter into the church of the Lord,' while in the Prophet the Lord says the opposite? . . . Now, the meaning of the term 'eunuch is not the same in both quotations. In the former it is to be understood literally, in the latter spiritually. Let us then enumerate the species of eunuchs. In the Gospel the Lord declares: 'There are eunuchs who were born so from their mother's womb, and there are eunuchs who have been made so by men, and there are eunuchs who have made themselves such for the kingdom of heaven' (Matt. xix, 12). This third eunuchry, because it is not achieved with a cutting instrument but rather through a purposeful chastity, is to be called spiritual, though not entirely so, because celibacy is made manifest in the flesh. And these, without doubt, are those laudable eunuchs to whom, according to the aforesaid Prophet, the Lord will give 'a place in his house and in his walls' . . .'

. . . He continues with an interpretation of the letter of the Law:

> Of all these types one cannot truly say that none enters the church of the Lord, but only that canonical authority forbids the sacred honors of the altar to the maimed and the castrate. We must therefore ask what kind of eunuch it is who may not enter into the church of the Lord. To those who ask this, another quotation offers itself: 'Cursed is every male who does not produce seed in Israel.' Neither quotation can rightly be understood without the other; though the words are different, the sense is the same. Thus, the eunuch who may not enter into the church of the Lord, who does not produce seed in Israel, and who ought to be cursed because he has not produced seed in Israel, is the man who, though able to edify his neighbor with his words, has kept silent, or who, though he has known good and useful things, loves idle and vain ones. Such a man is the opposite of the man who has made himself a eunuch for the kingdom of heaven's sake. The latter is to be praised because, having the natural power to beget sons, he is continent of his flesh for the kingdom of heaven. . . . The former is in the same degree detestable because, having had committed to him the talent of God's word, which he could invest well and barter usefully for the edification of many men, he lies idle and neglects the grace he has undeservedly received.[5]

This exposition may be valuable for an understanding of Chaucer's use of the idea of eunuchry in his description of the Pardoner. . . . Besides eunuchry thought of as voluntary chastity, we are presented with another figurative type which Rupertus characterizes as *detestabilis,* the antithesis of the laudable spiritual eunuchry. This eunuchry is also the result of an act of will, but of an opposite act in that this man, in full knowledge of the *bona et utilia,* chooses the worse part: the *otiosa . . . et vana.* This man, possessing the ability to inform his neighbor, remains silent; knowing the value of good works, he chooses idleness. Instead of cutting himself off from evil works, he cuts himself off from good works. He refuses offered grace. In short, he is the presumptuous man who, by *his* act of will, commits the unpardonable sin, not for the sake of, but in despite of, the kingdom of heaven. He holds a position in

Babylon exactly equivalent to that held by his opposite in Jerusalem. . . .

Besides the significant treatment of the idea by Rupertus, it is not difficult to find equally suggestive statements in other places. The *Glossa Ordinaria* itself reflects the opposition already noted. In the second class of eunuchs it places those false religious who deceptively put on the guise of religion, but in reality are not chaste: the wolves in sheep's clothing. "Inter hos computantur etiam hi qui specie religionis simulant castitatem."[6] Consonant with these remarks is also the opposition by Paschasius Radbertus between the *eunuchus Dei* and the *eunuchus non Dei.*[7] Rabanus Maurus gives a most significant account of the *eunuchi qui facti sunt:*

> Man-made eunuchs are produced by philosophers, or are softened into women for the worship of idols, or under the spell of heresy they simulate charity in order to counterfeit the truth of religion. But none of these will attain the kingdom of heaven; only the man who has made himself a eunuch for Christ.[8]

The *eunuchus non Dei*—the perverted, or perverse, churchman—is he who, according to Deuteronomic law, *non intrabit in ecclesiam Domini.* Commentaries on Deuteronomy xxiii, 1 also describe this type of eunuchry with clarity. The *Glossa Ordinaria* explains the prohibition thus: "All who live effeminately and do not do manly work cannot remain in the congregation of the saints, nor are they fit to enter the kingdom of heaven. . . ."[9] The false eunuch is the man who lives at ease (*vacat otio*, in Rupertus' words), and does not carry out "manly" works. That is to say, he is sterile in good works, impotent to produce spiritual fruit. Bruno Astensis is more specific yet: "By this is signified that no one will enter into the heavenly homeland who, sterile in good works, does not have the organs of spiritual generation and fertility."[10]

We may carry the metaphor one step farther. The spiritual fruits, or progeny, which the upright produce are, traditionally, as Bruno suggests, virtues or good works. St Augustine refers several times to the analogy by which good works represent spiritual offspring. For this idea the most obvious

Scriptural basis is Genesis, i, 28, in which the Lord, having created man in His own image, male and female, "blessed them and said: Increase and multiply and fill the earth. . . ." This benediction is usually distinguished from that given the beasts (Gen. i, 22) which was a precept for physical multiplication only. While man was granted the necessity of such increase, his blessing referred also to the soul by which he was superior to the beasts. For man, then, the precept instituted the state of honorable marriage, but further prescribed for the soul the multiplication of virtues by spiritual fertility. Common also is the interpretation according to which man is thus commanded to "increase and multiply" the congregation of the faithful that the number of the elect might be fulfilled. With respect to the concept of spiritual "multiplication" reference is also frequently made to Psalm cxxxvii, 3: "Multiplicabis me in anima mea, virtute" [literally, "Thou shalt multiply me with virtue in my soul"—Ed.].[11] By increase in good works and multiplication in virtues, or by augmenting the number of the faithful, the *eunuchus Dei* may properly be said to be fecund. "In the third kind of eunuchry, hope of the heavenly kingdom, engendered by faith, is brought forth by charity, by which many more children are begotten than by the flesh."[12] It is in just such spiritual multiplication that the *eunuchus non Dei* is sterile. As Rupertus said, he deliberately refuses to perform good works, and wilfully turns away from virtue.

II

If we look at Chaucer's Pardoner in terms of the Christian concept of eunuchry, both the utility of the image and the true character of this "noble ecclesiaste" are illuminated. According to these terms we should indeed expect him to be a eunuch. That is, the ecclesiastic is figuratively supposed to be the third type of eunuch distinguished in Matthew—one who by his own will has cut himself off from temporal pleasures. Castration or circumcision by the word of God is equivalent to cutting away the *vetus homo* that the *novus homo* might live:[13] this eunuch's will, says Radbertus, is "newly begotten in the Holy Spirit."[14]

The Pardoner, according to his own boast, is by no means a eunuch in this sense. The opposite, however, implicit in the developed Christian concept of eunuchry, provides a sense quite appropriate to the man as he presents himself in his prologue and tale; and this opposition itself implies a biting and bitter satire directed at the type of churchman he represents. It is evident that by *his* act of will he has cut himself off from virtue and good works, and that this act has been performed, not through charity, but through its antithesis, *cupiditas*. The animal symbols of lechery with which he is associated immediately suggest that, although he is perhaps physically frustrated, the inner man hardly "abides in chastity." If the *eunuchus Dei* is the *novus homo* of Scripture, the Pardoner, having cut away this possibility, lives impenitently the life of the *vetus homo*.

Upon such oppositions, basic to Scriptural imagery and exegesis, the portrait of the Pardoner is developed by Chaucer. The song of cupidity with which he is introduced, for example, strongly suggests the *vetus canticum* sung by the *vetus homo*, itself the reverse of the *canticum novum* which the new man sings.

More definite, however, is the comparison provided between the Pardoner and the parson whom he is said to gull with his false relics.

> But with thise relikes, whan that he fond
> A povre person dwellynge upon lond,
> Upon a day he gat hym moore moneye
> Than that the person gat in monthes tweye;
> 705 An thus, with feyned flaterye and japes,
> He made the person and the peple his apes.

The comparison seems to be purposefully introduced in order to play off the character of the Pardoner against that of the "povre PERSOUN OF THE TOUN" who yet was rich "of hooly thought and werk"—that is, of virtue and good deeds, the spiritual progeny of the true eunuch. The Parson, we recall, "also a lerned man, a clerk, That Cristes gospel *trewely wolde preche*," preaches in churches for motives other than *cupiditas;* his interest, as it should be, is in increasing and multiplying the congregation of the faithful:

> To drawen folk to hevene by fairnesse,
> By good ensample, this was his bisynesse.

He is a shepherd, not a mercenary. Of all these traits the Pardoner possesses the opposite, by his own rather proud admission. The Parson who with his "brother" may be said to live in "parfit charitee," like the true eunuch who has devoted his life to others *propter regnum coelorum* and thus multiplies spiritually, is a perfect foil to the Pardoner. By spiritual standards the best of all the pilgrims, he is ironically compared with one who, in his perfect cupidity, is possibly the worst of the lot.

The Pardoner does better the Parson in one respect: "he gat hym moore moneye." But to do this he subverts the Parson and all that he stands for. The analogy of his "Com hider, love," in Church, is the "offertorie," the purpose of which he reverses by applying it to his own benefit rather than to God's. Like the song he sings with the Summoner, this is the *vetus canticum* of cupidity rather than the *canticum novum* of charity. The increase of his money is typical of the Pardoner's *multiplicatio*. Sterile in the spiritual multiplication of heavenly treasure, he lays up his treasure on earth. Since Deuteronomy stated that such eunuchs shall not enter *in ecclesiam Domini*, it is ironic that the Pardoner is said to conduct most of his business "in chirches."[15] Here he advertises his own variety of multiplications with a calculated propaganda. The goodman who uses his 'sholdre-boon, Which that was of a hooly Jewes sheep," with the proper magic ritual, "As thilke hooly Jew our eldres taughte," (suggestive of the Old Law) will find "His beestes and his stoor *shal multiplye*." His marvellous mitten, equally useful to the man who wishes to get ahead in the world, will provide *"multiplying* of his grayn." The formula here is the offering of "pens, or elles grotes."

The Pardoner thus makes of the Church a kind of medicine show, and will promise to multiply earthly and material things, a function singularly appropriate to the particular type of sterility he represents.

'Multiplication' can be taken in many senses. There is that of earthly begetting, in accordance with that first blessing our

> nature received. . . . And such multiplication plainly is fruitful and comes only from the Lord's blessing. What of other multiplications? One man is multiplied in respect to gold; another, silver; another, cattle; another, his family; another lands; another, all of these. . . . And men are multiplied with burdens in their souls. He in whom vices are multiplied is multiplied in his soul. One is sensual only; another avaricious, proud, sensual: he is multiplied in his soul, but by his own evil. This is a multiplication of poverty, not of richness.[16]

Multiplicationes terrenae, the increase of earthly treasure, are those at which the spiritually sterile excel. The Pardoner in this activity uses his "relikes" to turn the mind of the goodman not to God through charity, but to his personal material wealth through cupidity: a reversal insidiously perverse with regard to his victim's eternal well-being. The increase he offers (and even this is "feyned") is that of the *vetus homo*—the opposite of the multiplyings of the *novus homo.* So far as the latter are concerned, the Pardoner is wilfully a sterile man. . . .

If the Pardoner may be analyzed in terms of the *eunuchus non Dei,* his nature and status among the pilgrims of the *Canterbury Tales* may be further clarified in terms of its equivalent—the *vetus homo.* The term "Old Man" is Paul's (cf. Col. iii, 1–10; Eph. iv, 17–24; Rom.. vi, 1 ff.), who also calls him the "body of sin." As an aspect of the nature of man, the *vetus homo* represents the flesh and its manifold lusts, opposed to the *novus homo:* that is, the spirit and reason, by which these are subdued. In terms of the Biblical history of man, the Old Man, in any human being, is the image of fallen Adam, unregenerate in accepted grace and unredeemed by Christ, Who is called the "New Man." As the result of original sin, all men are said to be born in the image of the *vetus Adam.* By baptism, however, we are said to die to sin and to be reborn in the image of Christ; and he who adopts this image is termed the New Man (sometimes the Young Man). As Christ's flesh was crucified and buried that the Old Law might be overthrown, so should the *vetus homo,* or the flesh, be crucified and buried, first in baptism (Rom. vi, 4–6) and later in penance, by a similar free act of will. Through this death man achieves life under the New Law, as the *eunuchus Dei,* by an analogous act, achieves spiritual potency.

This brief account of the *vetus homo* is intended to suggest a common cluster of ideas also utilized by Chaucer in his description of the Pardoner. Although this man thinks he deceives his fellows by putting on external "newness," his "newe jet" does not completely disguise the Old Man, sterile in charitable works, beneath.[17] That in his perfect cupidity he typifies the *vetus homo* (an identification strengthened by verbal hints) would have sufficiently condemned the Pardoner in the more perceptive minds of Chaucer's audience. What is worse, the man knows and freely admits the evil of his character. And worse yet, besides knowing the evil of cupidity and still practicing it, he is proud, even boastful, of his abilities. Acting out of neither ignorance nor frailty, he is recognizable as the man impenitent in sin. Thus there is no hesitation, in the confession of his prologue:

> But shortly myn entente I wol devyse;
> I preche of no thing but for coveitise.
> 425 Therefore my theme is yet, and evere was,
> *Radix malorum est cupiditas.*
> Thus can I preche agayn that same vyce
> Which that I use, and that is avarice.[18]

It is not difficult to recognize the theological type after which the Pardoner is figured. . . . His eunuchry, his *vetustas* and his pride, would easily have identified him as a man sinning vigorously against the Holy Ghost.

Presumption, or *peccatum in Spiritum sanctum*, is the one sin which is irremissible, since it involves the refusal of grace. St Augustine stressed final impenitence as the irremissible sin, for God is said not to pardon where penitence is absent. This sin is usually described in terms of malice, the opposite or absence of charity. The less serious sin against the Father arises through frailty (absence of power), and that against the Son through ignorance (absence of wisdom). Impenitence, or other aspects of this sin, are absolutely opposed to the remission of sins which is appropriated to the Holy Ghost. It refuses profferred grace, without which there can be no pardon. The grace of the Holy Ghost precedes contrition, the first requisite of penitence, as the Pardoner knows. Of the last requisite, penance, he sells partial indulgence.[19]

Again the contrast with the Parson, whose tale is a penitential manual, is evident. According to their offices, both the Pardoner and the Parson are *media* through which grace may be brought to the faithful; but the Pardoner, like Rupertus' *eunuchus detestabilis,* "acceptam indigne gratiam negligit" ["neglects the grace he has undeservingly received"]. A type of the impenitent man, the Pardoner accumulates temporal wealth by making a mockery of penitence and pardon. Like the eunuchs described by Rabanus Maurus, who "persuasione haeretica simulant charitatem, ut mentiantur religionis veritatem" ["simulate charity through heretical persuasion in order to counterfeit the truth of religion"], he knowingly perverts the function of his office. According to St Augustine, the duplicity characteristic of the sinner *in Spiritum sanctum* is likely to appear in a discrepancy between words and deeds—a concept which elsewhere forms part of his definition of a lie.[20] This characteristic obviously applies to the Pardoner, who stirs his hearers to devotion in order to increase his sales. In the bragging confession of his misdeeds there in not a sign of contrition. The same distinction, highly conventional, also forms part of the traditional exegesis of the *lignum aridum* with which Isaiah compared the eunuch. Of the sterile tree St Augustine remarks in another place, "It had only leaves; fruit it did not have. . . : even so are those who have words and have not deeds."[21]

III

I have tried thus far to indicate that the three terms suggested for identifying the character of the Pardoner—that is, consideration of the man as the conventional *eunuchus non Dei,* as the *vetus homo,* and as the sinner *in Spiritum sanctum* —are merely different emphases with respect to the same spiritual phenomenon. The eunuch is the *vetus homo,* who by wilfully cutting himself off from grace presumptuously sins against the Holy Spirit. Chaucer suggests this spiritual state by using the image of eunuchry, reinforcing his point by allusions to the concept of the *veteres homines* who, according to Paul, "have given themselves up to lasciviousness, unto the working of all uncleanness, unto covetousness" (Eph. iv, 19).

The significance of the concept of the *vetus homo* for an understanding of the character of the Pardoner can be grasped only by examination of all of Paul's statements in their full Scriptural and exegetical context. However, a few details may be mentioned with regard to the statement in Ephesians, iv, 17 ff. A specific reference to this text indicates its importance. To Paul's exhortation to those who have "put off the Old Man": "he that stole, . . . let him labor, working with his hands . . . that he may have something to give the needy" (iv, 25), the Pardoner retorts, "I wol nat do no labour with myne handes," and engages rather in thievery of spiritual offerings. . . .

In portraying the Pardoner of Rouncevale, then, Chaucer provides the *cortex* of his description with details which individualize his character, but which also expose for the reader a *nucleus* of deeper significance. By recalling the conventional concepts of the false eunuch and of the *vetus homo*, they help to identify the nature and enormity of the Pardoner's sin. He emerges as a type of the false ecclesiastic. Among the pilgrims of the *Canterbury Tales* he stands at the opposite pole from the Parson, the true leader in the Church, who strives

> To shewe you the wey, in this viage,
> Of thilke parfit glorious pilgrimage
> That highte Jerusalem celestial:

that is, the straight and narrow "wey" which Christ identifies with Himself. On the other hand, the Pardoner, dealing as he does with spiritual merchandise, commits the most vicious and dangerous hypocrisy possible. Of the characters on the pilgrimage to Canterbury he is the representative of the false leader within the Church, who "having had committed to him the talent of God's work, which he could invest well and barter usefully for the edification of many men, lies idle and neglects the grace he has undeservedly received." He will not make baskets nor counterfeit the apostles. Cloaked in the outward aspects of his office, he wilfully misdirects those whom he can move. As he says, he "saffrons" his speech with Latin

> . . . for to strike hem to devocioun.
> Than shewe I forth my longe crystal stones . . .

The shift in intent expressed between these two lines drama-
tizes his tactics, the gap between his *verba* and *facta*—his
"handes" and his "tonge." It parallels significantly his conclud-
ing effort with Harry Bailly. The relics in those "stones" turn
the love of his victim from God and into *amor sui*, reversing
the proper ladder of love, for they claim to provide increase in
temporal or earthly treasure. As a selling technique he makes
his hearers "soore to repente."

The "wey," therefore, that the Pardoner shows "in this
viage" is the opposite to that pointed out by the Parson. The
Parson's way is through penitence;[22] the Pardoner's, although
he knows the better path, through impenitence in evil. Sterile
in good works, wilfully sinning against the Holy Ghost, he
remains boastfully impenitent in full knowledge of his sin.
Chaucer has produced a daring and effective irony in creating
as his Pardoner the eunuch who presumptuously glories in the
one unpardonable sin.

IV

Rupertus' method in analyzing the concept of the eunuch
may be applied to a great variety of signs, with much the same
results. A case in point is Professor Robertson's illustration of
the mediaeval treatment of gardens, trees, flowers and related
symbols. As he says, "similar studies might be made of names,
numbers, animals, stones, or other things,"[23] and they might
be similarly documented. When the more familiar Scriptural
images appear literally in the *cortex* of Christian art, they im-
mediately suggest one of their spiritual analogies which are
themselves usually twofold, referring to their significance in
both Jerusalem and Babylon. We may often determine the
exact spiritual analogy only from context, since the opposite
spiritual equivalent is usually implied. Concepts such as the
concept of Death may be considered literally, as the rioters
themselves do in the tale, still preserving the spiritual opposi-
tion—in this case, death to sin (Rom. vi, 11) or death to Christ
or life (Col. iii, 4).[24] To use pertinent terms, the concepts of

either the death of the *vetus homo* or the death of the *novus homo* may be symbolized by physical death. Thus, taking an example from the *Pardoner's Tale*, the literal image of the treasure suggests the spiritual opposites of Matthew, vi, 19. In the context of the tale we recognize that the rioters do not find the "true" treasure (in which the "povre" Parson is "rich") they should have laid up in heaven, but the "false" earthly treasure which is itself the death they seek—as was understood by the hermit of the analogue in the *Cento Antiche Novelle*. The concept of the heavenly treasure, strongly implied, stresses how far down the "croked" way the rioters have gone.

In these terms I wish now to outline briefly an interpretation of the tale itself, in which the calculated description of the Pardoner may be seen to be functionally appropriate. Recognizing the importance of the form of the sermon (one of the effects of which is to throw the Pardoner into bolder contrast with the Parson) and of the theological subdivisions of its *expositio* for a detailed analysis of the *Pardoner's Tale*, I confine my attention here almost exclusively to the *exemplum* intended to illustrate his exposition of the theme: *Radix malorum est Cupiditas*. One of the best conceived stories in all literature, this *exemplum* possesses an undeniable universality, provocative despite any change in systems of values. I feel, however, that an interpretation based on Chaucer's use of Scriptural imagery, without precluding others, provides an additional dimension of philosophical importance.

The Pardoner—this *quaestor*—himself a seeker after the false treasure, tells a tale of seekers after Death. We should remember that the basic concern of the *exemplum* is Death. Death in the tale is the literal result of each of the aspects of *cupiditas* distinguished in the *expositio*. The tale is first an example showing the evils of drunkenness, that "verray sepulture Of mannes wit and his discrecioun." The rioters' day begins in drink, to the solemn background of their "fordronke"[25] comrade's funeral bell, and ends in death, brought to two of the three in a bottle of wine. They swear, furthermore, an oath of brotherhood, the breaking of which leads directly to death. After they find their treasure they

draw lots to decide who is to bring back the "breed and wyn,"
and *hasardrye* becomes involved in all the murders.

Ironically, the Pardoner, of course, is himself a chief
offender with regard to most of the vices he treats in his ser-
mon. He will not tell his tale until he has eaten and drunk his
fill.

> 320   "It shal be doon," quod he, "by Seint Ronyan!
>   But first," quod he, "heere at this al-stake
>   I wol bothe drynke, and eten of a cake."

He is a man of many oaths (*Ronyan*, in both French and
English a word for the "coillons," is an appropriate saint for a
eunuch to swear by). More generally, as the *vetus homo* and
the *aridum lignum* of spiritual eunuchry, he is the literal em-
bodiment of *cupiditas*, the larger theme of his sermon.

> 425   Therfore *my* theme is yet, and evere was,
>   *Radix malorum est Cupiditas.*

Death is conceived in the *exemplum* in the variety of senses
implicit in Christian thought. Death of either the *vetus homo*
or the *novus homo* is the *modus vivendi* of the other: a
phenomenon suggested by Chaucer's metaphor of eunuchry,
and expressed by the Pardoner himself:

> But, certes, he that haunteth swiche delices
> 548   Is deed, whil that he lyveth in tho vices.

In attempting to "slay" Death, then, the rioters do not engage
in an entirely meaningless quest. Adam's fall brought death,
both physical and spiritual, into the world, and all men after,
born in his image, have been mortal. The virtuous man *should*
slay Death, the inheritance of the Old Man. By crucifixion and
burial of this "earthly image"—the "body of sin"—the soul may
put on the image of Christ and achieve its heavenly treasure
in eternal life, the inheritance of the New Man. As Christ slew
Death upon the Cross, so his followers can gain eternal life
and cause the death of Death.

The symbolic quest of the rioters to cause their version of
the death of Death is significantly introduced.

> In Flaundres whilom was a compaignye
> Of yonge folk that haunteden folye,
> 465 As riot, hasard, stywes, and tavernes,
> Where as with harpes, lutes, and gyternes,
> They daunce and pleyen at dees bothe day and nyght,
> And eten also and drynken over hir myght,
> Thurgh which they doon the devel sacrifise
> 470 Withinne that develes temple, in cursed wise,
> By superfluytee abhomynable.

Like the Pardoner himself, they are classed ironically as "yonge folk." That these men are literally but not spiritually "young" is apparent from Chaucer's compact exposition. Dancing the "olde daunce," subjecting themselves to fortune in their play, engaging in the false banquet of sense, "they doon the devel sacrifise Withinne that develes temple."

> And right anon thanne comen tombesteres
> 478 Fetys and smale, and yonge frutesteres,
> Syngeres with harpes, baudes, wafereres,—

the purveyors of the "olde daunce," the false feast, the *vetus canticum*—"Whiche been the verray develes officeres." Into this atmosphere of spiritual death is introduced the spectre of physical death: "they herde a belle clynke Biforn a cors, was caried to his grave."

The irony of the situation is now heightened. One of the rioters tells his "knave" to ask the corpse's name. The "boy" provides not only this information, but also some suitable advice.

> 680 "And, maister, er ye come in [Death's] presence,
> Me thynketh that it were necessarie
> For to be war of swich an adversarie.
> Beth redy for to meete hym everemoore;
> Thus taughte me my dame; I sey namoore."
> 685 "By seinte Marie!" seyde this taverner,
> "The child seith sooth . . . .
> 690 To been avysed greet wysdom it were,
> Er that he dide a man a dishonour."

The advice of the "child" can be duplicated endlessly in sermons and moral tracts. One should be ready to meet death at all times in view of the judgment after death. The "truth" of the young man's assertion has been recognized, however, by few other than the taverner. As a point of departure for the tale the false "yonge folk" literalize (and thus pervert) the word of the true "young man,"[26] whose "dame" is the Church,[27] the source of such doctrine. They set out to seek a literal Death.

Having perverted the counsel of the *novus homo*, the rioters turn for advice to a mysterious "olde man" who directs them on their way. Their search is not fruitless. The Death they discover, however, is no literal "traytour," but *spiritual* death which their spiritual blindness prevents them from recognizing: the gold which turns their hearts from the life of their souls. It is clear that this is the false "treasure"—almost eight bushels of earthly treasure; the opposite of the eternal treasure which should be laid up in heaven. The quest of Death personified and the resultant physical death of the revellers emphasize the real spiritual death found under the oak tree to which the old man guides them. Physical death comes to all; but spiritual death is the root of all evil.

The circumstances in which the treasure is discovered reinforce this identification. Although he says that he seeks Death himself, the old man points the way:

> 760   "Now, sires," quod he, "if that ye be·so leef
> To fynde Deeth, turne up this croked wey,
> For in that grove I lafte hym, by my fey,
> Under a tree, and there he wole abyde;
> Noght for youre boost he wole him no thyng hyde."

Death, he says, lies up the "croked wey"—the opposite of the straight and narrow; "in that grove"—that is, in the false paradise of cupidity, and "under a tree"—*in medio ligni*, where Adam and Eve lost their true Eden and found Death first. In terms of mediaeval Christian imagery, this is surely the way to find death, but not the way to slay him. Furthermore, if the *exemplum* as a whole illustrates the Pardoner's theme, in a sense the oak tree under which the gold is discovered literally exemplifies the words of his text, *Radix malorum est Cupiditas.* For this tree may itself be regarded as the *arbor malorum*—the tree of evil (or of death)[28]—whose root is cupidity symbolized by the golden earthly treasure. This tree, whose *radix* is *cupiditas*, is also a version of the symbolic sterile tree to which the eunuch is compared by Isaiah.

It is finally appropriate that the director on the "croked wey" should be the old man, who thus assumes a position in the tale suggestively analogous to that of the teller.[29] Spiritual death is arrived at by failing to follow the counsel of the *novus homo* in preference to that of the *vetus homo*. The cupidinous desires of the fallen aspect of man not only point out the way of perdition, the false paradise and the tree of death, but in a sense create them. In the tale the figure of the old man stands as a symbolic opposite to that of the tavern boy.

Like the youth, the old man refers to his mother:

> Thus walke I, lyk a restelees kaityf,
> And on the ground, which is my moodres gate,
> 730 I knokke with my staf, bothe erly and late,
> And seye "Leeve mooder, leet me in!"

In contrast to the youth, he is of the generation of the earth, earthy. There is a broad suggestion of the "earthly image" of Adam, the *vetus homo*, the antithesis of the *imago Christi*, or *novus homo*. Like the wandering Jew, the Old Man of whom Paul wrote cannot die, and will not die so long as human nature does not change. Significantly the revellers refer to him as a spy of Death, an ally of Death, and he is dressed in a shroud—"al forwrapped" save his face: for the *vetus homo* represents the state of spiritual death. He desires "an heyre clowt to wrappe" himself in—i.e. the hair shirt of penance, and he wishes to be buried: for the Old Man must be crucified and buried that the New Man may live. The *vetus homo* may die only by the assumption of the *novus homo*. This familiar concept lies behind a significant passage which previous discussions of the old man have avoided: his response to the question of the rioters:

> "Why lyvestow so longe in so greet age?"
> 720 This olde man gan looke in his visage,
> And seyde thus, "For I ne kan nat fynde
> A man, though that I walked into Ynde,
> Neither in citee ne in no village,
> *That wolde chaunge his youthe for myn age;*
> 725 And therfore moot I han myn age stille,
> As longe tyme as it is Goddes wille."

Like the Pardoner, this old man can quote Scripture to his own purpose;[30] his mouth is full of verbal holiness. Like the Pardoner, too, in full knowledge he points the way to spiritual death, directing the "riotoures" up the "croked wey" into the garden of cupidity, just as the desires of the *vetus homo* lead any soul astray. Lacking that peace which passeth understanding, he wanders, a "restelees kaityf," in a manner reminiscent of a description provided by the Parson with respect to the Judgment of the *veteres homines*:

> Right so fareth the peyne of helle; it is lyk deeth for the horrible angwissh, and why? For it peyneth hem evere, as though they sholde dye anon; but certes, they shal nat dye. / For, as seith Seint Gregorie, "To wrecche caytyves shal be deeth withoute deeth, and ende withouten ende, and defaute withoute failynge. / For hir deeth shal alwey lyven, and hir ende shal everemo bigynne, and hir defaute shal nat faille." / And therfore seith Seint John the Evaungelist: "They shullen folwe deeth, and they shul nat fynde hym; and they shul desiren to dye, and deeth shal flee fro hem."[31]

The result of the old man's direction is death, both spiritual and physical. . . . The *convivium* under the oak, with its reversed sacramental "breed and wyn," serves to symbolize the subjection of these Cain-like "brothers" to their earthly treasure; and recalls the Pardoner's own repast at the "alestake." The *exemplum* pictures the discovery and the effect of the "root of all evil."

V

The extraordinarily tight-knit organization of the *Pardoner's Tale* does not permit full explication in a limited space. Other details of the *cortex* might be shown to be similarly significant. What should be clear, however, is the consistent philosophical pattern artistically presented through the manipulation of Scriptural images, the main points of which have here been suggested rather than defined. The import of the *nucleus* is thus a consistent exemplification of the Pardoner's text.

It should also be more evident how the *Pardoner's Tale* fits generally into a scheme of opposition between Charity and Cupidity in the *Canterbury Tales* as a whole. The extreme maliciousness of the Pardoner as a person sets him at the far end of the scale among the pilgrims. As a type he is even more definitely evil. He is the false eunuch who stands and points the way up the wrong road. He represents the way of cupidity, malice, impenitence, spiritual sterility—just the opposite of the way of the Parson and his spiritual brother, the Plowman. He is that Old Man as he lives and exerts his influence in the great pilgrimage of life. And as the *vetus homo* he is to be opposed to the Christlike figure of the *novus homo,* the true guide—the "povre PERSOUN OF A TOUN." . . .

Behind Chaucer's conception of the Pardoner and his tale lies the familiar Christian thesis that all men should be *quaestores*—not, like the Pardoner, for the material treasure, but for what the Pardoner should seek, the spiritual "offertorie." They should seek not the false pardons of which the Pardoner's wallet is so "bret-ful," but that pardon which Chaucer cannot forbear mentioning albeit in the words of the Pardoner: that is, the Pardon of "Jesu Crist, that is oure soules leche." Important also is the concept that all should be seekers of Death, too—but the death of that Old Man, through whose burial Death is really conquered; and who must be put down before we cease to find *confusio,* or disorder, such as that which literally breaks out between the Pardoner and Harry Bailly at the end of this tale. And it is clear that this is a spiritual matter. All the worthy Knight can do as representative of the temporal arm of the law is to make a temporary peace—an earthly equivalent of the *visio pacis.* But the Old Man still goes on wandering through the world, glaring with sterile lust out of his hare-like eyes.

Notes

[1] A. L. Kellogg, "An Augustinian Interpretation of Chaucer's Pardoner," SPECULUM, XXVI (1951), 465–481.

[2] Readers familiar with the recent work of Prof. D. W. Robertson, Jr, will recognize my indebtedness to his method of interpreting mediaeval vernacular poetry through its use of conventional Scriptural symbolism. For the distinction between *cortex* and *nucleus* see his "Some Medieval Literary Terminology, with Special Reference to Chrétien de Troyes," SP, XLVIII (1951), 669–692, esp. 671 ff. An interrelated series of specific Scriptural images is examined at length in his "The Doctrine of Charity in Mediaeval

Literary Gardens," SPECULUM, XXVI (1951), 24–49. A full analysis
of a mediaeval poem in accordance with these principles is found
in *Piers Plowman and the Scriptural Tradition* (Princeton, 1951)
by Professors Robertson and B. F. Huppé.

[3] W. C. Curry, *Chaucer and the Medieval Sciences* (New York,
1926), 54–70. See p. 61.

[4] Rupertus Tuitiensis, *De Trinitate et operibus ejus. In Deuter-
onomia*, I, xxii (*PL*, CLXVII, col. 941–942). [Translation substituted
for the Latin quoted in the original article.—Ed.]

[5] *Ibid.*

[6] To Matth. xix, 12 (*PL* CXIV, vol. 148) ["Among these are also
reckoned those who simulate chastity under the guise of religion"].
Cp. *Pard. prol.* 421–422.

[7] *Expositio in Matthaeum*, IX, xix (*PL*, CXX, col. 654–656).

[8] *Op. cit.*, *PL*, CVII, col. 1019. [Translation substituted.—Ed.]

[9] *PL*, CXIII, col. 477. Bede. *In Pentateuchum commentarii—
Deuteronomium* (*PL*, XCI, col. 391), and Rabanus Maurus, *Enar-
ratio super Deuteronomium*, III, vii (*PL*, CVIII, col. 929) make the
same statement almost verbatim. [Translation substituted.—Ed.]

[10] *Expositio in Deuteronomium* (*PL*, CLXIV, col. 526). Cf.
Haymo, *Comm. in Isaiam*, III, lvi (*PL*, CXVI, 1007): "This passage
does not speak of the seed of procreation but of the seed of good
work, . . . for they shall not be separated from the glory of the
elect if here below they produce spiritual seed, that is good
work. . . ." [Translations supplied.—Ed.]

[11] See St Augustine's exposition (*PL*, XXXVII, col. 1778).

[12] Radbertus, *op. cit.*, (*PL*, CXX, col. 655).

[13] See Rom. vi, 6–11; Col. iii, 7–10; Eph. iv, 22–23. This associ-
ated concept is treated more fully below.

[14] *Op. cit.*, col. 655.

[15] *Gen. Prol.* 707 states: "He was *in chirche* a noble ecclesiaste."
The first line of the Pardoner's prologue runs: " 'Lordynges,' quod
he, 'in chirches whan I preche' " (329; cf. 378).

[16] St. Augustine, *Enarratio in Psalmum CXXXVII*[:3] (*PL*,
XXXVII, col. 1778). Compare his *Enarratio in Psalmum IV*[:8]
(*PL*, XXXVI, col. 82).

[17] In fact, as elsewhere, by Scriptural echo Chaucer calls our at-
tention to the reality. In the Latin of Eph. vii, 24, the terms is
"induite novum hominem," literally used with reference to putting
on articles of dress or ornament. The Pardoner has also, ironically,
"put off" his hood, which may be thought of as symbolizing the
New Man (and in any case his proper ecclesiastical office). The
hood of the Austin Canon symbolized death to the vanities of the
world (See M. P. Hamilton, "The Credentials of Chaucer's Par-
doner," *JEGP*, XL (1941), 63.

[18] It should be noted that Faux-Semblant, disguised as a friar,
makes a similar false confession in the *Roman de la Rose* (see
D. S. Fansler, *Chaucer and the Roman de la Rose* [New York,
1914], p. 162 ff.). Confession is said to be false if unaccompanied
by contrition.

[19] Technically, the Pardoner receives a free gift of alms, itself
effective as penance (cf. Kellogg and Haselmeyer, *op. cit.*, p. 252).
According to the rule of opposites, almsgiving is usually specified

for the sin of *coveitise*. It is impossible, within the limits of this article, to elaborate the full irony of the situation. The Pardoner's false confession—perversion of the second requisite in penitence; the full significance of his refusal to "bye it on [his] flessh so deere," or of his own impenitence in relation to his official duties; his character and activities in the light of the theology of indulgence and of preaching—all deserve investigation and can only be suggested here.

[20] Some idea of the pervasive significance of duplicity may be gained from Augustine's tractate, *de mendacio*. See also Col. iii, 9; Eph. iv, 25; and n. 29, above. The Parson is, again, just the opposite: "first he wroghte, and afterward he taughte."

[21] *Enarratio in Psalmum CXXVIII*[:6] (*PL*, xxxvii, col. 1688). Compare *PL*, xxxvi, col. 334. So with the Pardoner's "preaching," in contrast to the Parson's, only part of the office is fulfilled—the "letter" rather than the "spirit." *A Late Medieval Tractate on Preaching* states: "Jesus undertook to do and to teach, or rather, first to do and then to teach. To denote this, each faithful preacher today is held to preaching first by deed and then by sermon. Would indeed that each preacher were to become such a diligent imitator of Jesus Christ, that he should preach not with the word alone but also with works!" [trans. Harry Caplan, in *Studies in Rhetoric and Public Speaking in Honor of James A. Winans* (New York, 1926) p. 72: cited by C. O. Chapman, "Chaucer on Preachers and Preaching," *PMLA*, xliv (1929), 184].

[22] Cf. *ParsT*. 75–80.

[23] *Op. cit.*, Speculum, xxvi (1951), 25.

[24] Cf. *ParsT*. 183–184.

[25] Drunkenness tropologically symbolizes blindness, love of temporalia: i.e., spiritual death. Cf. Robertson and Huppé, *Piers Plowman, op. cit.*, pp. 40, 52, 110–111.

[26] The figure of the "youth" as man spiritually regenerate is as traditional as that of his opposite, the Old Man. Alanus defines "*Juvenis*, proprie dicitur renovatus per gratiam" ["A *youth* is what the man renewed by grace is properly called"] (*Distinctiones, PL*, ccx, col. 825); "*Juventus*, proprie, innovatio virtutum" ["*Youth* is properly a renewal of virtues (powers)"] (*ibid.*). The *Allegoriae in sacram Scripturam* of Rabanus Maurus (*PL*, cxii, col. 975) defines "*Juventus*, reversio ad bonum, ut in Psalmis: 'Renovabitur ut aquila vita tua [Ps. cii, 5],' id est ad instar aquilae a pravi vetustate." ["*Youth* is return to goodness, as in the psalms: 'Thy life shall be renewed as the eagle,' that is, like the eagle, from a vicious old age"]. Isidore's *Etymology* includes the following: "*Puer* . . . pro obsequio et fidei puritate" ["*Boy* is said to indicate obedience and purity of faith"] (*PL*, lxxxii, col. 416).

[27] Cf. Gal. iv, 26.

[28] The Parson describes the *lignum vitae*, its opposite, in some detail: cf. *ParsT*. 112–126. Cf. Roberston, *op. cit.*, Speculum, xxvi (1951), 25–27.

[29] The old man has been variously identified: as the personification of Death; as the personification of Old Age; as the Wandering Jew—that remnant of the Old Law who wanders through Christendom seeking to die; and most recently as just an aged man. Identification as the *vetus homo* has not previously been made.

[20] He quotes the Old Law: Leviticus, xix, 32, according to the letter.

[21] *ParsT*. 213–216. The Scriptural citation is to Apoc. ix, 6. "Kaityf" etymologically derives from *captivus* (i.e., in context, thrall to sin).

13

Chaucer's Prioress: Mercy and Tender Heart

R. J. SCHOECK

I WANT to reconsider the conventional reading of the Prioress's Tale. That there is some irony in Chaucer's portrayal of the Prioress is now, I take it, generally accepted, though obviously there is something less than agreement on the degree of that irony. Yet, despite this recognition of the ironic portraiture of the Prioress, there seems still to be a widespread reading of her Tale as uniformly devout religious poetry, univocal and unisonous. By examining the complex of attitudes towards Jews and toward Christian-Jewish relations that is embodied in Chaucer's poem, I should like to suggest another reading of this tale.

JEWS IN CHAUCERIAN ENGLAND

There is no need to document the sad lot of the Jews in medieval England and Western Europe during the thirteenth and fourteenth centuries. European Jews were in effect excluded from Christian society. Viewed from within, their refusal to accept the Cross was a challenge to the growing

Reprinted, by permission, from *The Bridge, A Yearbook of Judaeo-Christian Studies*, Vol. II, ed. John M. Oesterreicher (New York: Pantheon Books, 1956), pp. 239–55. Copyright, 1956, by the Institute of Judaeo-Christian Studies. Text altered by the author for this reprinting.

sense of the essential unity of Christendom: no other group, in fact, posed so special a challenge to the Christian revelation. Viewed from without (as Toynbee describes their situation, in an objective phrase that cuts deeply), theirs was the unfortunate fate to be a fossil remnant in an alien culture. But however viewed, the Jews were allowed no place in Christendom in the late thirteenth and the fourteenth centuries; under Innocent III it was made clear that their place was outside the Pale, and their exclusion was marked by the Badge.

But can this be the full explanation of the Prioress's cruelly anti-Semitic Tale within Chaucer's Canterbury framework? Can the reader close his eyes to the unmistakable reality of the anti-Jewish theme and concern himself only with the literary form in which that theme finds expression? Can he be content with analyzing the twenty-seven and more analogues of the miracle of the Virgin as a literary type,[1] or with performing similar functions of literary analysis, necessary, but meaningless when divorced from life? I think not. The interpretation which I am about to suggest is that in the Tale which Chaucer assigned to the Prioress, the widely circulated ritual murder legend is held up for implicit condemnation as vicious and hypocritical.

THE PRIORESS

We must begin with the teller of the Tale, the Prioress herself, and look with some care at Chaucer's portraiture of her. One recent commentator has declared that the mere fact that she "is one of the Canterbury pilgrims is the first point of satire in a portrait that is satiric,"[2] for prohibitions of nuns' going on pilgrimage were frequent. Of course, as a prioress, the head of her house, she would have found that a great deal of business took her outside the nunnery.

A gentlewoman by birth, yet there is a sense of straining in her manner—

> And peyned hire to countrefete cheere
> Of court, and to been estatlich of manere,
> And to ben holden digne of reverence. (GP, 139–41)

Much of the phraseology that colors her portrait is taken deliberately from the medieval romance, particularly when she is said to be "simple and coy." Years ago Professor Lowes pointed out that this phrase set the stage for the many secularizing nuances of the Prioress which fourteenth-century readers "must have been quick to gather." Then her very name, Eglantyne, "exquisitely incongruous," for in each of the romances known to the century, "the lady bearing the name of Chaucer's Prioress is a beautiful, romantically worldly figure far removed from a nun." Her sparkling eyes, her small soft mouth, her beautifully broad forehead, her shapely nose—all these attributes are conventional in the cataloguing descriptions of medieval heroines.[3] The point is double: not merely that she is physically attractive, but that the reader should be cognizant of that attraction. The Prioress could not help being beautiful, but the reader is being presented with her attractiveness in the mode of the medieval romance with all its worldliness and sentimentalizing falseness of values.

Her manners are carefully those of polite society, and to the attentive fourteenth-century listener there was subtle but effective irony in Chaucer's evocation, for the manners described are taken from a famous account in the *Roman de la Rose* of what wiles a woman is to use to attract and hold her lover. But what is perhaps the most ironic touch of all, richly ambiguous and controversial, is the brooch whose significance is still debated by some Chaucerians. Hanging from her rosary, it is of shining gold, engraved with a crowned A and the motto *Amor Vincit Omnia*. In the earlier Middle Ages, this originally profane motto had been endowed with a connotation of sacred love, but by the fourteenth century the motto was again employed in its original sense— while of course the sacred connotation was still current. Lowes's questioning of the meaning of this brooch is justly famous:

> Now is it earthly love which conquers all, now heavenly; the phrase plays back and forth between the two. And it is precisely that happy ambiguity of the convention—itself that result of an earlier transfer—which makes Chaucer's use of it here, as a final

summarizing touch, a master stroke. Which of the two loves does "amor" mean to the Prioress? I do not know; but I think she thought she meant love celestial.[4]

One may wish to be chivalrous to the Prioress, but (and this is really the issue) how did Chaucer's audience see her? At the moment of their first viewing her in the dramatic narrative, there was no certitude but only ambiguity: from the first hint in "simple and coy" of the discord between the woman and the nun so subtly suggested by the two contradictory sets of associations to the summarizing touch of the magnificently ambiguous brooch, we have a nun who is something less than the fulfillment of the spiritual ideal.

One final point:

> But, for to speken of hire conscience,
> She was so charitable and so pitous
> She wolde wepe, if that she saugh a mous
> Kaught in a trappe, if it were deed or bledde.
> Of smale houndes hadde she that she fedde
> With rosted flessh, or milk and wastel-breed.
> But soore wepte she if oon of hem were deed,
> Or if men smoot it with a yerde smerte;
> And al was conscience and tendre herte. (GP, 142–50)

In middle English, "conscience" had our primary denotation (the faculty which pronounces upon the moral quality of one's actions or motives), but also the secondary meaning, now largely lost, of "tenderness of feeling": both meanings are bound up in Chaucer's use of the word here. "To speken of hir conscience," "to speak of her conscience," Chaucer says—but we get nothing of her moral faculty, only her emotional tenderness. Moreover, the object of that tenderness, of her "charitable" nature, is not the neighbor but pets; and there seems little disputing that it was contrary to ecclesiastical regulations for a nun to have such pets as the Prioress's "little dogs"[5] (though earlier, to be sure, such religious as those addressed in the *Ancrene Riwle* were permitted them). The Dominican Bromyard, late fourteenth-century theologian of Cambridge, thundered from his pulpit against the wealthy who indulged themselves in pampered pets, especially at a time when food was scarce. One may well ask what kind of "charity" it is that Chaucer chose to describe as lavished on animals. The point is not (as one scholar has suggested recently) that this is "the sort of woman who would weep even over a dead mouse or a whipped dog"; it is that she weeps only over such sentimentalized suffering and apparently ignores the human suffering so prevalent around her. It is that warped quality, as we shall see, which dominates her tale.

Only this far does Chaucer go in the General Prologue, but with superbly controlled irony and devastating tact he has contrived to leave shadows of doubts, several kinds of uncertainty, and some strong implications about the Prioress in the mind of his audience. Beyond that, at this stage of Chaucer's developing portrait of this religious woman, we cannot declare.

THE PRIORESS'S TALE

Preceding the Prioress's tale is a Prologue which in Professor Robinson's words "contains many ideas and expressions drawn from the Scriptures, the services of the Church, and other religious poetry." As would be most appropriate to the Prioress, it recalls in particular certain passages of the Office of the Blessed Virgin; "it was a regular literary convention to prefix to a miracle or saint's legend an invocation to Christ or the Blessed Virgin." A carefully wrought prayer, this Prologue of hers, and rich in symbolism; the attentive reader may well be struck by the irony of having an anti-Semitic legend prefaced by a prayer rich in images from the Old Testament. The Prioress invokes Christ:

> in laude, as I best kan or may
> Of thee and of the white lylye flour
> Whiche that the bar, and is a mayde alway,
> To telle a storie I wol do my labour . . . (B. 1650–3)

Then she calls Mary:

> O mooder Mayde! o mayde Mooder free!
> O bussh unbrent, brennynge in Moyses sighte . . .
> (B 1657–8)

and implores her:

> Help me to telle it in thy reverence! (B 1663)

Against this note of seeming sincerity and the subtly sug-
gested backdrop of the Old Testament roots of the Christian
faith, we hear the Prioress's Tale: how the "wicked Jews"
slew a happy child for no reason other than his joyful singing
of the praise of Mary, and how the murder was revealed
when, from the privy drain into which he had been cast,

> This gemme of chastite, this emeraude,
> And eek of martirdom the ruby bright,
> Ther he with throte ykorven lay upright,
> He *Alma redemptoris* gan to synge
> So loude that al the place gan to rynge. (B 1799–1803)

Having expanded on this "miracle" with great unction, the
Prioress gratuitously links it with the thirteenth-century leg-
end of the choir-boy Hugh of Lincoln:

> O yonge Hugh of Lyncoln, slaynd also
> With cursed Jewes, as it is notable,
> For it is but a litel while ago . . . (B 1874–6)

It has long been remarked that her Tale displays a "fierce
bigotry" (as Wordsworth put it). This is how she begins:

> Ther was in Asye, in a greet citee,
> Amonges Cristene folk, a Jewerye,
> Sustened by a lord of that contree
> For foule usuer and lucre of vileynye,
> Hateful to Crist and to his compaignye . . . (B 1678–82)

And this is how she accounts for the alleged murder of a
Christian child by Jews:

> Oure firste foo, the serpent Sathanas,
> That hath in Jues herte his waspes nest . . . (B 1748–9)

That the Prioress's own words should convict her of
bigotry is not enough; they must be seen as a clear contra-

diction of the mind of the Church, and to this end Dunn's comments in his *Chaucer Reader* can be of help:

> Her tale is derived from a vague but ancient and widespread libel, already current in England before Chaucer was born, that Jews were accustomed to murder Christian children for ritualistic purposes. She does not, it is true, claim any firsthand acquaintance with the Jews and is, in fact, unlikely to have had it, for they were expelled from England in 1290 and were not readmitted until the seventeenth century; and she sets the scene of action in an unidentified part of disant Asia. But she accepts without question the validity of the legend underlying her tale and, in her epilogue, quite gratuitously cites an equally legendary English story of the boy named Hugh of Lincoln, who was reported in the thirteenth century to have been murdered by the Jews. . . .*

Let us single out these points for emphasis, so that later reference can easily be made to them: (1) the vague but widespread belief that Jews were accustomed to murder Christian children for ritualistic purposes; (2) the acceptance of the validity of the report without question, and the retelling of this report or legend; (3) implicit approval of the action taken against the Jews; and (4) the continuing or stirring up of old prejudices.

These points are specifically covered by several popes in bulls condemning the ritual murder libel and offering to the Jews the protection of the Holy See.' I should like to quote here passages from that of Gregory X in 1271, not in the order in which they appear in the original but in accordance with the four points.

POINT 1:

> It sometimes happens that certain Christians lose their Christian children. The charge is then made against the Jews by their enemies that they have stolen and slain these children in secret, and have sacrificed the heart and blood. The fathers of the said children, or other Christians who are envious of the Jews, even hide their children in order to have a pretext to molest the Jews, and to extort money from them so as to pay their dues. They assert thereupon, most falsely, that the Jews have taken away these children and slain them, and have sacrificed the heart and blood. Yet their Law expressly forbids the Jews to sacrifice or to eat or to drink blood: even though it be of animals which have the hoof cloven. This has been

confirmed in our *curia* on many occasions by Jews converted to the Christian faith. None the less, on this pretext many Jews have frequently been seized and detained, against all justice.

POINT 2:

Inasmuch as the Jews are not able to bear witness against the Christians, we decree furthermore that the testimony of Christians against Jews shall not be valid unless there is among these Christians some Jew who is there for the purpose of offering testimony.

POINT 3:

No Christian shall presume to seize, imprison, wound, torture, multilate, kill, or inflict violence on [the Jews]: furthermore, no one shall presume, except by judicial action of the authorities of the country, to change the good customs in the land where they live for the purpose of taking their money or goods from them or from others.

POINT 4:

We decree that no Christian shall stir up anything new against [the Jews].
Moreover, if any one, after having known the content of this decree, should—which we hope will not happen—attempt audaciously to act contrary to it, then let him suffer punishment in his rank and position, or let him be punished by the penalty of excommunication, unless he makes amends for his boldness by proper recompense.[8]

At the end of the thirteenth and during the fourteenth centuries, the charge of ritual murder became more frequent; yet the popes had proclaimed the truth and set up an ideal against which these excesses and tortures and false charges should have been seen for what they were.

Doubtless most of the company hearing Madame Eglantyne's Tale would not have seen a Jew in England—the situation is very much like that of the Shakespearean audience and Shylock—but most of them would have traveled in France, some of them perhaps as widely in Europe as Chaucer had traveled on the king's business, and the likelihood of acquaintance or contact with Jews would be correspond-

ingly greater, for in England it seems fairly certain that only
the smallest pockets of Jews were left after their expulsion
in 1290.

By such a sophisticated court audience the disparity be-
tween the Prioress's professed devotion and her bigotry
could doubtless have been more easily seen than by a county
audience of less broadening travel and of narrower views.
While not all could have measured the great distance of that
disparity, surely readers have always recognized that other
Tales (like the Pardoner's) present hypocrisy, or (like the
Shipman's) knavery and deceit. For those who did discern
the pious hypocrisy of the Prioress, there is a level of irony
in the symbolism that reinforces this startling incongruity
and develops the irony of her portrait in the Prologue. There
is for example the reference to Rachel:

> His mooder swownynge by the beere lay;
> Unnethe myghte the peple that was theere
> This newe Rachel brynge fro his beere. (B 1815–7)

The allusion is to the weeping of Rachel for her children—
the sons of Jacob in captivity (Jer. 31:15)—used by the
Prioress, we may be sure, as a conventional figure of lamen-
tation and weeping. There is deep meaning in the fact that
the First Nocturn of Matins on the feast of the Holy Inno-
cents gives Jeremiah's poetical representation of Rachel, with
its magnificent consolation in a bitter time: "Let thy voice
cease from weeping and thy eyes from tears" (31:16). But
this (like the Old Testament symbolism in the Prologue to
her Tale, of which she is, I take it, unaware) is lost on the
Prioress and is without influence on her conscience or charity.
There is even more. Rachel's weeping is interpreted in the
New Testament (Mt. 2:18) as a prophetic parallel to the
lamentation of the mothers whose children were slain at
the command of Herod the Great. The Third Nocturn on this
day is from a homily by St. Jerome:

> When he took the Child and His mother, and fled into Egypt,
> he took them by night, and in darkness. And that darkness sig-
> nified the night of ignorance in which he left the unbelievers
> from whom he fled. But when he returned into Judaea, the

Gospel makes no mention of night or darkness; for at the end of the world the Jews shall be enlightened, and shall receive the faith again as once they received Christ returning from Egypt.

In all this evocation of Old and New Testaments there is a compassion beyond the Prioress's reach of soul: bland and unmoved, indeed with merciless satisfaction in "the evils they deserve," she tells of the torturing of the Jews, how they were drawn apart by wild horses and then hanged (p. 198; lines B 1822–4). The culminating irony of her last lines is the echoing of her petition for a mercy of which she is herself incapable:

> Preye eek for us, we synful folk unstable,
> That, of his mercy, God so merciable
> On us his grete mercy multiplie . . . (B 1877–9)

Though I do not wish to make too much of it, the Prioress's story is followed by Chaucer's own story of Sir Topaz, the *Tales'* one unmistakable burlesque, a satiric jousting with decadent knight-errantry of late medieval romances. Perhaps it is introduced in order to clear the air: the Prioress's Tale had left the company "sobered" for a moment, but then the Host began to "japen," he "again began his jokes." There might well be more than one reason for him to feel that the company should be cheered up at once. In any case, his reaction to the Prioress's story is most ambiguous.

Within the larger framework of the *Tales* one has only to look to the Plowman for a true model of the Christian, for here is one who follows Christ in loving, in true charity:

> . . . lyvynge in pees and parfit charitee.
> God loved he best with al his hoole herte
> At alle tymes, thogh him gamed or smerte,
> And thanne his neighebor right as hymselve.
> He wolde thresshe, and therto dyke and delve,
> For Cristes sake, for every povre wight,
> Withouten hire, if it lay in his myght. . . . (GP, 532–8)

Or take his brother, the Parson:

> He was a shepherde and noght a mercenarie.
> And though he hooly were and vertuous,

> He was to synful men nat despitous,
> Ne of his speche daungerous ne digne,
> But in his techyng discreet and benygne.
> To drawen folk to hevene by fairnesse,
> By good ensample, this was his bisynesse. (GP, 514–20)

There are, then, within the poem models of right conscience, true charity, and proper tenderness to human needs and suffering.

JEWS AND THE FOURTEENTH-CENTURY MIND

It might be objected that Chaucer was a man of the fourteenth century and shared its limitations: how could we expect him to transcend them, to shatter the wall of prejudices?

I do not know what most Englishmen of the century thought about Jews. The answer may well be that for them there could be only "Jews," not a Jew, and that they were to be found in unidentified distant regions or, as the Prioress places them, in the past. But certainly, there were those who did not hate them; there was at least one honest chronicler, William of Newburgh, who saw two sides to the slaughter of the Jews in York, and he was not afraid to speak the truth as he saw it.[9] Converted Jews like the fourteenth-century Strassburg banker Merswin followed Nicholas of Lyra in pleading that Jews could be saved. On the other hand, Mannyng, an Austin canon of Bourne, complains in his early fourteenth-century *Handlyng Synne*, a realistic picture of medieval living, rich in its detailing of virtues and vices, that not only some of the "lewd folk" but even some priests say of the Jews that "we wot not whether they be saved or no." He attempts to controvert this, for "certes," he writes, "they are all in error."[10] Mannyng would doubtless not have charged as he did that the layfolk and priests erred in supposing it possible for Jews to be saved if there had not been quite a few who thought so.

In Langland's *Piers Plowman* later in the century, we find the thought defended that there must somehow be a place in heaven for the good Jew and for the good pagan, for if there is truth in a man, "the true God would never allow his truth to be dishonored." Along with such passing allusions as suggest the conventional ideas about Jews as usurers, at times connected with the Lombards, we see Langland hold up their kindness to each other as a measure against which he can charge his fellow Christians with lack of charity:

> Allas! that a Cristene creature · shal be unkynde till an other,
> Sitthen Iuwes that we Iugge · Iudas felawes,
> Ayther of hem helpeth other · of that that hym nedeth.

And then the poet speaks of Jews as our teachers, our "loresmen":

> Whi nel we Christene · of Cristes good be as kynde
> As Iuwes, that ben owre lores-men? · shame to vs alle![11]

There was not only Langland but also the quiet current of mysticism and scriptural study that owed much to the rabbinical tradition. (Though this influence would seem to have been strongest in the thirteenth century, there is much evidence of its continuing through the fourteenth.) When we look at the theological work of the Victorine school, and against the evidence of Mannyng's *Handlyn Synne* read the pleadings of Langland (and on the Continent, of Merswin and others) for a more tolerant, a more loving, view of the Jews, and add to all this the work of the Premonstratensians—then the view I am suggesting as the implicit framework within which the Prioress and her Tale are fitted is, I think, not implausible.

A fourteenth-century Englishman such as Chaucer or Langland could scarcely have questioned the laws and social forces that had excluded the medieval Jew from Christian society. The time had not yet come to condemn anti-Semitism in the way Pius XI was to do: by reminding men that the Christian faith, and hence our civilization, were born with Abraham's loving sacrifice and that, in the spirit, Abraham is every Christian's father. But there is in Chaucer's treatment of the Prioress a clear-eyed recognition of the inhumanity of her Tale, its violation of the deepest sense of charity which fourteen centuries of Christianity had been laboring to develop, and its failure to carry the burden of charity which is enjoined on all Christians but especially on religious. The Prioress is not condemned, however; rather is the poem's objective view one of understanding pity of her: further than this all of Chaucer's compassion could not go.

But how great a thing it was in such a complex social and cultural environment for a poet to insist that anti-Semitism could be viewed through the recognizable frame of such a woman as the Prioress, one who succumbed too easily to the worldly concern with things and manners, and whose charity was too much of this world.

Notes

[1] This analysis—by Carleton Brown in *Sources and Analogues of Chaucer's Canterbury Tales*, ed. W. F. Bryan and Germaine Dempster (Chicago: University of Chicago Press, 1941), pp. 447–485, and by Margaret H. Statler, "The Analogues of Chaucer's Prioress' Tale: The Relation of Group C to Group A," *Publications of the Modern Language Association*, LXV (1950), 896–910—is painstaking and necessary scholarship: I do not mean to condemn it in itself. From his study of the analogues, Carleton Brown attributes the detail of making the child a seven-year-old to Chaucer: aside from obvious significations of the age, it is well worth noting how heavily Chaucer stresses the diminutive throughout the Prioress's Tale; this is consonant with the Prioress's excessive and false charity over her "little dogs."

[2] Muriel Bowden, in her *Commentary on the General Prologue to the Canterbury Tales* (New York: Macmillan, 1948), p. 93.

[3] John Livingston Lowes, "Simple and Coy," *Anglia Zeitschrift für Englische Philologie*, XXXIII (1910), pp. 440–451; cf. his *Convention and Revolt in Poetry* (Boston: Houghton Mifflin, 1919), pp. 60–65.

[4] *Convention and Revolt in Poetry*, p. 66.

[5] See Eileen Power, *Mediaeval English Nunneries* (Cambridge: Cambridge University Press, 1922) pp. 305–309, and Note E ("Convent Pets in Literature"); also her *Medieval People*, pp. 90–91, 194. J. M. Manly, in his edition of the *Canterbury Tales* (New York: Henry Holt, 1928, p. 506), cites an order of 1345, quoted in William Dugdale's *Monasticon Anglicanum* (II, 619, no. xi): "Also we command that neither birds [perhaps falcons] nor dogs nor little birds be kept by any abbess or nun within the walls of the abbey or within the choir, especially while they should be engaged in divine services."

[6] Charles W. Dunn, *Chaucer Reader* (New York: Harcourt Brace, 1952), pp. 41–2.

[7] One of the earliest and most weighty papal condemnations of the blood accusation was addressed by Innocent IV to the Arch-

bishops and Bishops of Germany in 1247: "We have received a mournful complaint from the Jews of Germany, telling how some princes, both ecclesiastical and lay, together with other nobles and powerful persons in your cities and dioceses, devise evil plans against them and invent various pretexts in order to rob them unjustly of their goods, and gain possession thereof. This they do without stopping to consider prudently that it is from the archives of the Jews, so to speak, that the testimonies of the Christian faith came forth. Holy Scripture pronounces among other injunctions of the Law 'Thou shalt not kill', forbidding them when they celebrate the Passover even to touch any dead body. Nevertheless, they are falsely accused that, in that same solemnity, they make communion with the heart of a slain child. This is alleged to be enjoined by the Law, whereas in fact such an act is manifestly contrary to it. Moreover, if the body of a dead man is by chance found anywhere, they maliciously ascribe the cause of death to the action of the Jews. On this, and many other fictitious pretexts, they rage against the Jews and despoil them of their possessions, against God and Justice and the privileges mercifully granted to them by the Holy See; notwithstanding that they have never been tried for these crimes and have never confessed them and have never been convicted of them. By starvation, imprisonment and many heavy persecutions and oppressions they harass them, inflicting upon them divers kinds of punishment, and condemning large numbers to a most shameful death. Hence the Jews, who are under the power of the aforesaid nobles, lords and princes, are in a worse condition than were their fathers in Egypt, and are compelled to go into exile from localities where they and their ancestors have dwelt from time immemorial." Quoted by Cecil Roth, *The Ritual Murder Libel and the Jew* (London: Woburn Press, n.d.), pp. 97–98.

⁸ For Point 1, see *ibid.*, pp. 21–22. Points 2, 3 and 4 are quoted from *The Jew in the Medieval World*, ed. by J. R. Marcus, pp. 151–4. Regarding such a decree there is always the twofold question of how effective it is and how generally known. The bull quoted could not have been very widely effective, and it may well be that the Prioress had not seen this bull; it was not her office to. Nor is it likely that Chaucer's listening audience would have had firsthand experience with a document like this, for it was the direct concern of ecclesiastical chanceries. But the view expressed was doubtless known.

⁹ Cf. H. M. Colvin, in *The White Canons in England* (Oxford: Clarendon Press, 1951), pp. 165–6.

¹⁰ *Handling Synne*, Early English Text Society, 119 (1901), p. 298.

¹¹ *The Vision of William concerning Piers the Plowman* . . . edited W. W. Skeat (Oxford: Clarendon Press, 1886), I, 270. (B IX. 83–7).

14

The *Canon's Yeoman's Tale*

CHARLES MUSCATINE

THE ABRUPTNESS of the Canon's arrival among the pil-
grims, his equally abrupt flight, and the breathless, vehement
urgency of his Yeoman's subsequent discourse, have led most
critics from the poem to the facts that may have inspired
it. Tyrwhitt's conjecture—"that some sudden resentment had
determined Chaucer to interrupt the regular course of his
work, in order to insert a Satire against the Alchemists"—has
not been generally accepted. But scholarship still tends to
class the poem as a "current event." If not autobiographical,
it is journalistic, and something like biographical interest still
lurks in the much-debated question of Chaucer's attitude to-
ward alchemy. Was Chaucer a credulous, medieval dupe, or
an initiate into alchemical mysteries, or was he modern, a
skeptic? Speculation on questions such as this has robbed the
poem of the critical interest due it. The story is widely re-
garded as a good one, a good piece of realism, and not much
more. Let it be admitted that there is hardly another poem
of Chaucer's that seems so compact of fact, so little ulterior

Reprinted, by permission of author and publisher, from *Chaucer
and the French Tradition* (Berkeley: University of California Press,
1957), pp. 214–21. Copyright, 1957, by the Regents of the Uni-
versity of California.

in its design. Its surface argument is determinedly simple; it is a warning against alchemy. Its materials are so solid as to seem to defy further "interpretation." If there is a philosophical pattern to the *Canterbury Tales,* this seems to be its one unassimilable lump. I am emboldened to present the following rather hypothetical reading partly by the conviction that journalism is un-Chaucerian, partly by the virtual absence of previous literary criticism, and partly by the enigmatic nature of the poem itself. The reader will have to judge how much to allow in it for the peculiar preoccupations of our own age, and how much for my own conviction, already expressed in these pages, that Chaucer's realism is ultimately symbolic.

The poem divides itself into three parts which do not quite coincide with the formal, textual divisions. The first part (the *Prologue* and *prima pars* of the text, i.e., verses 554–971) describes the arrival of the Canon and Yeoman, the Canon's flight, and the Yeoman's revelation of their alchemical activities. Its style is dramatic: all of the *prima pars* is, indeed, dramatic monologue. The second part (*pars secunda* to verse 1387) is the Yeoman's tale proper, of another swindling canon-alchemist. The narrative here, though it contains some rhetorical formalism, is so highly dramatized with interjections and asides that it harmonizes closely with the tone of the first part. In the third part (1388–1481) the stance of the narrator changes. Whereas before he has been represented as unlearned, and his very proverbs are accredited to hearsay, now his voice carries its own authority. He cites Arnaldus de Villanova and the rather mysterious "Senior" without embarrassment, and ends with a sober, philosophical statement that deepens the context of the entire poem. We must recognize here—what we have seen in the *Roman de la Rose,* in the *Troilus,* and elsewhere—the convention of philosophical amplification. The characterization of the speaker is suspended in favor of comment on the wider meaning of his position:

> Thanne conclude I thus, sith that God of hevene   [1472]
> Ne wil nat that the philosophres nevene
> How that a man shal come unto this stoon,

I rede, as for the beste, lete it goon.
For whoso maketh God his adversarie,
As for to werken any thyng in contrarie
Of his wil, certes, never shal he thryve,
Thogh that he multiplie terme of his lyve.
And there a poynt; for ended is my tale.

This philosophical postscript expresses the ruling attitude
toward alchemy in the poem. In the light of it, the poem
expresses neither credulity nor skepticism, but rather a dis-
tinction between false alchemy and true, between men's
alchemy and God's. The body of the poem, the first two
parts, is an exposure of the alchemy without God, of faith
in earth. Its skepticism is that of the believer, not of the
scientist, who sees in technology another secular religion, as
seductive in its way as the religion of Love:

This sotted preest, who was gladder than he?   [1341]
Was nevere brid gladder agayn the day,
Ne nyghtyngale, in the sesoun of May,
Was nevere noon that luste bet to synge;
Ne lady lustier in carolynge,
Or for to speke of love and wommanhede,
Ne knyght in armes to doon an hardy dede,
To stonden in grace of his lady deere,
Than hadde this preest this soory craft to leere.

The poem's dualism of attitude is conventional. It corresponds
to the division of the science between the charlatans and
puffers on the one hand, and the philosophers and mystics
on the other. Medieval alchemical texts from about the early
thirteenth century discuss pro and con the doubts already
raised concerning the possibility of transmutation, and the
Christian alchemical tradition is full of both practical "skep-
ticism" and the thoroughly orthodox but hardly credulous
notion that to God all things are possible.[1]

As with other philosophical poems of Chaucer, we are
more interested in the poetry than in the conclusion. The
poetry everywhere evokes a profound sense of the futility,
the cursedness, of a soulless striving with matter. The trickery
of alchemical swindlers, illustrated by the "tale" proper,
stands also for the nature of the science itself. The chantry
priest is swindled by the alchemist in the second part just
as the alchemist is swindled by the science in the first. That

the victim is a priest and the alchemists also canons may be
owing to current events, for all we know. But the poetic
effect is to suggest that their activity is a deep apostasy, a
treason, a going over to the devil himself. They are Judases
(1003). The falseness of mere deceit is not enough to account
for the Yeoman's passionate insistence on "this chanons
cursednesse," and the ubiquity of "the foule feend" in the
Yeoman's discourse. The following rhetorical invocation to an
undistinguished victim can be anticipated only by our seeing
something infernal in "this chanoun,"

>   roote of al trecherie,   [1069]
> That everemoore delit hath and gladnesse—
> Swiche feendly thoghtes in his herte impresse—
> How Cristes peple he may to meschief brynge.
> God kepe us from his false dissymulynge!
> Noght wiste this preest with whom that he delte,
> Ne of his harm comynge he no thyng felte.
> O sely preest! o sely innocent!
> With coveitise anon thou shalt be blent!
> O gracelees, ful blynd is thy conceite,
> No thyng ne artow war of the deceite
> Which that this fox yshapen hath to thee!
> His wily wrenches thou ne mayst nat flee.

Religious overtones are suggested equally by the context.
The poem follows the *Second Nun's Tale*. There is perhaps
something more than coincidence in the contrast between
St. Cecilia, unharmed in her bath of flames, conquering fire
through faith, and the blackened, sweating believers in earth,
whose fire blows up in their faces. Cecilia, in her retort to
the pagan prefect, curiously anticipates the Yeoman's teach-
ing:

> "Ther lakketh no thyng to thyne outter eyen   [2NT 498]
> That thou n'art blynd, for thyng that we seen alle
> That it is stoon, that men may wel espyen,
> That ilke stoon a god thow wolt it calle.
> I rede thee, lat thyn hand upon it falle,
> And taste it wel, and stoon thou shalt it fynde,
> Syn that thou seest nat with thyne eyen blynde."

> Though ye prolle ay, ye shul it nevere fynde. [CYT 1412]
> Ye been as boold as is Bayard the blynde,
> That blondreth forth, and peril casteth noon.
> He is as boold to renne agayn a stoon

As for to goon bisides in the weye.
So faren ye that multiplie, I seye.
If that youre eyen kan nat seen aright,
Looke that youre mynde lakke noght his sight.
For though ye looken never so brode and stare,
Ye shul nothyng wynne on that chaffare.

The extremely naturalistic characterization of the Yeoman
serves the conception of alchemy as a blind materialism. He
is a simple, unlearned soul. His greatest gift is a dogged
sense of the world of matter. There is not the faintest glim-
mer of spirituality or mysticism about him. Screened through
this personality, everything is lost but the world of rocks
and stones. Thus his idiom is ruggedly dramatic. His nar-
rative can be trusted to describe the slightest motions in the
physical world:

But taketh heede, now, sires, for Goddes love!   [1176]
He took his cole of which I spak above,
And in his hand he baar it pryvely.
And whiles the preest couched bisily
The coles, as I tolde yow er this,
This chanoun seyde, "Freend, ye doon amys.
This is nat couched as it oghte be;
But soone I shal amenden it," quod he.
"Now lat me medle therwith but a while,
For of yow have I pitee, by Seint Gile!
Ye been right hoot; I se wel how ye swete.
Have heere a clooth, and wipe away the wete."
And whiles that the preest wiped his face,
This chanoun took his cole—with harde grace!—
And leyde it above upon the myddeward
Of the crosselet, and blew wel afterward,
Til that the coles gonne faste brenne.
"Now yeve us drynke," quod the chanoun thenne;
"As swithe al shal be wel, I undertake.
Sitte we doun, and lat us myrie make."
And whan that this chanounes bechen cole
Was brent, al the lemaille out of the hole
Into the crosselet fil anon adoun;
And so it moste nedes, by resoun,
Syn it so evene aboven it couched was.
But therof wiste the preest nothyng, alas!
He demed alle the coles yliche good;
For of that sleighte he nothyng understood.

His commentary, on the other hand, is dully repetitive; it is
analysis frustrated and strangled by a limited vision. Blear-

eyed, he has come to see only, as his modern counterpart
might put it, that alchemy "don't work":

> "We blondren ever and pouren in the fir,   [670]
> And for al that we faille of oure desir,
> For evere we lakken oure conclusion."
>
> For alle oure sleightes we kan nat conclude.   [773]
>
> Noght helpeth us, oure labour is in veyn.   [777]
>
> For lost is al oure labour and travaille.   [781]
>
> Al is in veyn, and pardel muchel moore.   [843]
>
> This is to seyn, they faillen bothe two.   [851]
>
> The pot tobreketh, and farewel, al is gol   [907]
>
>   be it hoot or coold, I dar seye it,   [956]
> That we concluden everemoore amys.

Beneath the Yeoman's unconscious simplicity, this insistent
chorus voices a frustration beyond that of mere mechanical
failure. It registers a failure of vision. It says that dealing
with matter as matter has no end, that is, no teleology.
Medieval philosophical alchemy was nourished on hylozoism,
on the feeling that matter was instinct with life. The Yeo-
man's recitation, however, evokes an opposite feeling, of
matter spiritless and contingent, of that primordial impurity,
"corrupt," "floterynge," from which only God can raise man.
To expect an end, a "conclusioun," to the cooking of this
hopeless stuff is the real irony of the alchemist's failure.

The technical imagery of the poem is very powerful in
evoking the feeling of matter as matter. The Yeoman's recita-
tion is dramatically motivated; now that the Canon is gone
he will tell all that he can. The ensuing list of materials and
equipment answers to a tradition of inventory in the alchemi-
cal writings themselves, but, given certain changes of tone,
it answers also to the literary convention of the *parade*, the
list of wares or drugs vaunted in the *Herberie* and in the
mercator scenes of the passion plays. Chaucer read alchemy
for the matter. The manner belongs more to the tradition of
Rutebeuf. Nowhere else in Chaucer is there such a solid, un-
spiritual mass of "realism," and nowhere is its artistic func-
tion less to be doubted:

> Ther is also ful many another thyng   [784]
> That is unto oure craft apertenyng.

Though I by ordre hem nat reherce kan,
By cause that I am a lewed man,
Yet wol I telle hem as they come to mynde,
Thogh I ne kan nat sette hem in hir kynde:
As boole armonyak, verdegrees, boras,
And sondry vessels maad of erthe and glas,
Oure urynales and oure descensories,
Violes, crosletz, and sublymatories,
Cucurbites and alambikes eek,
And othere swiche, deere ynough a leek.
Nat nedeth it for to reherce hem alle,—
Watres rubifiyng, and boles galle,
Arsenyk, sal armonyak, and brymstoon;
And herbes koude I telle eek many oon,
As egremoyne, valerian, and lunarie,
And othere swiche, if that me liste tarie;
Oure lampes brennyng bothe nyght and day,
To brynge aboute oure purpos, if we may;
Oure fourneys eek of calcinacioun,
And of watres albificacioun;
Unslekked lym, chalk, and gleyre of an ey,
Poudres diverse, asshes, donge, pisse, and cley,
Cered pokkets, sal peter, vitriole,
And diverse fires maad of wode and cole;
Sal tartre, alkaly, and sal preparat,
And combust materes and coagulat;
Cley maad with hors or mannes heer, and oille
Of tartre, alum glas, berme, wort, and argoille,
Resalgar, and othre masteres enbibyng,
And eek of oure materes encorporyng,
And of oure silver citrinacioun,
Oure cementyng and fermentacioun,
Oure yngottes, testes, and many mo.

The *Wife of Bath's Prologue*, as we have seen, has a notable collection of concrete, material images. But compared to this, it is spiritual and airy. If art and not journalism is at work in the *Canon's Yeoman's Tale*, this chaos of matter, refuse, excrement, represents the universe of technology.

In the context of this kind of interpretation, the headlong entry of the Canon and Yeoman cannot be read as Chaucer's afterthought. It seems thoroughly, artistically, premeditated. These men are not introduced with the other pilgrims, because they are not within Christian society. They do not go on pilgrimages; they are not headed for Canterbury, or rather, for the City of God that it represents. Their entry is dramatically motivated, to be sure. They see the pilgrims leave town and must therefore gallop to catch up. But Chaucer's emphasis on the haste and the hot sweat, like the Yeoman's stridency of tone, seems to call for a more-than-dramatic explanation. It is very well for the sympathetic Chaucerian Narrator to find an earthy zest in it all: "But it was joye for to seen hym swete!" (579).We must ask, nevertheless, whether the hot gallop and the high temperature are not at the same time precisely characteristic of the Canon's way of life, the way of technology. The Canon doubtless intends to swindle the pilgrims, but this is only one stage in the greater pursuit:

> "To muchel folk we doon illusioun,   [673]
> And borwe gold, be it a pound or two,
> Or ten, or twelve, or manye sommes mo,
> And make hem wenen, at the leeste weye,
> That of a pound we koude make tweye.
> Yet is it fals, but ay we han good hope
> It for to doon, and after it we grope.
> *But that science is so fer us biforn,*
> *We mowen nat, although we hadden it sworn,*
> *It overtake, it slit awey so faste."*

The Canon is described as carrying peculiarly little baggage. Dramatically, this is explainable by the traditional poverty of alchemists. Poetically, it says what the Yeoman in a brief moment of reflection says later on:

> I warne you wel, it is to seken evere.   [874]
> That futur temps hath maad men to dissevere,
> In trust thereof, from al that evere they hadde.

The pathetic gravity of these lines suggests that the "al that evere they hadde" is more than money and clothing and a fresh complexion. It is also, perhaps, the spiritual tradition that a community of men takes with it along the way, and that gives purpose and direction to the journey. Marie Hamilton remarks that the Canon was apostate, or else "guilty of that *instabilitas loci* forbidden to monastics."[2] Surely his flight, while it is dramatically motivated by "verray sorwe and shame" (702), poetically symbolizes an apostasy from the human congregation, an instability of place in life. Like the canon of the Yeoman's story, he abides nowhere.

Chaucer could make fun of the complacent ignorance that despises knowledge. The carpenter of the *Miller's Tale* is a victim of this vice:

"I thoghte ay wel how that it sholde be! [3453]
Men sholde nat knowe of Goddes pryvetee.
Ye, blessed be alwey a lewd man
That noght but oonly his bileve kan!"

The *Canon's Yeoman's Tale* deals with an ignorance that is less funny: that complacent faith in science that despises God. Dante's Hell has its place for those who "wished to see too far ahead."[3] Chaucer is no less conservative. In attitude the poem is as medieval as the *Knight's Tale*. The dogged refusal to admit the intractability of matter, one of the virtues to which we owe so much of our civilization, is here represented by a group of sooty figures sifting and picking for salvage in a pile of refuse. He who cheers them on is a fool. In the light of later history, indeed, the poem is reactionary. This kind of alchemy gave us chemistry. Yet there is still time to judge whether the poem has not a germ of wry prophecy in it, whether already in the fourteenth century an acute consciousness could not have caught the future of technology in a single line:

The pot tobreketh, and farewel, al is go!

Notes

[1] See M. Berthelot, *La Chimie au moyen âge,* I (Paris, 1893), pp. 238–239, 281, 344–345; Arthur John Hopkins, *Alchemy Child of Greek Philosophy* (New York, 1934), pp. 213–215; and the illustrative materials printed by John Webster Spargo in *Sources and Analogues,* pp. 691–698.
[2] "The Clerical Status of Chaucer's Alchemist," *Speculum,* XVI (1941), 107.
[3] *Inferno* XX, 38.

15

Chaucer and the Rhetoricians

JOHN MATTHEWS MANLY

IN THAT charming Canterbury Tale which reveals the family life of Chauntecleer the cock and his favourite wife, Dame Pertelote, there is a passage to which I invite your attention. The pride and confidence of Chauntecleer have just been betrayed by the subtle flattery of Dan Russell the fox, and Chauntecleer, having closed his eyes the better to imitate the crowning of his revered father, has been seized by the throat and is being hurried away to destruction on the fox's back. It is the most tragic moment of the delightful mock-heroic tale and calls for all the resources of the most accomplished rhetoric. In accordance with the best theory and practice of the art, the narrator of the tale bursts forth into a series of apostrophes, first to Destiny, then to Venus, upon whose day, Friday, the tragic event occurred, and finally, climactically, to a person whose name means nothing to the uninstructed modern reader:

> O Gaufred, deere maister soverayn,
> That, whan thy worthy king Richard was slayn
> With shot, compleynedest his deeth so soore,
> Why ne hadde I now thy sentence and thy loore

Warton Lecture on English Poetry. Reprinted, by permission, from *The Proceedings of the British Academy*, XII (1926), 95–113.

The Friday for to chide, as diden ye?
Than wolde I shewe you how that I coude pleyne
For Chauntecleeres drede and for his peyne.

The commentators tell us that the appeal and the allusion
are to Master Gaufred de Vinsauf—Galfridus Vinosalvensis—
and a section of his *Nova Poetria,* in which the death of
Richard Coeur de Lion, who received his fatal wound on a
Friday, is lamented with all the artifices of medieval rhetoric,
and the fateful Friday is reproached in terms which, though
highly ingenious, are distinctly ludicrous.

But the prosperity of a jest lies as much in the readiness
of the hearer as in the facetiousness of the jester. Why did
Chaucer expect his hearers to recognize the literary gem
alluded to, and to enjoy the allusion? Nearly two hundred
years had passed since King Richard was slain, and only a
few less since the Latin poet wrote his intentionally serious
but actually comic lamentation. And yet Chaucer assumed
that his audience would understand at once, without even
mention of the surname of this Master Gaufred. He could
not have alluded more trippingly to the best known among
his own contemporaries. And his confidence was justifiable.
Every educated man remembered Master Gaufred and some
perhaps knew by heart his famous lamentation, for the *Nova
Poetria* was one of the principal text-books on rhetoric and
was studied in the schools with a zeal devoted perhaps to
few modern school books.

That Chaucer's intention here was satirical admits of no
doubt. He felt and he made his readers feel the enormous
absurdity of Gaufred's rhetorical outburst. Are we to infer
that he regarded rhetorical theories in general only as objects
of ridicule and, like the author of Hudibras in a later age,
held that

> All a rhetorician's rules
> Teach nothing but to name his tools?

There are a score of other passages in which he or the char-
acters through whom he speaks profess to care little and
know nothing about rhetoric. Says the Franklin:

> I lerned never rethoric certeyn;
> Thing that I speke, it mote be bare and pleyn.
> I sleep never on the Mount of Pernaso
> Ne lerned Marcus Tullius Scithero.
> Colours ne knowe I none, withouten drede,
> But swiche colours as growen in the mede,
> Or elles swiche as men dye or peynte.
> Colours of rethoryk been to me queynte.

In like manner the Host says contemptuously to the Clerk of Oxenford:

> Youre termes, youre colours, and youre figures,
> Keepe hem in stoor til so be ye endite
> Heigh style, as whan that men to kynges write.

With most writers, medieval or modern, such passages would be conclusive as to the writer's scorn of rhetoricians and rhetorical theory, but the interpretation of Geoffrey Chaucer is not so simple a matter. One is not always safe in taking his words as having only their plain and obvious meanings. When, for example, he denies the Summoner's view that the archdeacon's curse need not be dreaded by anyone who was willing to pay, and says:

> Of cursing oghte ech gilty man him drede,
> For curs wol slee, right as assoillyng saveth,

many scholars think he was speaking ironically and meant that neither curse nor absolution had any validity. And certainly the humorous citation by Chauntecleer and Pertelote of 'Daun Catoun', and 'the hooly doctour Augustyn, or Boece or the bishop Bradwardyn' does not imply any lack of respect for those eminent authorities. Moreover, in the passages adduced above from the Host and the Franklin, it is clear that we have the views of those two characters, not the views of Chaucer himself, for the Clerk responds to the admonition of the Host not only by telling a tale he had learned from that excellent rhetorician Francis Petrarch, but by delivering a panegyric on Petrarch's 'heigh style' and 'rethoryke sweete'; and the very terms of the Franklin's disclaimer of rhetorical skill are derived from that most rhetorical of Latin poets,

Persius, no doubt through the medium of some medieval treatise on rhetoric.

To any student of his technique, Chaucer's development reveals itself unmistakably, not as progress from crude, untrained native power to a style and method polished by fuller acquaintance with rhetorical precepts and more sophisticated models, but rather as a process of gradual release from the astonishingly artificial and sophisticated art with which he began and the gradual replacement of formal rhetorical devices by methods of composition based upon close observation of life and the exercise of the creative imagination. His growth in artistic methods and in artistic power—a growth unequalled so far as I am aware among medieval authors— seems inexplicable unless we admit that he had thought long and deeply upon the principles of composition, the technique of diction and phrasing, methods of narration, description, and characterization, and numberless other details of the writers' art. The astonishing advance from the thin prettinesses of the *Boke of the Duchesse* to the psychologic depth of *Troilus and Criseyde*, the swift tragic power of the *Pardoners' Tale*, the rollicking exuberance of the tales of the Miller and the Reeve, the matchless humour of the first half of the *Summoner's Tale*, and the incomparable portraiture of the *Prologue* is inconceivable as mere vegetative growth. The great debt of Chaucer to the Italians—and I suspect that his debt to Dante was as great as that to either Petrarch or Boccaccio—was perhaps not so much because they furnished new materials and new models for imitation, as because they stimulated his powers of reflection by forms and ideals of art different from those with which he was familiar.

Without arguing this point, I shall merely suggest certain evidences of his fondness for experimentation. Unfortunately —or perhaps fortunately—most of his early writings have perished. The balades, roundels, virelayes, and other hymns to the god of Love testified to in *The Legend of Goode Women* are gone, but two of the extant minor poems are obviously experimental. The fragment entitled *A Compleynte to his Lady*, possibly written when he was in search of a suitable form for narrative verse, preserves an experiment in *terza rima,* the measure of Dante's great poem. The much discussed and little understood *Anelida and the False Arcite* seems also purely an experiment in versification and is of interest, chiefly if not solely, because the formal Complaint is an even more remarkable *tour de force* in rhyming than the famous translations from Sir Otes de Granson.

In investigating the sources of Chaucer's notions of literature and his conceptions of style, scholars have hitherto discussed only the writings of other authors which may have served as models for imitation. The possibility of his acquaintance with formal rhetorical theory and the precepts of rhetoricians has not been considered, notwithstanding the hint that might have been derived from the allusion to Gaufred de Vinsauf and the other passages of rhetoric scattered through his works. Even *a priori* there would seem to be a high probability that Chaucer was familiar with the rhetorical theories of his time, that he had studied the text-books and carefully weighed the doctrines. Whatever modern scholars may have said of the errors in his references and the shallowness of his classical learning—and there are few of his critics whose errors are less numerous than his—he was a man of scholarly tastes and of considerable erudition. His works bear witness to no small reading in astronomy, and astrology, in alchemy, in medicine, and in philosophy and theology, as well as in classical authors current in his day. The ancient tradition that he was educated, in part at any rate, in the law school of the Inner Temple has recently been shown to be possible, if not highly probable. The education given by the inns of court seems to have been remarkably liberal. What more likely than that the formal study of rhetoric not only was included in his academic curriculum, as one of the Seven Arts, but also occupied much of his thought and reflection in maturer years?

What, then, was medieval rhetoric? Who were its principal authorities in Chaucer's time? And what use did Chaucer make of methods and doctrines unmistakably due to the rhetoricians?

To the first two questions satisfactory answers can be

readily given. Professor Edmond Faral has recently printed the chief rhetorical texts of the thirteenth and fourteenth centuries, with illuminating biographical and bibliographical notes and excellent summaries of the doctrine. To answer the third question fully would require a volume, but a provisional view of the matter can be obtained from a rapid survey of Chaucer's best-known work.

Fortunately for our inquiry, the Middle Ages knew only one rhetorical system and drew its precepts from few and well-known sources. Morever, there was little development of the doctrines or variety in the mode of presentation. The principal sources of the doctrines were three: the two books of Cicero entitled *De Inventione,* the four books entitled *De Rhetorica, ad Herennium* and the Epistle of Horace to Piso. Treatises based upon these were not uncommon in the earlier Middle Ages, but after the beginning of the thirteenth century the practical spirit of the time tended in the universities to substitute instruction in letter writing and the *artes dictaminis* for more theoretical and supposedly less useful study of general rhetorical principles. It is perhaps for this reason that the treatises of Matthieu de Vendôme and Gaufred de Vinsauf, written early in the thirteenth century, retained their vogue in the time of Chaucer. These treatises are the *Ars Versificandi* of Matthieu, and the *Documentum de Arte Versificandi* and the *Nova Poetria* of Gaufred. The first two are prose treatises, carefully defining and discussing all processes and terms and illustrating them by examples, in part drawn from earlier writers, such as Virgil, Horace, Ovid, Statius, and Sidonius, and in part composed by the rhetorician himself, either to show his skill or to pay off a grudge. For example, Matthieu is tireless in the composition of verses attacking the red-haired rival whom he calls Rufus; Gaufred, illustrating the beauties of *circumlocutio,* says it is of special value when we wish to praise or diffame a person: thus if any one were speaking of William de Guines, the disreputable butler of the king, he might, instead of his name, more elegantly use this circumlocation, *Regis ille pincerna, pudor et opprobrium, pincernarum faex, et inquinamentum domus regiae.*

The doctrine taught by these two authorities, the common medieval doctrine, falls logically and naturally into three main divisions or heads: (1) arrangement or organization; (2) amplification and abbreviation; (3) style and its ornaments.

Of arrangement they had little to say, and that little was purely formal and of small value. They treated mainly of methods of beginning and ending, distinguishing certain forms as natural and others as artificial. Artificial beginnings consisted either of those which plunge *in medias res* or set forth a final situation before narrating the events that led up to and produced it, or of those in which a *sententia* (that is, a generalization or a proverb) is elaborated as an introduction, or an *exemplum* (that is, a similar case) is briefly handled for the same purpose. It will be readily recognized that all these varieties of beginning are familiar use at the present day; and, curiously enough, in recent years writers for the popular magazines have shown a special fondness for beginning with an elaborately developed *sententia*.

We have not time today for a detailed examination of Chaucer's methods of beginning, but this is hardly necessary. The moment one undertakes a survey of his poetry in the light of rehtorical theory, one is struck by the elaborate artifice of its beginnings and the closeness of their agreement with rhetorical formulae. This artificiality has long been recognized but has been mistakenly ascribed to the influence of the poems upon which he drew for his materials. His French sources, however, are hardly responsible for these elaborate beginnings: they furnish only the raw materials which Chaucer puts together in accordance with the instructions of his masters in rhetoric. The apparent simplicity with which the *Boke of the Duchesse* begins disappears under examination: the reader is led through several long and tortuous corridors—totaling one-third of the poem—before he arrives at the real subject, which in turn is developed with amazing artificiality. The long failure of the mourning knight to make clear the nature of his loss may be regarded as an expanded form of the rhetorical figure called *occupatio*.

The *Parlement of Foules* admirably illustrates the method of beginning with a *sententia:*

The lyf so short, the craft so long to lerne

This is expanded into two seven-line stanzas. Then comes, not the narrative itself, but a preliminary narrative, interspersed with various rhetorical devices, including generalizations, an apostrophe, and an outline of Cicero's *Somnium Scipionis,* in all 119 lines, before the story proper begins.

This method is even more elaborately developed in the *Hous of Fame.* In fact the poet is within twenty lines of the end of Book I before he begins to tell his story. There are sixty-five lines on dreams, sixty-five more of invocation, and more than 350 telling in outline the entirely unnecessary story of Dido and Aeneas.

Even when the narrative begins in a natural manner, as in *Anelida and Arcite,* the poem is given an artificial character by prefixing an invocation or by some other rhetorical device. The beginning of the *Legend of Goode Women* combines the methods of *sententia* and *exemplum:* our belief in the joys and pains of heaven and hell, says the poet, is based, not upon experience, but upon the acceptance of the sayings of 'these olde wise'; in like manner we must accept the testimony of books—those treasuries of wisdom—about the existence of good women, though we have never known them. A few of the separate legends begin inartificially, but it was not until late in his career that Chaucer developed the method of beginning used with such masterly skill in the tales of *Miller, Reeve, Summoner,* and *Pardoner.*

Methods of ending are treated by the rhetoricians even more summarily than beginnings, the preferred forms being the employment of a proverb or general idea, an *exemplum,* or a brief summary. Chaucer is fond of some sort of explicit application of his stories. In the *Reeve's Tale* this takes the form of a proverb:

And therefore this proverbe is seyd ful sooth
Him thar nat wene wel that yvele dooth:
'A gylour shal hymself bigyled be.'

And the *Manciple's Tale* ends in a stream of proverbs and proverbial sayings. But the more common form of application is a generalization or an exclamatory comment. Very common also is the ending summarizing the situation at the end of the tale. On the other hand, notwithstanding Chaucer's fondness for *exempla*, the *exemplum*-ending is very rare; perhaps the only instance, and that a doubtful one, is in the *Friar's Tale*:

> Herketh this word, beth war, as in this cas:
> 'The leoun sit in his awayt alway
> To sle the innocent, if that he may.'

Peculiar to Chaucer are the references to other writers for further information—as in several of the legends—and the triple *demande d'amours* with which the *Franklin's Tale* ends.

The technical means of passing from the beginning to the body of the work—*prosecutio,* as it is called— are treated with much formality by Gaufred, though he remarks with great good sense that the prime requisite is to get on with the subject: *In ipsa continuatione, primum est continuare.*

In Chaucer, after a rhetorical beginning, the transition to the narrative itself is usually clearly and formally indicated; so, for example, in *Troilus and Criseyde:*

> For now wol I gon streight to my matere.

The amount of attention devoted by the rhetoricians to the second main division, that of amplification, is to the modern reader surprising, but it results quite naturally from the purely mechanical character of the art of rhetoric as conceived by them. To them the problems of composition were not problems of the creative imagination but problems of 'fine writing'—*l'art de bien dire*. They had no conception of psychological processes or laws. The questions they raised were not questions of methods by which the writer might most perfectly develop his conception or of the means by which he might convey it to his audience. The elaborate system of technical devices was discussed only with reference to the form and structure of each device, never with reference to its emotional or aesthetic effects. As the rhetoricians conceived the matter, if a writer had something new to say, rhetoric was unnecessary; the novelty of the material relieved him of any concern for its form. But alas! this situation seldom arose. Practically everything had already been said. All the tales had been told, all the songs had been sung, all the thoughts of the mind and feelings of the heart had been expressed. The modern writer, they held, could only tell a thrice-told tale, only echo familiar sentiments. His whole task was one of finding means and methods of making the old seem new. He might therefore well begin his task of composition by choosing some familiar but attractive text—some tale, or poem, or oration, or treatise—or by making a patchwork of pieces selected from many sources. His problem would be that of renewing the expression and especially of making it more beautiful—*ornatior* is the common term.

Let no one scoff at this method as incapable of producing interesting and attractive writing. It has been practised very commonly by writers in all lands and epochs. It is recommended and taught in a widely used series of French text-books. It is the method recently revealed as pursued by that most charming of stylists, Anatole France, and is perhaps the only method by which he or Laurence Sterne could have produced such effects as they achieved.

Medieval rhetoricians assume that the writer, having chosen his subject, will find his material either too great or too small for his purpose. His problem will almost necessarily be one of amplification or abbreviation. The methods of amplifying and abbreviating are derived from the technique of style. They are therefore dealt with in their proper places when style and its ornaments are under discussion, but for the sake of clearness they are also expounded elaborately with special reference to their uses and values as means of amplification and abbreviation.

The principal means of amplification are six—some writers say eight:

Description, though perhaps not the most important, may be named first, as receiving fullest attention from both Matthieu de Vendôme and Gaufred de Vinsauf. Eleborate patterns and formulas are given for describing persons, places, things, and seasons. If the description applies to externals, the features to be described are enumerated and the order in which they are to be taken up is strictly specified; if it concerns a character, the characteristics to be mentioned are listed, and those appropriate to each sex, age, social status, employment, temperament, and career are set forth in detail. Specimens are given to illustrate the doctrines. These descriptions are not like those in Chaucer's later work, determined by the requirements of the situation in which they occur. Their use is purely conventional, for the purpose of amplifying the material, and their construction is purely mechanical. They are merely opportunities for the writer to display his rhetorical training. It is very enlightening to compare Chaucer's later descriptions—such, for example, as those of Alysoun and Absalon in the *Miller's Tale*—with the early ones; for example, with that of the Duchess Blanche, which, with the exception of one or two possibly realistic touches, is nothing more than a free paraphrase of lines 563–597 of the *Nova Poetria*, composed by Gaufred de Vinsauf as a model for the description of a beautiful woman. The features described in the two passages are the same, they are taken in the same order, and the same praise is given to each. The resemblance is still further heightened by the fact that, like Chaucer, Gaufred declines to guess at the beauties hidden by the robe—a trait hitherto regarded as characteristically Chaucerian.

There seems little doubt, indeed, that Chaucer's character sketches, widely as they later depart from the models offered by the rhetoricians, had their origins in them. An American scholar has recently attempted to show that Chaucer derived them from the treatises on Vices and Virtues, with their descriptions of character types. The possibility of an influence from this source I will neither deny nor discuss, but the specimen sketches given by the rhetoricians seem entirely sufficient to account for Chaucer's interest in this type of description.

The next most important device was digression, of which two subdivisions were recognized: first, digression to another part of the same subject, anticipating a scene or an event which in regular course would come later; second, digression to another subject. Digression may obviously be made in many ways and may include many special rhetorical devices. Prominent among the special forms are the development of a *sententia* and the introduction of *exempla*, illustrating the matter in hand. These two devices are of the utmost importance for Chaucer in particular and for the Middle Ages in general. The temper of the Middle Ages being distinctly practical and its literary valuations being determined, not by the criteria of art but by those of edification, *sententiae*, proverbs, and *exempla* were used with an ardour now difficult to appreciate. The use of *exempla* was strongly inculcated by the rhetoricians. Matthieu de Vendôme urges the writer to provide an abundance of *exempla*. With an amusing anticipation of the Wife of Bath's remark,

> I hold a mouses herte not worth a leek
> That hath but oon hole for to sterte to,

he declares: '*Etenim mus intercipitur facile muscipulae detrimentis, cui propinat refugium crepido singularis*'. But the precepts of the rhetoricians on this point had already been heeded by other writers, and in Chaucer's poems it is difficult to separate the direct influence of rhetorical theory from that of the practice of Guillaume de Machaut, whose first use of *exempla* was in his *Dit de l'Alerion* and whose later use of them gave them a vogue attested by the imitation of all his successors. Chaucer was unfortunately as much seduced by this astonishing fad as was any of the French imitators of Machaut. They are familiar from the series of twenty-one consecutive instances in the *Franklin's Tale* and the humorous accumulation of them in the controversy between the Cock and the Hen.

Third in importance among the devices of amplification may be placed apostrophe, with its rhetorical colours *exclamatio, conduplicatio, subiectio,* and *dubitatio.* It would be difficult to exaggerate the importance of apostrophe in medieval literature. Addresses to persons living or dead, present or absent, to personified abstractions, and even to inanimate objects are to be found in almost every composition with any pretensions to style from the eleventh century onward; and a special form, the *Complainte,* developed into one of the most widely cultivated types of literature. Chaucer's use of apostrophe is so frequent that no examples need be cited. Almost every tale contains from one to a dozen examples of it. Among the colours, his favourites seem to be those known as *exclamatio*—simply a passionate outcry addressed to some person or thing present or absent—and *dubitatio,* that is, a feigned hesitation what to say, a rhetorical questioning as to which of two or more expressions is appropriate to the idea and situation. Like Wordsworth's—

> O Cuckoo, shall I call thee Bird
> Or but a wandering Voice?

Fourth in order may come *prosopopeia* or *effictio,* the device which represents as speaking persons absent or dead, animals, abstractions, or inanimate objects. Widely used for purposes of amplification, this figure often furnished forth the whole of a piece of literature. Examples are numerous. A charming one contemporary with Chaucer is the *débat* in which Froissart represents his dog and horse as discussing their master and the journeys which he compels them to make with him. Chaucer uses it briefly many times, and elaborately in the principal scene of the *Parlement of Foules.*

Less important than the foregoing are the devices of *periphrasis* or *circumlocutio,* and its closely related *expolitio.* *Circumlocutio* was highly regarded as one of the best means, both of amplifying discourse and of raising commonplace or low ideas to a high stylistic level. It is too familiar to require discussion, but Master Gaufred seems not to have distinguished clearly between a statement expanded for the mere sake of amplification and one which expresses some important detail or phase of an idea. For example, he calls the opening lines of Virgil's *Aeneid circumlocutio* and declares, 'This is nothing else than to say, I will describe Aeneas'. And, after quoting from Boethius three lines of the metre beginning,

> O qui perpetua mundum ratione gubernas,

adds,

Quod nihil aliud est quam, 'O Deus'.

These remarks and the similar ones by Matthieu de Vendôme
will doubtless recall Chaucer's sly comment in the *Franklin's
Tale* on his own rhetorical description of the end of the day:

> Til that the brighte sonne lost his hewe,
> For thorizonte hath reft the sonne his lyght,—
> This is as much to seye as it was nyght.

The colour *expolitio* includes the repetition of the same idea in
different words (one form of *interpretatio*) and also the
elaboration of an idea by adding the reasons or authorities,
pronouncing a generalization with or without reasons, dis-
cussing the contrary, introducing a similitude or an *exemplum*,
and drawing a conclusion. Although these two figures are of
minor importance, they nevertheless play a considerable part
in the writings of Chaucer, as of most other medieval authors.

Other devices for amplification existed, but I will spare you
even the enumeration of them.

Abbreviation is joined by the rhetoricians with amplifica-
tion, but is obviously of much less practical interest. The
medieval writer is, as a rule, not so much concerned to ab-
breviate as to amplify. Master Gaufred, however, instructs his
readers that in treating a well-worn subject the best means of
creating an appearance of novelty is to survey the whole sub-
ject and then run quickly over the parts that predecessors
have dwelt upon and dwell upon parts they have neglected.
The principal means of abbreviation recommended are certain
of the figures of words: asyndeton, reduction or predication,
and the like. Chaucer's favourite methods are two:

(1) The use of absolute constructions—perhaps the most
striking and beautiful example of this is the opening line of
the second book of the *Troilus:*

> Out of these blake wawes for to saile,
> O wind, o wind, the weder ginneth clere!

the second line furnishing an instance of the figure called
epizeusis.

(2) The figure called *occupatio,* that is, the refusal to
describe or narrate—a figure used with special frequency in
The Squire's Tale, as for example:

> But for to telle yow al hir beaute
> It lyth nat in my tongue, nyn my konnyng

and

> I wol not tellen of hir straunge sewes

or

> I wol nat taryen yow, for it is pryme

or

> Who koude tellen yow the forme of daunces
> So unkouth, and so fresshe countenaunces?
>
> No man but Launcelot, and he is deed.

Into the vast and tangled jungle of the medieval treatment
of Style and its Ornaments we cannot venture now. Its extent
may be inferred from the fact that, notwithstanding the in-
clusion of very long specimens of apostrophe, prosopopeia, and
description (328 lines in all) the portion of the *Nova Poetria*
devoted to the important subjects of 'Art in General,' 'Organi-
zation', and 'Amplification and Abbreviation' occupies only
674 lines, whereas that devoted to the 'Ornaments of Style'
occupies 1125. The tangle is suggested by the fact that there
are recognized, defined, and discussed thirty-five colours, or
figures of words, twenty figures of thought, and ten varieties
of tropes, with nine more sub-varieties. These figures fall into
two very distinct classes: first, those in which human emotion
and aesthetic feeling have always found utterance—metaphor,
simile, exclamation, rhetorical questions, and the like; and
second, a vast mass of highly artificial and ingenious patterns
of word and thought, such as using the same word at the end

of a line as at the beginning, heaped-up rhymes, and alliteration.

Like other writers in all ages, Chaucer makes extensive use of the first class of figures; of artificial patterns he makes only a limited use, and that solely in highly rhetorical passages, like the *Monk's Tale*, certain parts of the *Boke of the Duchesse*, and in the apostrophes, exclamations, and *sententiae* of other serious compositions. The humorous tales, for which the rhetoricians forbid the use of *colores*, are entirely free from special rhetorical devices, with the single and striking exception of the *Nun's Priest's Tale*, a mock-heroic composition so full of rhetoric and so amusingly parodying the style of the *Monk's Tale*, which immediately precedes it, as to invite the suggestion that the 'high style' and its parody were purposely juxtaposed. It is possible that Chaucer's desire to carry out this amusing contrast explains the otherwise puzzling changes of the Monk from the spectacular huntsman and hard rider of the *prologue* to the bookish pedant of the hundred lamentable tragedies who greets our astonished ears when he is called upon for a tale?

As no one ever pays any attention to statistics and percentages, they rest the mind. This may therefore be a fitting time to introduce a few. If we list the *Canterbury Tales* according to the percentages of the larger rhetorical devices which they contain, they form an interesting descending series, ranging from nearly 100 per cent to 0. Highest, as might be expected, stands the *Monk's Tale*, with nearly 100 per cent. of rhetoric. Next comes the *Manciple's Tale* with 61 per cent.; then the tales of the *Nun's Priest* and the *Wife of Bath* with 50 per cent. The tales of the *Pardoner* and the *Knight* have 40 and 35 per cent. respectively; while those of the *Man of Law*, the *Doctor*, the *Prioress*, the *Franklin*, the *Second Nun*, and the *Merchant* fall between 30 and 20 per cent. The half-told tale of the *Squire* stands alone with 16 per cent., and slightly below it comes the tales of the *Clerk* and the *Canon's Yeoman*, with 10 per cent. Quite in a class by themselves stand the tales of the *Reeve* and the *Shipman*, with about 5 per cent. of rhetoric, and those of the *Miller*, the *Friar*, and the

Summoner, in which the rhetorical devices do not occupy more than 1 per cent. of the text.

Although some of these percentages are just what we should expect from the character of the tales and their probable dates, some are rather surprising. It is natural that the *Monk's Tale* should head the list, for it is professedly a collection of tragedies. But that some of Chaucer's freest and most delightful work should contain twice as much rhetoric as some of his least inspired compositions is a puzzle that demands investigation.

Let us begin by examining one of the least known and least interesting of the tales, that of the *Manciple.* It is in fact so insignificant and so little read that I cannot even assume that all of you recall the plot. 'When Phebus lived here on earth, we are told, he had a fair young wife, whom he loved dearly, and a white crow, whom he had taught to speak. But the wife was unfaithful and took a lover. This was observed by the Crow, who upon Phebus's return home told him. Phebus in sorrow and anger slew his wife, and then, repenting of his deed and disbelieving the charge brought against her, plucked the white feathers from the bird and doomed all crows to be black.'

We may note in the first place that the tale is not particularly appropriate to the Manciple or indeed to any other of the pilgrims, and that no effort is made to adapt it to him. It consists of 258 lines, of which 41 are devoted to describing Phebus, his wife, and the crow, and 50 to telling the incidents of the story. The remaining 167 lines—61 per cent. of the tale—are patches of rhetoric. Even this high percentage is perhaps too low, for the 25 lines of description devoted to Phebus are so conventional, so much in accordance with rhetorical formulas, that they might fairly be added to our estimate of the percentage of rhetoric. No effort was made by the author to conceive any of his characters as living beings or to visualize the action of the tale. The action, to be sure, seems in itself unpromising as the basis of a masterpiece of the story-teller's art, but so, if we consider them closely, are the basic narratives of the *Nun's Priest's Tale* and the tales of the *Miller,* the *Reeve,* and the *Friar.* If Chaucer had been as well inspired when he wrote this tale as when he wrote his masterpieces, Phebus might have been as real to us as the Oxford Carpenter or the Miller of Trumpington, his wife as brilliant a bit of colour as the Carpenter's wife, and the Crow as interesting a bird as Chauntecleer or Pertelote. But he developed the tale, not imaginatively, but rhetorically. Instead of attempting to realize his characters psychologically and conceive their actions and words as elements of a dramatic situation, he padded the tale with rhetoric. Thus he thrust into it and around it 32 lines of *sententiae,* 36 of *exempla,* 18 of *exclamatio,* 14 of *sermocinatio,* 3 of technical transition, 17 of *demonstratio,* and 63 of *applicatio*—all external and mechanical additions, clever enough as mere writing, but entirely devoid of life. If the tale had been written as a school exercise, to illustrate the manner in which rhetorical padding could be introduced into a narrative framework, the process of composition could not have been more mechanical or the results more distressing.

But Chaucer was endowed with the temperament, not of the rhetorician, but of the artist; and in some way he arrived at the memorable discovery that the task of the artist is not to pad his tales with rhetoric, but to conceive all the events and characters in the forms and activities of life. For this he was well prepared by native endowment and by a habit of close observation which developed early and which redeems even his earliest poems from entire banality. Owing to the loss of so much of his prentice work and the uncertain chronology of what has been preserved, we cannot trace in detail the displacement of the older rhetorical by the new psychological methods. But certain lines in the *Hous of Fame* indicate that when he was writing that poem he at least had formed an idea of the new methods, even though he may long have continued in some respects under the dominance of the old. The lines in question are in the poems of the second and third books:

> O thought that wroot al that I mette,
> And in the tresorie it sheet
> Of my brayn, now shal men se
> If any vertu in thee be

and more specifically:

> And if, divyne Vertu, thou
> Wilt helpe me to shewe now
> That in myn hede y-marked is.

These passages, although the first is translated from Dante, seem to me to express Chaucer's growing conviction that narration and description, instead of being mere exercises in clever phrasing, depend upon the use of the visualizing imagination.

But in spite of this recognition of the true method, and in spite of his ability later in the *Nun's Priest's Tale* to parody the whole apparatus of medieval rhetoric, Chaucer did not free himself at once—and perhaps never entirely—of the idea that writing which pretended to seriousness and elevated thought was improved by the presence of apostrophes and *sententiae* and *exempla,* as he had been taught by the rhetoricians. Nor could it be expected that he should. The whole weight of the medieval conception of literature was against him—the conception, I mean, that literature, like history, is of value only in so far as it can be profitably applied to the conduct of human life, a conception which not only remained in full vigour through the Middle Ages and the period we are accustomed to call the Renaissance, but even now lies at the basis of much critical theory.

Chaucer's greatness arose from his growing recognition that for him at least the right way to amplify a story was not to expand it by rhetorical devices, but to conceive it in terms of the life which he had observed so closely, to imagine how each of the characters thought and felt, and to report how in this imaginative vision they looked and acted. And if he felt obligated, as apparently he still did, in writings of serious and lofty tone, to supply *sententiae,* proverbs, *exempla,* and other fruits of erudition, he came more and more to make only a dramatic use of these rhetorical elements, that is, to put them into the mouths of his *dramatis personae* and to use only such as might fittingly be uttered by them.

It is this dramatic use of rhetorical devices which we must learn to recognize in the later and more artistic poems, and which must be taken into account in our examination of the percentages of rhetoric in the separate tales of the Canterbury pilgrimage. The mere fact that the percentage in two such masterpieces of narrative art as the tales of the *Nun's Priest* and the *Wife of Bath* is nearly twice as great as in the less successful tales of the *Man of Law* and the *Doctor* would be very misleading, if taken without further investigation. But the difference in manner of introduction and use appears immediately and is of fundamental significance. In the tales of the *Doctor* and the *Man of Law* the rhetoric is prevailingly, indeed almost exclusively, used by the narrator; that is, it is not incorporated and used dramatically but stands apart from the tale. There is even a difference the *Doctor's Tale* and that of the *Man of Law* in manner of handling. In the *Man of Law's Tale* the narrative is, for the most part, broken into comparatively brief sections and the rhetoric of the narrator is freely interspersed in the forms of *apostrophe, exclamatio, collatio, sententiae* and *exempla*, with various digressions on astrology. In the *Doctor's Tale*, on the other hand, the narrative comes in a solid block of 172 lines, preceded by 109 lines, all but 39 of which are purely rhetorical utterances of the narrator, and followed by 10 lines of rhetorical application. But both stories are, as artistic compositions, pretty crude and show no fusion of rhetorical elements. In the tales of the *Nun's Priest* and the *Wife of Bath* the situation is very different. In the *Nun's Priest's Tale*, although the rhetoric is scattered through the narrative as in the *Man of the Law's Tale*, it is not the external comment of the narrator but the vitally dramatized utterance of speakers whose actions, and attitudes, and sentiments we accept as belonging to a world of poetic reality. In the *Wife of Bath's Tale* there are two main masses of rhetorical devices: one of them is the famous oration on 'gentilesse', poverty, and age uttered by the Fairy Wife to her humbled husband, the other is the long *exemplum* on woman's inability to keep a secret, uttered by the garrulous Wife of Bath herself. But in the latter instance no less than in the former the rhetoric is dramatic, is conformed to the character, and is motivated.

The tales of the *Prioress* and the *Second Nun* differ very

slightly in percentage of rhetorical devices or in the placing
of them. If we could isolate the tales—disconnect them from
their narrators and the circumstances of their telling—we
should probably agree that they show the same style of work-
manship and may belong to the same period, a comparatively
early one. But the difference between them in effect is very
great. Why is this? Apart from the mere difference in appeal
of the material of the two stories, is it not because in the one
tale Chaucer has failed to visualize or to make his readers
see the principal characters—Cecilia, Valerian, and Pope
Urban remain to him and to us mere names—whereas both
he and we have a vivid and charming picture of the little
choir boy as he goes singing to his death? Is it not also be-
cause through some freak of chance the Second Nun herself
is a mere name in the *Prologue* and by the little episode of
conversation with the Host the Prioress is endowed with last-
ing beauty and sympathetic appeal? Chaucer himself seems to
have felt this. When the prioress's tale is ended he tells us of
its profound effect upon the whole party including himself;
after the other tale he says, drily,

> When toold was al the lif of Seint Cecile
> Er we had ridden fully fyve mile,

we were overtaken by two men.

The tales of the *Franklin* and the *Merchant* differ only
slightly in percentage of rhetorical devices from those of the
Prioress and the *Second Nun,* but in the placing and handling
of these devices, as well as in other respects, they seem to
belong to a much later period of Chaucer's workmanship. The
dramatis personae are vividly conceived and the action is
clearly visualized. Both tales show, however, the persistence
of the rhetorical habit and training. In the *Merchant's Tale*
most of the rhetoric is introduced dramatically as forming the
speeches of January and his advisers, but there is a long un-
dramatic passage—inappropriate either to the Merchant or to
the clerical narrator for whom the tale appears to have been
originally composed. In the *Franklin's Tale* a fine story finely
told is nearly spoiled by one hundred lines of rhetorical

exempla. The fact that they are put into the mouth of Dorigen in her complaint against Fortune indicates that Chaucer was trying to motivate them dramatically. But what reader, modern or medieval, would not have been more powerfully and sympathetically affected if Chaucer, with the psychological insight displayed in *Troilus and Criseyde,* had caused his distressed and desperate heroine to express the real feelings appropriate to her character and situation?

It may be noted that the tales showing a low percentage of formal rhetorical devices are, with a single exception, humorous tales and all are tales which on other grounds are regarded as of late date. The exception is the *Clerk's Tale,* a pretty close translation from Petrarch. The small amount of rhetoric added by Chaucer in making this translation from Petrarch is in curious contrast to the large amount added in translating the *Man of Law's Tale* from Trivet. Can it be that his rivalry with Gower in the latter case was responsible for the rhetoric?

The absence of rhetorical devices from the humorous tales may be due in part to the specific declaration of the rhetoricians that rhetorical ornament of all sorts should be strictly excluded from such tales. But surely Chaucer's growing power of artistry, his vast observation of life, and his newly devised method of imaginative reconstruction of the scenes, characters, and events of his stories gave him such a wealth of significant detail that there was no need and no space for the older methods of amplification. *Sententiae* are reduced to single lines, mostly proverbs; *exempla* to passing allusions; apostrophes and exclamations to the briefest of utterances. For it is not only in the humorous tales that his advanced method is displayed. The most tragic of them, the *Pardoner's Tale* of the three roysterers who sought Death, is as vividly imagined as the tales of the *Miller* and the *Reeve,* and the long passages of rhetoric, placed between the opening twenty lines, which so wonderfully create background and atmosphere, and the narrative itself, are thoroughly explained and justified by their function as part of the Pardoner's sermon.

The survey we have made of Chaucer's work, hasty as it has necessarily been, has, I think, shown that he began his career, not merely as a disciple and imitator of a thoroughly artificial school of writing, but as a conscious exploiter of the formal rhetoric taught by the professional rhetoricians, and that it was only gradually and as the result of much thought and experiment that he replaced the conventional methods of rhetorical elaboration by those processes of imaginative construction which give his best work so high a rank in English literature. To treat his poems as if they all belonged to the same stage of artistic development and represented the same ideals of art is to repeat the error so long perpetrated by students of Shakespeare.

If today I have contributed in any measure to making more intelligible the nature of Chaucer's early work and the path traversed in achieving his freedom and his mastery of narrative and descriptive art, I shall feel that the result is in harmony with the aims and accomplishments of that first historian of our poetry, to honour whose memory this lectureship was established. I am very grateful for the opportunity which has been granted me of presenting this first sketch of an unwritten chapter in the development of one of England's greatest poets before an assemblage of England's most authoritative, and, I may add, most sympathetic students of literature.

16

Was Chaucer A Laodicean?

ROGER S. LOOMIS

In an essay on Chaucer and Wyclif, published in 1916, Tatlock remarks of the poet, 'He was not such stuff as martyrs are made of, but something of a Laodicean.' With this statement and with the substance of Tatlock's article as a whole I agree; no one nowadays would present the portly poet, pensioner of three orthodox but far from immaculate kings, composer of love allegories and racy fabliaux, as a zealot, a reformer, a devotee of causes. *Something* of the Laodicean there is about him, but was he wholly lukewarm, wholly neutral in the warfare of principles which went on in his day as it does in ours? Can it be said of him, as it was said of the Laodiceans, 'I know thy works that thou art neither cold nor hot'?

The question is a real once since some of the most eminent of Chaucer scholars and literary critics have expressed the conviction that the poet was wholly indifferent or noncommittal as to moral, social, and religious issues. The authority of Lounsbury lies behind the following statements: 'He looks

Reprinted, by permission of author and publisher, from *Essays and Studies in Honor of Carleton Brown* (New York: New York University Press, 1940), pp. 129–48. Copyright, 1940, by New York University.

upon all social and political phenomena of his time from the comparatively passionless position of a man of letters who happened to be also a man of genius.' It was not religious sympathy but intellectual clearness 'that led him to draw his famous portrait of the Parson.' 'For his religious rascals he seems, in fact, to have had a sort of liking.' 'Many of the tenets of Wycliffe found favor with the class with which he had become affiliated. . . . It is certainly only in this way that Chaucer can be characterized as a follower of Wycliffe.' 'He speaks with contempt of the gentility that is based upon position and descent, and not upon character. But his contempt is invariably good-humored and little calculated to provoke resentment.'[2]

Coulton writes in similar vein. 'Where Gower sees an England more hopelessly given over to the Devil than even in Carlyle's most dyspeptic nightmares—where the robuster Langland sees an impending religious Armageddon . . . there Chaucer with incredible optimism sees chiefly a merry England to which the horrors of the Hundred Years' War and the Black Death and Tyler's revolt, are but a foil. The man seems to have gone through life in the tranquil conviction that this was a pleasant world, and his own land a particularly privileged spot.'[3]

Root has much the same to say: 'Chaucer is never touched by the spirit of the reformer. . . . He sees the corruption of the Church and clearly recognizes the evil of it; but who is he to set the crooked straight? . . . The good is always admirable; and the evil, though deplorable, is so very amusing. . . . Let us cleave to what is good and laugh goodnaturedly at what is evil.'[4]

Mr. Christopher Dawson observes that Chaucer 'is a courtier and a scholar who looks at the English scene with the humorous detachment of a man of the great world. . . . Chaucer took the world as he found it, and found it good.'[5] Miss Hadow remarks that Chaucer's 'object is to paint life as he sees it, to hold the mirror up to nature, and as has justly been said, "a mirror has no tendency."'[6] Kuhl asserts: 'Chaucer's rollicking humor and his apparent indifference towards existing conditions give point to his philosophy in *Vache* [*Balade de Bon Conseil*]."[7]

In that indispensable and judicious guide to Middle English literature, Wells's *Manual*, we find the following pronouncements: 'His [Chaucer's] work is always the product of poise and control; it is tolerant; it is cool; it is the utterance of an amused spectator, not a participant.' 'Among a nation of writers who had been and were concerned especially for the welfare of their fellows and society, in a period when the literature was responding particularly to the impulse of great political and religious and social needs and movements, Chaucer exhibits scarcely a sign of any reforming spirit, or indeed any direct reflection of those needs and movements.' 'The dependence of the poet's fortunes on royal and noble patrons may have made wise a diplomatic silence in regard to contemporary conditions; but the silence remains.' 'Slyly he exposed the worldliness and hypocrisy of monk and friar and pardoner and summoner. But it is the individuals that he exposed, not what fostered and lived by such agents. He did not take the matter to heart. . . . He expresses no indignation.' 'As regards religious views Chaucer is as noncommittal as he is regarding most others. . . . Much vain effort was formerly expended in arguing that he was a Lollard, or at least of strong Lollard leanings.'[8]

This conception of Chaucer's bland unconcern with the great issues of his day, thus expressed by eminent scholars, is also to be met with in the work of modern critics who, though making no pretense to specialized knowledge, are deservedly influential. Miss Eleanor Chilton writes: 'There is no conviction in reading him . . . that he was ever more than an amused bystander at the comedy.'[9] Aldous Huxley speaks of Chaucer's 'serenity of detachment, this placid acceptance of things and people as they are.'[10] 'Peasants may revolt, priests break their vows, lawyers lie and cheat, and the world in general indulge its sensual appetites; why try and prevent them, why protest? After all, they are simply being natural, they are all following the law of kind. A reasonable man, like himself, "flees fro the pres and dwelles with soothfastnesse." '[11]

Here, then, is an array of testimony from some of the best

critical minds united in the belief that Geoffrey Chaucer looked upon the stormy spectacle of English life with a smiling tolerance, was merely amused by abuses in church and state, was inclined to believe that this was the best of all possible worlds. If cross-examined, he would doubtless be, like Calvin Coolidge's minister, against sin; he would also be in favor of virtue; he pitied suffering in remote times and places; he doubtless expressed with sincerity the more sentimental forms of religious emotion. But, according to this view of his nature, he never was moved to indignation by any contemporary evil, never took sides on any issue of moment, never lifted a finger to set the crooked straight. Lounsbury frankly concedes that the influence of environment and an eye to the main chance controlled Chaucer's pen; Coulton lays the major emphasis on his congenital optimism; Root attributes this unruffled surface to his serene Boethian philosophy; while Huxley finds the explanation in an attitude of fatalistic naturalism. But though these critics disagree widely as to why Chaucer remained a neutral observer of the events of his day, they agree that he was a neutral, that he must have seemed to those involved in the struggle a sitter on the fence, a Laodicean.

In this paper I am not at all concerned with rendering a moral judgment on a great genius; I am but slightly concerned with probing into the obscure matter of motives; I am mainly concerned with a question of fact. Did Chaucer show an amiable and universal tolerance in dealing with contemporary men and affairs; or did he on more than one occasion make it quite clear on which side he stood?

There would, of course, be no debate if there were not some evidence to support the view that the poet was a neutral by temperament, or by philosophical conviction, or from a discreet regard for his personal fortunes. He was in daily contact with men on opposite sides of the bitter struggle for power between King Richard and his uncles, and yet, as Professor Hulbert has brought out,[12] he seems to have kept the friendship of both factions. Kuhl has suggested that Chaucer's selection of the five guildsmen in the General Prolog was dictated by the consideration that these guilds were neutral in the conflict between the victualers and the nonvictualers, and so gave no offense to either party.[13] To retain, as Chaucer did, his pensions and perquisites during the last years of Richard's reign and to have them immediately confirmed by Richard's foe and conqueror implies a prudent neutrality and superlative tact. But, when all this has been said, does Chaucer's character suffer? Was there any reason why in any of these quarrels a man was bound to declare himself? In a conflict of interests, not of principles, a man of sense will try to keep out of trouble and is not to be censured if he can keep on good terms with both sides. If Chaucer accepted favors from men as little admirable as King Richard and John of Gaunt, he might well plead in extenuation that even a man of stern principle, John Wyclif, owed much of his early power and influence to these same questionable supporters. We can hardly expect the poet to be squeamish where the reformer was not. We may be sure that Wyclif's relations to Richard and his uncle involved no downright betrayal of his principles, and, if the question be raised as to Chaucer, we may well give him the benefit of the doubt. There is no evidence that in his public career or in his relationships with public men he was guilty of dishonorable conduct. If, in the midst of these factional struggles and personal rivalries, the diplomat in Chaucer prescribed for him the unheroic role of a friend to both sides, that is all to his credit as a man of sense.

When we consider his attitude on matters of greater moment, there is still some confirmation for the view that he avoided controversy and played safe. His references to the Hundred Years' War and to the Peasants' Revolt are purely casual, and indicate no attitude whatsoever.[14] Here are two topics on which, we may be sure, every tongue was loosed. Chaucer twice served as a soldier in the war, and twice acted as ambassador to bring it to a termination. During the Peasants' Revolt he must have counted some of his fellow students at the Inner Temple among the victims, the palace of his friend John of Gaunt was sacked, and the Princess Joan of Kent, who, as Miss Galway has given us some reason to believe,[15] was the object of his Platonic devotion, was insulted by the mob. But scholars have repeatedly observed that there is not one serious and specific comment on either the great war or the revolt in all his extant work. Though Minot had written his jingoistic jingles to celebrate the early triumphs of King Edward, and though Gower had loosed his invectives against the insurgent peasantry, Chaucer maintained a neutrality which was certainly not dictated by his personal interests.

In regard to the events of 1381, it is not possible to interpret that silence with certainty. But is it not possible that his failure to match the violent denunciations of his friend Gower is to be explained by the fact that, as a humanitarian and a just man, he knew too well that Jack Straw and his 'meynie' had serious grievances and that the revolt had been crushed only because Richard had broken his solemnly pledged word to the people? On the other hand, the mob had beheaded the innocent archbishop and massacred the harmless Flemings. May not Chaucer have reasoned that, where there was much wrong on both sides, there was no obligation to offer his career as a vain sacrifice to the cause of the oppressed? Once more it is arguable that Chaucer's neutral attitude, even on a great public question, was dictated not by artistic detachment or cowardice, but by a feeling that right and wrong were so mixed that to tell the whole truth would merely bring down on his head the curses of both sides. At any rate, his reticence on the matter proves that he was not one of those gentlemen of property who became more voluble on the sins of the unemployed and the arrogance of labor than on any other subject. And surely it is little short of amazing that, writing the General Prolog within six years of the Peasants' Revolt, this poet of the court should sketch for us a representative peasant, the Plowman, not as a loafer, a scamp, a boleshevik, a sower of class hatred, but as a model of all the social and Christian virtues.

This interpretation of Chaucer's attitude toward the great rising becomes the more plausible when one realizes that one of his favorite topics is the responsibility of the gentleman to behave like one. As Chesterton has acutely remarked, 'Though Chaucer is called a courtier, it is Chaucer, much more than Langland, who is always saying that true nobility is not in noble birth but in noble behaviour; that men are to be judged by worth rather than rank; and generally that all men are equal in the sight of God. And similarly, though Langland is treated as a revolutionary, it is Langland much more than Chaucer who is always saying that upstarts have seized power to which their birth does not entitle them; that the claims of family have been disregarded through the insolence of novelty, and that men are bragging and boasting above their station."[16] Not to mention the passage which Chaucer translated from Boethius and the evidence that he had also carefully noted what Dante and Jean de Meun had to say on the subject,[17] he inserted in his Parson's Tale, as Professor Patch has observed in his discerning article on 'Chaucer and the Common People,'[18] remarks not found in Peraldus to the effect that 'of swich seed as cherles spryngen, of swich seed spryngen lordes.' He dragged into the Wife of Bath's Tale a long and vigorous discourse on the text that he is 'gentil that dooth gentil dedis.' He wrote one of his best balades on the same theme. It is, of course, true, as Professor Robinson asserts, that these ideas were official doctrines of the Church. But surely the poet did not reiterate and go out of his way to introduce them because they were harmless platitudes, but rather because he thought that, if repeated often enough, they might make some impression on the snobs and titled cads whom he counted among the readers. After all, the sentiment is precisely that of Burn's *A Man's a Man for A' That,* which critics have not been wont to treat as a rhetorical commonplace. Was Chaucer less revolutionary than Burns because he harped on the same theme in the fourteenth instead of the eighteenth century?

As for the Great War, though he voiced no judgment on it specifically, he does have a good deal to say about war in general. We must discount the lines in *The Former Age* which proclaim among the blessings of an ideal society that 'No flesh ne wiste offence of egge or spere,' 'No trompes for the werres folk ne knewe.' For other blessings of the Golden Age enumerated in the same poem are a diet of mast, haws, and water of the cold well, and the enthusiasm of the vintner's paunchy son for a vegetable and teetotal diet is open to grave suspicion. But we may take far more seriously

the Melibeus. True, Chaucer, introduces it jestingly as a little
thing in prose. But it is incredible that he should have de-
liberately set himself at his desk and spent good days and
weeks translating a work of edification only in order that he
might bore himself and his readers. He did not translate the
Rose or the *Boethius* or the *Astrolabe* or the Parson's Tale
with any such ponderously subtle effort at humor. Chaucer,
the humorist, like Mark Twain, Dickens, Thackeray, and
many another master jester, had his grave aspect, and was
capable of translating a work of instruction for no more
recondite a purpose than instruction. Robinson rightly avers[19]
that for the poet and his age the Melibeus was an interest-
ing treatment of a very live topic—the practical futility of
force, the wickedness of revenge, the beatitude of the peace-
maker. We may agree with G. H. Cowling that 'its appear-
ance amongst the *Canterbury Tales* seems to indicate that
the strain and loss in blood and treasure due to the Hundred
Years' War with France had caused the prudence and pacifism
of this allegory to appeal to others besides Chaucer.'[20]

The portrait of the Knight in the General Prolog also car-
ries its meaning. As Legouis has remarked, 'The virtues of
his [Chaucer's] Knight, of his Clerk, of his Parson are in
fact so many hidden sermons.'[21] In all these we have ob-
viously ideal portraits, and it is noteworthy that the ideal
knight as depicted by Chaucer had devoted his military
career, incidentally perhaps to 'his lordes werre,' wherever
that may have been, but mainly and specifically to fighting
for our faith against the heathen on all fronts. This emphasis
was probably deliberate. In the single volume of Wyclifite
writings collected by Matthew there are seven direct attacks
on war waged by Christians on Christians.[22] Of Wyclif him-
self, Workman writes that he maintained that wars waged
for 'God's justice,' 'in the cause of the Church or for the
honour of Christ,' are right, and no other.[23] If Chaucer's
listing of the campaigns of the Knight, if the phrases
'foughten for oure feith' and 'again another hethen' are a
part of the doctrine implied in the description of the Knight,
that doctrine coincides with the doctrine of Wyclif on the
subject of war.

Chaucer's attitude toward the Hundred Years' War may also be inferred from his silences. Legouis makes the statement, startling but true: 'There is not a single patriotic line in his work.'[24] There is no disparaging reference to Frenchman or Italian or German as such. He was a better Wyclifite, a better Catholic, a better internationalist than the great majority in his day. He believed that Christendom must at least defend itself by the sword against Islam—and what agnostic of today would deplore the victory of Charles Martel at Tours?—but within the bounds of Christendom Chaucer believed profoundly in peace. The mature Chaucer of 1387 must have been convinced of the futility of war, except for some high cause far transcending the territorial pretensions of monarchs, and must have deplored the waste and destruction and barbarity that characterized the conflict between his own people and a people whom he had all the reasons of a poet to admire. His protest he put into the Melibeus and the portrait of the Knight, where his contemporaries, I feel sure, caught his drift more easily than do most of his interpreters today.

Readers or hearers of the General Prolog in the year 1387 would also have felt that on another vital controversy of the time Chaucer was deliberately taking sides and shaping the evidence. Three years after Wyclif's death Lollardy was still powerful and popular in London; though partially suppressed at Oxford, it was still alive there; it found favor with a party of the lesser nobility and knights, including Sir Lewis Clifford, Sir Richard Stury, and other friends of Chaucer's. Now if Chaucer displays any bias in his selection of characters for idealization or satiric treatment, it is in this very matter. I am not going to revive the legend that Chaucer was an avowed Wyclifite and propagandist,[25] nor am I proposing that his attacks on the vices of the clergy proclaim him unorthodox. It has not been brought out, however, so far as I am aware, how heavily the scales are weighted in the General Prolog in favor of the supporters of Wyclif and against the classes who opposed him. Who are the ideal types depicted?

There is the Knight, who has already stood for Chaucer's protest against warfare between Christians. But he was also a member of a class notorious at this time for their support of Lollard preachers and anti-clerical doctrines. Under date of 1382 we read that Sir Thomas Latimer, Sir Lewis Clifford, and Sir Richard Stury forced their tenantry to attend Lollard sermons and stood by armed to see that the evangelists were unmolested.[26] In the very year of the General Prolog, 1387, the attack of Pateshull on the morals of the friars pleased, we are told, these same knights, as well as Sir John Clanvowe, Sir William Neville, and Sir John Montague.[27] This group was called the *milites capuciati*, or 'hooded knights,' because they did not doff their hoods at the sacrament of the altar. The Lollard document of 1388 known as the *XXV Points* concludes with the prayer that God will light the hearts of lords to know and destroy the heresies of the official church.[28] The protest to the pope in 1390 against the corruption of the clergy and the usurpations of the papacy might be construed as an answer to this prayer, since it was signed by John of Gaunt, the Earl of Salisbury, and the knights, Clifford and Stury. Clifford, Stury, Latimer, and Montague formed a group of knights who in 1395 attempted to bring the whole issue before open parliament. As late as 1399 Archbishop Arundel warned convocation against certain knights in parliament whose identity is obscured since all the knights formerly prominent had been by this time reduced to silence by royal and ecclesiastical pressure.

There is a special significance in these facts, for five of these most conspicuous Lollard knights were at one time or another members of Richard's privy council: Clifford, Stury, Neville, Clanvowe, and Montague. They were not humble country gentlemen or mere soldiers; they were powers in the land. Moreover, of these five knights all but Montague were Chaucer's close friends. The witness of their contemporaries makes it abundantly clear that knights as a class were suspected of anticlericalism and some were regarded as outstanding supporters of Lollardy during the decade after Wyclif's death. We know that the poet was linked by ties of friendship to leaders of this group. In idealizing the Knight he was not only flattering a class with which he had close associations, but he may have deliberately held up to admiration a class which because of certain prominent members was popularly identified with the cause of Lollardy.

It is, of course, fair to object that Chaucer's Knight had been on a crusade and was going on a pilgrimage—both practices of which Lollards disapproved, and that therefore his author could not have conceived him as in any sense a representative of the cause. It is true, nevertheless, that four conspicuous Lollard knights fought for the faith against the infidel in Tunis in 1390: Clifford, Montague, Neville, and Clanvowe. Montague, it would seem, continued his crusading career in 1391 by service in 'Lettow' and 'Pruce.' In 1394 or 1395 Clifford joined the Order of the Passion founded for the recovery of the holy places. All these crusading activities, it is important to note, took place while Clifford and Montague were still prominently identified with the Lollard cause and before there were any signs of defection among the other knights. Wyclif himself, we remember, had declared that wars waged in the cause of the Church and for the honor of Christ were right. The crusading career of Chaucer's Knight, though it might have been denounced by Lollard extremists, does not remove from him the associations with Lollardy that attached to his class. On the other hand, that he should promptly on his return from his 'viage' seek the shrine of 'the hooly blisful martir' does disqualify him as a good Wyclifite. For the Reformer and his disciples were consistently opposed to pilgrimages. It cannot be maintained—and I do not maintain—that the Knight was a Lollard. Nevertheless, no matter how orthodox the individual, knights as a class were in the public mind of 1387 tinctured with Wyclifite sympathies. . . . Chaucer's unrestrained laudation of the Knight might be taken as an expression of sympathy with a suspect class.

This supposition is reinforced by the fact that Chaucer next chooses for serious and unqualified laudation a secular clerk of Oxford. Though nothing identifies him individually as a disciple of Wyclif, yet it was the secular clerks of Oxford who till 1382 had been open supporters of his teachings. Though the University in that year condemned the heretical doctrines, and they were studied henceforth surreptitiously, in the western counties in the year 1387 three of Wyclif's foremost disciples, all secular clerks who had been associated with the master at Oxford, Purvey, Hereford, and Aston, were active in propaganda. It is reasonable to suppose that in 1387 a secular clerk of Oxford would still, in spite of all appearances to the contrary, belong to a highly suspect group. And Chaucer portrays for us such a man as a wholly admirable type.

The third idealized figure is the Parson. He is not labeled a Wyclifite; he is not one of the itinerant poor priests; but not only his fellow pilgrims, the Host and the Shipman, smell of a 'loller' in the wind, but many a modern scholar as well. Moreover, he never denies the accusation. If there was one fundamental thought characteristic of Wyclif, it was the authority of the Bible and especially the gospels as opposed to the Fathers, philosophers, councils, and all commentators and canonists whatsoever. Dr. Workman writes: 'Wyclif's insistence on the supreme authority of Scripture was not less than that of Luther and won for him at an early date the proud title of "doctor evangelicus," while he desired that the title of "viri evangelici," "men of the Gospel," should be given to his adherents. How close was the association in orthodox circles between reference to the gospel's authority and heresy, we know from the witness of Margery Kempe, who, when she pleaded before the Archbishop of York that 'the Gospel giveth me leave to speak of God,' was promptly answered by one of the Archbishop's clerks, 'Here wot we well that she hath a devil within her, for she speaketh of the Gospel.'[29] Now three times Chaucer hammers home the point that the Parson took his doctrine from the gospel. He 'Cristes gospel trewely wolde preche.' 'Out of the gospel he tho wordes caughte.' 'Cristes loore and his apostles twelve/ He taughte, but first he folwed it hymselve.'

In this final couplet there is a further hint that Chaucer intended his ideal priest to be recognized as a Lollard—a hint which no one seems to have publicly exposed though doubtless some scholars have realized its significance. If there is one phrase which occurs inevitably and often monotonous-

ly in the English writings of Wyclif and his followers, it is
the phrase 'Crist and his apostles.' It is a phrase notably
absent from the contemporary writings of the orthodox,
though a diligent search would presumably turn up a few
examples. But in the literature of Lollardy it is to be found,
with variations, as a familiar leitmotif. In the *De Papa* of
1380 Wyclif wrote, for example, in the space of two para-
graphs: 'Thes prelatis blasfemen in Crist and in His hooly
apostlis'; 'Crist forsok it in word and dede, and bi His lore
His apostlis'; 'Crist ordeynede that His apostlis . . . shulden
be scaterid'; 'thus may Cristen men lerne bothe of Crist and
His apostles.'[20] The so-called *Complaint* of 1382 is full of
references to Christ and the apostles.[21] In *The Church and
Her Members*, written by Wyclif in the last year of his life,
we find: 'Crist . . . movede apostlis to do his dedes'; 'apostlis
of Crist'; 'Crist or his apostlis'; 'thus lyvede Crist with his
apostlis'; 'so diden Cristis apostlis.'[22] . . . It is safe to say that
when Chaucer spoke of the Parson as teaching Christ's lore
and that of his apostles, he left no doubt in the minds of
contemporary readers that here was the ideal parish priest
conceived according to the Lollard view.

The Parson's later reproof to the Host in the matter of
swearing confirms this interpretation. Wyclifite opposition to
this practice was notorious.[23] It was, for instance, one of the
accusations of heresy against Margaret Backster in 1428
that she warned her neighbor to abstain from all swearing,
either by God or by any saint. The Parson's Prolog, probably
composed after the disintegration of the Lollard party in
1395, still contains two suggestions of Lollard puritanism.
Bluntly, the priest declares in response to the Host's invita-
tion, 'Thou getest fable noon ytoold for me'; and later, 'I
kan not geeste "rum, ram, ruf," by lettre,/ Ne, God woot,
rym holde I but litel bettre.' Both these views regarding the
use of 'fables' and of rime in sermons can be matched in
the Lollard *De Officio Pastorali*, in which we read: 'Certis
that prest is to blame that shulde so frely haue the gospel,
and leeueth the preching therof and turnyth hym to mannus
fablis. . . God axith not dyuysiouns ne rymes of hym that
shulde preche.'[24] But though Chaucer consistently maintains

the definitely evangelical coloring of his Parson through the
Parson's Prolog, the Tale one must acknowledge is wholly
conventional and orthodox. Here is no talk of 'Cristes lore
and his apostles twelve,' but much concerning the seven
deadly sins and the formalities of confession—topics sanc-
tioned, even specifically prescribed, by the hierarchy.[35] Un-
fortunately, there is no clue to the date of the Parson's Tale,
and we are left to conjecture for an explanation of the in-
congruity between all Chaucer had led us to expect of the
man and all that finds expression in the sermon. One con-
jecture which may be as good as any other is that the sermon
belongs to the last years of the century, when Lollardy was
patently a lost cause. Chaucer was approaching the mood in
which he arranged for his interment in Westminster Abbey
and wrote his *Retractions.* This was no time for him to round
off his *magnum opus* with a heretical sermon, which would,
even if he felt inclined, get him into trouble and might
rouse an indignant hierarchy to burn every copy of the
Canterbury Tales.

If Chaucer's relation to Lollardy followed the evolution
thus outlined, it would parallel that of two of his oldest
friends, Sir Richard Stury and Sir Lewis Clifford. As has
been noted above, under the date of 1382 they are named
as active supporters of the poor priests; and thirteen years
later, in 1395, they are still listed as advocates of the ex-
tremist *XII Conclusions.* But Stury was promptly forced to
recant under royal pressure, and soon after died. Clifford
in 1402 not only recanted but also informed on his associates
in the movement; and in his will, two years later, spoke of
himself as a false traitor to God, unworthy to be called a
Christian man, and directed that his body be buried in the
furthest corner of the churchyard, unmarked by any stone
whereby one might know where his stinking carrion lay.
These two intimates of the poet fell away after 1395 from a
movement that had become dangerous. Their motives we
do not know and cannot judge. The difference between the
decidedly free-spoken Chaucer of the General Prolog and
the entirely correct Chaucer of the Parson's Tale and the
Retractions may be attributable likewise to the ebb of the

Wyclifite tide. But he who would apportion the degree of
policy and the degree of sincere contrition which motivated
Chaucer's change of front would be a bold man.

The General Prolog of the *Canterbury Tales,* then, fur-
nishes three wholly ideal portraits; of these one is plainly
sketched in accordance with Wyclif's ideas, and the other
two represent members of classes known to be sympathetic
to his program. On the other hand, the Prolog furnishes
portraits of several rascals. The rascality of the Miller and
the Merchant is briefly and lightly touched upon; that of the
Shipman is offset by admiration for his hardihood and sea-
manship; and that of the Reeve and the Manciple is offset
by admiration for the cleverness with which they cheated
their wealthy masters. But there are three rascals whom
Chaucer seems to have labored to make morally repulsive—
the Friar, the Summoner, and the Pardoner—and the two
latter he made physically loathsome as well. The Friar would
cajole a farthing out of a widow in barefoot penury. The
Summoner's face was covered with white-headed pustules,
and he was so generous that he would let a man keep his
doxie for a whole year in return for a quart of wine. The
Pardoner sold sham relics of Our Lady and St. Peter, was a
pompous hypocrite, had glaring eyes, and a goatlike voice;
'I trowe he were a geldyng or a mare.' If contempt and
loathing can be expressed in words, they are found in these
three portraits. Now, of course, satire on clerical scoundrels
was no monopoly of the Lollards; Catholics in good stand-
ing were loud in their denunciation of these same traitors to
the faith. But the fact remains that Wyclifite literature is
full of attacks on the mendicant orders, ecclesiastical courts,
and the veneration of relics. As Tatlock puts it: 'Everybody
assailed the clergy, but the reformer's club and the poet's
rapier made for the same points; there is a striking resem-
blance in what they say, and they clearly thought much
the same.'[36]

To be sure, laughter is mingled with the scorn, and ap-
parently it is this laughter which caused Lounsbury to speak
of Chaucer's liking for religious rascals and of his contempt
as 'invariably good-humored and little calculated to provoke

resentment.' Certainly Chaucer, as an artist, relished to the full the 'entertainment value' of successful, as well as of unsuccessful, knavery. But if anyone really thinks that his treatment of the Friar and the Pardoner was 'good humored,' let him read again the Summoner's Prolog and Tale and the Host's response to the Pardoner's invitation to kiss his relics, and let him ask himself how he would feel if he had been the Friar or the Pardoner. And he might well ponder these words of Franklin P. Adams, who was no mean judge of humor.[37] 'The expression of the social consciousness as articulated in the "Dooley" sketches [by Finley Peter Dunne] would never have been printed unless they had been written in dialect. . . If pretense and hypocrisy are attacked by the [newspaper] office clown, especially in dialect, the crooks and shammers think that it is All in Fun. And when the Dunnes and the Lardners die, the papers print editorials saying that there was no malice in their writing and no bitterness in their humor. Few writers ever wrote more maliciously and bitterly than Lardner and Dunne. They resented injustice, they loathed sham, and they hated the selfish stupidity that went with them.' It is a shallow estimate of Chaucer's fun which fails to detect the underlying earnestness.

The impression made by the General Prolog on the public of Chaucer's day may perhaps be appreciated if we imagine a novel published in 1936, say, in which three characters were idealized—a Middle Western farmer, a college professor, a Democratic politician of liberal views—and three characters were pilloried—a journalist in the employ of Hearst, a syphilitic banker, a homosexual stockbroker. Though the novel contained no downright New Deal propaganda, would a modern reader have any doubt as to where the author's sympathies lay? Neither can there be much doubt as to where Chaucer's sympathies lay when he wrote the Prolog of the *Canterbury Tales*.

Finally, there is a subject which Chaucer thrice treats in passages for which he has no source and in which he seems to be expressing his own mind. That subject is the use and the abuse of the royal power. The balade, *Lack of Stead-*

fastnesse, which is undeniably a humble remonstrance on the part of the poet to his sovereign, Richard II, depicts in general terms the lawlessness and confusion of the times, and calls on the king to show forth his sword of castigation, dread God, do law, and wed his folk again to steadfastness. Again, since in the Prolog to the *Legend of Good Women* we find Alceste urging a course of mercy and justice on the God of Love, who is also a king, many scholars have been inclined to see here another tactful reminder to Richard. Such an interpretation does not necessarily involve any complete identification of the God of Love with Richard or of Alceste with any queen or princess. When we note that Alceste recommends to the god-king some courses of action which seems to have little to do with the immediate situation—for example, to keep his lords in their rank, to do right to both poor and rich, not to listen to envious tattlers—then we may reasonably surmise that the poet had in mind not only the fantastic and half-humorous situation of his dream, but also the real situation of the realm. The poem was to be sent to Queen Anne; doubtless her husband would see it too, and it is quite like Chaucer to offer a little advice to his king in a form which might prove palatable and which could surely not give offence.

A few years before, in what was to be the Knight's Tale, Chaucer had created a situation which had marked analogies with the scene of Alceste's intercession for the poet. Theseus, it will be remembered, discovers Palamon and Arcite in mortal combat, is resolved to execute them, is swayed to clemency by the entreaties of his queen and Emelye, and then reflects, 'Fy/ Upon a lord that wol have no mercy. . . . That lord hath litel of discrecioun/ That in swich cas kan no divisioun,/ But weyeth pride and humblesse after oon.' Here it is possible that Chaucer is gently hinting that Richard is doing well to heed the pleas of Queen Anne for a policy of magnanimity and mercy. We know, then, that Chaucer undertook to advise his sovereign openly once; and it is more than likely that in these two other passages he sought in more indirect ways to guide the royal will into the right channels.

The facts and the inferences which I have adduced in this paper justify our rejecting any notion of Chaucer as either a sycophantic timeserver, who merely echoed the sentiments of his patrons and associates, or of a cheerful philosopher who looked upon the follies and struggles of mankind with an amused detachment. Needless to say, he was no martyr for any cause; he never, in modern parlance, 'stuck his neck out' too far or kept it out after it became dangerous. Perhaps it was his modesty which led him to feel that nobody would be much concerned or much the better if he sacrificed his pensions or his person for a principle. In the *Balade de Bon Conseil,* addressed to the son-in-law of his Lollard friend, Clifford, a poem in which he seems to have distilled the essence of his practical philosophy, he frankly advises Vache not to meddle in situations where he can only harm himself and achieve nothing. 'Stryve not as doth the crokke with the wal. . . . Be war also to sporne ayeyns an al.' But Chaucer does not counsel his younger friend to remain a detached spectator of life if we are to judge by his own practice. He did speak out, we have seen, on various controversial subjects more than once, presumably when he thought his efforts would not prove vain. The line in the same balade, 'Tempest thee noght al croked to redresse,' should therefore be read with some stress on the 'al.' For certainly on some occasions Chaucer did exert himself to set the crooked straight.

If in the light of the foregoing facts any one chooses to point the finger of scorn at Chaucer as something of a Laodicean and a trimmer, if any one living in a country where speech on political and religious questions is still free chooses to adopt an attitude of moral superiority to a poet of the Middle Ages who observed for the most part a politic discretion in his utterances, 'lordynges, by your leve, that am not I.'

Notes

[1] *MP,* xiv (1916), 67. For another discussion of Chaucer's moral earnestness see G. R. Stewart, Jr., 'The Moral Chaucer,' *Univ. of California Publications in English,* i, 89–109.

[2] T. R. Lounsbury, *Studies in Chaucer* (New York, 1892), II, 469, 482, 470, 479, 473.

[3] G. G. Coulton, *Chaucer and His England*, 2d ed. (London, 1909), p. 11.

[4] R. K. Root, *The Poetry of Chaucer* (Boston, 1906), pp. 28 f.

[5] C. Dawson, *Mediaeval Religion* (New York, 1934), pp. 160 f.

[6] G. Hadow, *Chaucer and His Times* (New York, 1914), p. 156.

[7] *MLN*, 40 (1924), 338, n. 90.

[8] J. E. Wells, *Manual of Writings in Middle English* (New Haven, 1916), pp. 602, 603, 604.

[9] E. Chilton, H. Agar, *The Garment of Praise* (New York, 1929), p. 121.

[10] A. Huxley, *Essays New and Old* (New York, 1927), p. 252.

[11] *Ibid.*, p. 254.

[12] J. R. Hulbert, *Chaucer's Official Life* (Menasha, 1912), pp. 70 f.

[13] *Transactions of the Wisconsin Academy of Sciences*, XVIII, 652 ff.

[14] Like Tatlock, I cannot detect a slurring allusion to the Peasants' Revolt in *Troilus*, IV, vv. 183 f. Cf. *MLN*, 50 (1935), 277 f.

[15] *MLR*, 33 (1938), 145–199.

[16] G. K. Chesterton, *Chaucer* (London, 1932), p. 247.

[17] J. L. Lowes, "Chaucer and Dante's *Convivio*," *MP*, 13 (1915), 19–27.

[18] *JEGP*, 29 (1930), 379.

[19] See also Professor Lawrence in *Essays and Studies in Honor of Carleton Brown* (New York, 1940), pp. 100–110.

[20] G. H. Cowling, *Chaucer* (London, 1927), p. 162.

[21] E. Legouis, *Geoffrey Chaucer*, trans. L. Lailavoix (London, 1913), p. 155.

[22] *English Works of Wyclif*, ed. F. D. Matthew, *EETS* (London, 1890), pp. 73, 91, 99, 100, 132, 152, 176.—The view is not, of course, exclusively Wycliffe. Cf. Gower, *Vox Clamantis*, Bk. III, vv. 663-666, 945–947; Bk. VII, vv. 491 f.

[23] H. B. Workman, *John Wyclif* (Oxford, 1926), II, 28.

[24] Legouis, *op. cit.*, p. 31.

[25] H. Simon, *Chaucer a Wycliffite*, Essays on Chaucer, Ser. 2, Chaucer Society (1876).

[26] Henry Knighton, *Chronicle* (Rolls Series), II, 181. On the Lollard Knights, cf. Workman, *op. cit.*, II, 380–404, and W. T. Waugh, "The Lollard Knights," *Scottish Historical Review*, XI, 55 ff.

[27] *Chronicon Angliae*, 1328–88, ed. E. M. Thompson (London, 1874), II, 377. Cf. G. M. Trevelyan, *England in the Age of Wycliffe* (London, 1925), p. 327.

[28] Workman, *op. cit.*, II, 390.

[29] *The Book of Margery Kempe*, ed. W. Butler-Bowden (London, 1936), p. 189. Cf. Workman, *op. cit.*, II, 150, n.2, 198.

[30] Wyclif, *Select English Writings*, ed. Winn, pp. 72 f.

[31] Wyclif, ed. Arnold, III, 509–522.

[32] Wyclif, *Select English Writings*, ed. Winn, pp. 121 f., 130, 133, 138.

[33] Workman, *op. cit.*, II, 27 f. Pollard, *op. cit.*, pp. 149–153. Wyclif, ed. Arnold, III, 332, 483. The objection to swearing was,

of course, not confined to Lollards. Cf. Coulton, *Medieval Pano-rama*, pp. 465 f.; *The Book of Margery Kempe*, ed. W. Butler-Bowdon, pp. 64, 150, 186, 189; G. R. Owst, *Literature and Pulpit in Medieval England* (Cambridge, 1933), pp. 414–425.

[34] Wyclif, ed. Matthew, pp. 438, 532. Cf. Wyclif, ed. Arnold, III, 147.

[35] D. Wilkins, *Concilia Magnae Britanniae et Hiberniae*, III (London, 1737), 59.

[36] *MP*, XIV, 264.

[37] Foreword to *Mr. Dooley at His Best*, ed. E. Ellis, pp. xvii–xviii.